universal web design

crystal waters

New Riders Publishing, Indianapolis, Indiana

universal web design

Senior Acquisitions Editor
John Kane

Senior Editors
Sarah Kearns
Suzanne Snyder

Development Editor
Linda Laflamme

Project Editor
Jennifer Eberhardt

Copy Editors
Wendy Garrison, Cricket Harrison,
Matt Litten, Michelle Warren,
Molly Warnes

Technical Editor
Kim Scott

Software Specialist
Steve Flatt

Acquisitions Coordinator
Stacey Beheler

Administrative Coordinator
Karen Opal

Manufacturing Coordinator
Brook Farling

Cover Designer
Sandra Schroeder

Cover Illustrator
©Nicholas Wilton/SIS

Cover Production
Aren Howell

Book Designer
Sandra Schroeder

Director of Production
Larry Klein

Production Team Supervisors
Laurie Casey
Joe Millay

Graphics Image Specialist
Oliver Jackson

Production Analyst
Erich J. Richter

Production Team
William Huys Jr., Linda Knose,
Elizabeth SanMiguel, Pamela Woolf

Indexer
Robert Long

Universal Web Design
By Crystal Waters

Published by:
New Riders Publishing
201 West 103rd Street
Indianapolis, IN 46290 USA

Printed in the United States of America 1 2 3 4 5 6 7 8 9 0

Library of Congress Cataloging-in-Publication Data

```
Waters, Crystal, 1964-
    Universal web design  :  Crystal Waters.
        p.    cm.
    Includes index.
    ISBN 1-56205-738-3
    1. Web sites--Design.     I. Title.
TK5105.888.W363    1997
025.04--dc21                            97-8937
                                          CIP
```

warning and disclaimer

This book is designed to provide information about web design. Every effort has been made to make this book as complete and as accurate as possible, but no warranty or fitness is implied.

The information is provided on an "as is" basis. The author and New Riders Publishing shall have neither liability nor responsibility to any person or entity with respect to any loss or damages arising from the information contained in this book or from the use of the discs or programs that may accompany it.

Publisher	Don Fowley
Associate Publisher	David Dwyer
Marketing Manager	Mary Foote
Managing Editor	Carla Hall
Director of Development	Kezia Endsley

about the author

Crystal Waters writes about, creates, consults on, teaches about, reviews, and tests web sites and web technologies. She's formerly been editor at a number of publications, and writes regularly for magazines. Her web site, www.typo.com., has received recognition as a Project Cool Site and as a Best of the Web site from c|net, among others.

Crystal is the author of *Web Concept & Design*, also by New Riders.

trademark acknowledgments

All terms mentioned in this book that are known to be trademarks or service marks have been appropriately capitalized. New Riders Publishing cannot attest to the accuracy of this information. Use of a term in this book should not be regarded as affecting the validity of any trademark or service mark.

dedications

This book, like the first, is dedicated to my mom, **Leona Schultz Waters**, who means more to me than any ink on paper can express.

acknowledgments

After listing about a billion people in the first book, I swore I'd try to keep this list short. But there are so many people who have supported, encouraged, and helped me during this writing blitz that I really can't help but try to list as many people as possible:

From left to right: Eddie, Crystal, Lois, Bob, Diane, & T.R.

Thanks to my cool sisters and brothers: **Lois**, **Diane**, **Bob**, **T.R.**, & **Eddie**. Without you all… well, I'd be an only child.

Überthanks to **Jack Lyon** for tons of support, and for writing and researching the bulk of the sound and downloadables chapters. I couldn't have done it without you. Well, maybe I could have, but it would have taken a lot longer. ;-)

Life as we know it would not be possible without **Lynda Weinman** (http://www.lynda.com) and **Bruce Heavin** (http://www.stink.com). Thanks for everything, as always, my pets.

And speaking of pets, special pats on the head to my feline family members, **Internet** and **Ginger**.

Thanks to **Barbara Bergesen** and **Lauren Guzak** for their many hours of work on the CD-ROM and various other book-related labors. They happen to be great friends, too.

I have tons of gratitude for the endless patience, support, and cheerleading from **Cheryl Thomas**, **Denise Finn** (yes, Denise, it's finally done!), **Cynthia Hoffman**, **Mary Ellen Doyle**, **Jordyn Mitchell**, **Coco Jones**, **Ben Templin**, **Annette Armbruster**, **Jean LeTarte**, **Evelyn Tracey**, **Cheryl Dematteis**, **Susan Jones**, **Gail** and **Winona Ross**, **Joe Lambert**, **Nina Mullen**, **Dana Atchley**, **Denise Aungst**, **Mark Frost**, **Heather Walsh**, **Jack Lyon** (again), **Trent Ward**, **Ray Vincenzo**, **Joe Scalmanini**, **Neil West**, **Minda Sandler**, and approximately 400 other people… you know who you are (I hope).

Many thanks for the encouraging words from some of my fellow (and favorite) industry writers: **Nan McCarthy**, **Robin Williams**, **Roger Parker**, **Kay Nelson**, **Lisa Napoli**, and dahling **Jeff Dawson**.

Oh, and thanks to **Jim LeValley** who helped get me into this mess, and **Jennifer Eberhardt** and **John Kane** of New Riders who have patiently helped me wade my way through it.

And many thanks to the many web designers and artists who make this medium worthy of lots of attention and the work it takes to cover it. Plus thanks to **Chank Diesel** (http://www.chankstore.com/) for the hipster fonts used on my site and in some of the examples in this book; **wayneb** of beatthief (http://www.beatthief.com/); **Jim Tobias** of Inclusive Technologies for his evaluation of WebTV hardware; **Peter Duke** of dukemedia (http://www.dukemedia) for his WebTV color palette; and everyone else who has written with comments, info and tips… not to mention the many people out there who keep pushing the limits of technology to bring it back to as many people as possible.

contents at a glance

   introduction *1*

1   *elements of the web experience* *15*

2   *navigational rules & options* *39*

3   *graphic enhancements* *49*

4   *page sizes* *65*

5   *text transformations* *81*

6   *forms & functionality* *103*

7   *putting it on the table* *117*

8   *frames* *133*

9   *sound bytes* *145*

10   *movin' & shakin'* *161*

11   *color & contrast* *181*

12   *the importance of HTML* *195*

13   *the text-only option* *207*

14   *downloadables* *229*

15   *accessibility review & resources* *243*

16   *WebTV* *261*

17   *assistive technology & legislation* *277*

   i   *connections* *283*

   index *293*

Table of Contents

intro designing sites for everyone 1

non-web examples...2

accessible by mistake 3

will design be sacrificed?...4

the sticklers—common site elements that cause problems 5

additional access advantages 6

    "forced quiet" environments....................................6

    slow modems or older equipment limitations 7

    timed access 7

how accessible do you have to be?....................................7

evaluating your audience..7

is this book for you? 8

what you need to know...9

how you'll benefit 9

what's in this book..10

about the cd-rom..12

the end is in site 13

1 elements of the web experience...**15**

what you can and can't control 15

the access method..16

the platform and configuration 16

    monitors and displays..18

speed and location 19

the person using the web...19

    comfort levels...19

    language barriers 20

    money matters..24

    time limits 24

    dislikes..25

    disabilities 25

your site—the only factor you can control....................25

    the web designer as educator.................................29

    the web designer as student—listening to your audience..........33

market research resources 36

summary...38

2 navigational rules & options **39**

guidelines for getting around 39

icons & metaphor 40

symbols & symbolism 42

navigation bars 44

the imagemap conundrum 44

text navigation 45

    clicking required 45

    when clicking isn't an option 46

summary 47

3 graphic enhancements **49**

making a picture-perfect web site 49

use the right graphic format 50

    gif 50

    jpeg 52

think smaller 53

    check your colors 53

    physical image size 54

    save images as 72 dpi 55

    make images smaller 56

    thumbnails 57

    specify image size 59

    be descriptive 60

    providing ALTernatives 60

    proposed D tag standard 62

captions 63

    imagemaps 63

summary 64

4 page sizes **65**

if it don't fit, fix it 65

smallest common denominator 65

popular screen sizes 67

paper versus screen 69

using javascript to resize browser screens to your specifications 74

monitor tests without the monitor 77

what's inside 79

    text and page size 79

navigational and organizational cues for oversized pages 80

summary 80

5 text transformations **81**

the words have it 81

reading and writing 83

speaking of punctuation… 84

break up text 84

use headlines and subheads 94

keep it simple 98

icons and links 98

multipage formats 100

links and readability 101

summary..102

6 forms & functionality **103**

accessible forms & alternatives 103

form alternatives 106

mousing around...106

form design 108

the right element for the content 108

give direction 111

consistency and logic 112

problems with standard form printing....................................112

summary..115

7 putting it on the table **117**

getting the place settings right...117

how tables work...117

tableless browsers 121

line breaks 121

paragraph breaks 123

extra space 124

how tables load 127

"table-like" pages for text browsers 127

tables and screen readers 132

summary..132

8 frames...**133**

the great cubicle debate 133

scroll annoyance..134

noframes..136

frames and people with impairments......................................138

backing out...139

other access lessons 140

summary..143

9   sound bytes **145**

do you hear what I hear? 145

the thrill is gone 146

getting in the mix..146

the classics: wav, aiff, au 147

digital tunes: midi and mod......................................150

midi 150

mod 151

super audio: mpeg 1 & 2..151

webcentric sounds: RealAudio, Shockwave, Voxware, and Talker 153

RealAudio 153

Shockwave 155

Voxware and Talker...156

resist temptation 157

not-so-stupid sound tricks 157

smaller is better...157

options are standard 158

links, links, links 158

sound off 159

transcripts 159

summary 160

10   movin' & shakin' **161**

adding descriptions & captions to movies....................161

offering alternatives..161

movie thumbnails 163

creating descriptive transcripts..................................163

captioning movies 165

summary..179

11   color & contrast **181**

the eyes have it 181

importance of contrast 181

multicolored backgrounds 183

picking out colors..186

readable blends..188

type size and style 192

color blindness 192

summary..193

12   the importance of html...**195**

the multi-accessible standard 195

sgml: the basis of html..196

logic and structure 196

the significance of function 197

where tags belong 198

html checkers 200

summary 206

13   the text-only option **207**

ASCII doesn't have to be boring 207

the benefits of text-only sites 207

text appearance 207

controlling text function and size 209

   headings 209

   font attribution tags 212

character styles 215

   logical type style tags 215

   physical type style tags 216

other text appearance tags 216

looks the same to me 218

coloring fonts 220

paragraphs defined 221

   more breaks 222

getting listed 222

   unnumbered, or unordered, lists 222

   numbered, or ordered, lists 223

   definition lists 223

   nested lists 224

cascading style sheets 224

summary 228

14   downloadables **229**

choose the right file format 229

compressed downloadables 230

   the exceptions 230

   finding the right format 231

the great debate: graphics 234

   moving right along: video 235

   sound and fury: audio 237

   words to the wise: documents 237

best bets 239

download options 242

summary 242

15   **accessibility review & resources** **243**

     41 things to check, fix, or try 243

         upload and test 243

         try your site with images off...............................244

         how's it look in other browsers? 244

         how's it look on other platforms? 247

         check your code 247

         keep text and links readable on the background...247

         color by numbers 248

         are images as small as they can be? 248

         title bar matching 248

         spelll czech!!! 249

         how fast is fast? 250

         navigation...250

         alignment 250

         window resizing 251

         is your "cool stuff" gratuitous?...........................252

         do all links work? 252

         making contact..252

         are links and icons consistent?...........................253

         size warnings 254

         turn off blinking...255

         clarity factors 256

         caption jpeg images 256

         provide sound & movie transcripts.....................257

         limit links 257

         html purity 257

         D tagging 257

         noframes...257

         sound choices 258

         forms 258

         multilingual 258

         site map..258

     summary..260

16   **WebTV** **261**

     designing for the TV generation.............................261

     arguments about televising the web.........................261

     how WebTV works...262

     accessibility issues...263

the remote and keyboard 263
navigational interface 264
design issues..265
available real estate...265
color challenge 266
font size..267
shuddering lines..272
downloadables 272
image size 272
WebTV-specific html tags 272
<sidebar>...</sidebar>..272
<nosmartquotes> 274
summary..275

17   assistive technology & legislation..277
are you legally olbigated to make your site accessible?...................277
Americans with Disabilities Act...277
for your employees..278
government availability 279
access to the world...279
the big question 280
summary..281

i   connections 283

index...293

designing sites for everyone

You may have heard the term "universal design" in regard to making technology, products, and places accessible to people with visual, hearing, cognitive, and physical impairments. Although making your site accessible to visually impaired web surfers is most certainly covered here, universal design is not limited to one "group" or another—hence the word "universal." The goal of universal design is to design a site for as many people as possible, serving everyone regardless of who they are or what limitations they may have.

The universal design concepts examined in this book follow the same universal design concepts suggested and implemented in architecture, home products, and other widely used products and places. One research organization, The Center for Universal Design at North Carolina State University, defines universal design as "the design of products and environments to be usable by all people, to the greatest extent possible, without the need for adaptation or specialized design."

The coolest aspect of making your web site accessible through universal design is that nearly everyone can benefit from the enhanced structure.

Access is also about *choice*. Offering your customers choices makes them happy and makes good business sense. If you went to a grocery store and had the choice of one brand of food only, you probably wouldn't shop there for long. And a tube top, for example, has the dubious honor of offering the feature of "one size fits all," but that doesn't mean everyone's going to rush out and buy

"It must be acknowledged that the principles of universal design in no way comprise all criteria for good design, only universally usable design. Certainly, other factors are important, such as aesthetics, cost, safety, gender, and cultural appropriateness, and these aspects should be taken into consideration as well when designing."

—The Center for Universal Design at North Carolina State University, http://www2.ncsu.edu/ncsu/design/cud/.

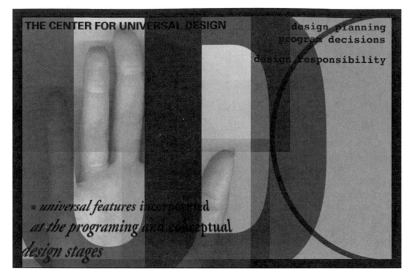

one, or that it will fit everyone, or that it's particularly flattering to everyone's figure. Luckily, we have the choice of many different fashions to choose from, in different sizes, at different prices, and different styles.

On the web the universal design approach lets you offer more choices. In some cases, just fixing a missing code or adding one line of text can make the difference as far as keeping someone at your site.

non-web examples

For an example of how universal design serves everyone, look no further than your TV. Although closed-caption television technology was developed for people with hearing impairments, studies show that many other people also benefit from and appreciate this feature. For example, people who don't want to wake others in the household turn on the closed-caption function. It's helped people new to English—and other languages—learn the dialect, and also has helped children to learn to read. Although it took a long time for closed-captioning to become a standard enhancement to television programs (the Television Decoder Circuitry Act of 1990 helped a bit, as well), now many television programs are close-captioned, as are a good deal of commercials.

Most televisions out of the box now support closed-captioning. Even if you're not hearing impaired, try turning it on sometime. My mother is deaf in one ear and extremely hearing impaired in

the other. Sometimes she's able to read the lips of people talking on television, but wide-angle shots, or those shots that don't show a person's mouth, mean she misses out. On my last visit home, I just pushed a couple of buttons on her remote control. Now she has access to all of the voices she was missing, along with tags such as [applause] or [western music in background playing through-out]. As I expected, the amount of character action and speech she could understand increased exponentially.

What surprises me is how much *I* use it. When I'm on the phone, I mute the TV, but I can still read to find out what's going on. When a loud vehicle drives by, I might miss hearing what some-one says, but it's there in text format on-screen. Sometimes I can't figure out what someone mumbles, and the caption clears it up.

Other examples of access design have become so prevalent that you and I might not even notice them. Okay, so you're hurrying through the airport, and you just gotta… you know… *go*. You're carrying four pieces of luggage, and you don't want someone to steal them while you're… *going*… so what stall do you go into? The wheelchair accessible bathroom, right? How many of you have used easy-grip-n-turn or easy-push door handles? Automatic sliding doors? Sidewalk curbcuts when you're roller skating or pushing a baby carriage or grocery cart? The point here is that these enhancements—just like closed-captioning—have grown to be appreciated by audiences other than those they were intended for. And often, we're not even aware that we're using them for our own benefit.

The web is the same. Even those of us who might have T1 access to the web and free accounts occasionally turn images off or want to know more about an image or don't feel like spending a bunch of time downloading a sound or video file just to find out a bit of information—especially if its not clear whether the want-ed information is even in there. We all want choices, and the more viable ones we offer our site visitors, the better we serve them.

accessible by mistake

I recently did a survey of professional web site designers and asked them whether their sites were accessible to those with visual, hear-ing, physical, or cognitive impairments. Most said that they didn't know, but that they either have or are contemplating creating a text version or low-graphics site for those viewers with slower modems or less-than-Netscape-capable browers. It has been a

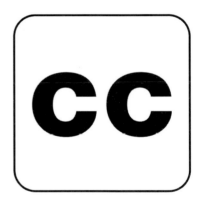

Closed-captioning, although devel-oped and implemented for those people with hearing impairments, is also helpful to those without hear-ing impairments. For example, one of my editors pointed out that her father watches the trivia game show *Jeopardy*, which happens to display the answers at the same time as the clues appear. He then gets on the phone to her sister who's also watching the show, and proves to her how smart he really is. Unless she reads this, she'll remain none the wiser.

4

widely accepted design issue to consider creating a low-bandwidth version of a site for people whose browsers don't support graphics and forms, and yet, nearly all of the site designers who answered the survey said they never considered that a text version of a site might benefit a web surfer who is visually impaired. One person asked me whether blind people can use computers. No, not all of them can, and not all of them want to. But if a person who is blind or otherwise visually impaired wants to access your info and he can't get at it, I think there's a problem not on the user's side, but in the site publisher's attitude toward serving its public.

The series of steps necessary to make a site accessible to a university student using LYNX, or to someone using a 14.4 modem and the AOL browser, are very much the same as those that assist viewers with learning disabilities or visual limitation in accessing a site. Similarly, adding text to an inline QuickTime movie gives a person with a hearing impairment access to information about the sounds and words happening in the clip, while offering the same benefits as closed-caption televisions. Learning to think through the steps that make a site universally acceptable helps to serve everyone who comes to your site.

will design be sacrificed?

This book is not about sacrificing those elements on your site that you've worked so hard to implement. It's not about removing graphics or JavaScripts, or creating sites that contain text only. It's not about avoiding new tags or standards. It's about optimizing a site for better navigation, viewing, content access, and enjoyment of the site overall.

I think most people would be surprised that the appearance of a site needn't change all that much in order to accommodate accessibility for all of its visitors. Working within the limits of the web has taught designers a great deal about creating images that are gorgeous yet low in file size, and browser text limitations have spawned creative ways of presenting text on sites.

There's no doubt that graphical user interfaces and multimedia have enhanced general human/computer interaction. However, for those using text browsers or who are visually impaired, graphically inclined applications can be virtually unusable. Screen readers and speech synthesizers can't read pictures. Some of the visually impaired can't focus on, or see, animations that are meant to direct the next move of a seeing person. Those with slow

modems or older browsers, or people who are deaf or hard of hearing, can't appreciate inline audio or movies with sound that explain an action on-screen.

However, there is no rule that you have to omit beautiful images or sacrifice innovative design or hot techno-gizmos when creating a site. Even minor touch-ups, such as image captions or text descriptions (such as those in the following D-tagging example), can take a site quite a few steps closer to being universally accessible. This example added one unobtrusive letter to my entire page.

It took only a couple minutes to make this image from my web site accessible. Note the underlined "D" link to the right of the image. This D-tagging is a standard suggested by the National Center for Accessible Media (http://www. boston.com/wgbh/ncam) and is a cue that there is information about this image available with a simple click on the letter.

Whenever users click on my D-tag, they're taken to a separate page that lists concise descriptions of each image. I also included a direct link back to the area in which the image appears. Those unable or unwilling to view images get an idea of what the [IMAGE] tag represents. Those who are surfing with images turned off are now better educated about potential images and can make a more informed choice of whether the image is worth downloading.

Okay, so I know there are designers out there who may feel that even that one letter is distracting, especially when there are multiple images on a web page. There are other ways of making your site accessible, and we're going to dig into many of them.

the sticklers—common site elements that cause problems

All of the elements discussed in this book—graphics, text, animations, forms, tables, imagemaps, colors, movies, audio, Java, JavaScripts, frames, style sheets, and so on—have all helped to inspire and challenge both browser developers and web designers to continually drive to create more interactive, all-purpose, informational exchange and entertaining sites. Designers demand a feature; a developer responds. A developer improves a browser's capabilities; designers push it as far as it can go, sometimes even beyond expectations.

6

Technology is just plain cool, but it can leave behind some people as the number of enhancements quickly grow, and the demands made of the user grow just as fast. We designers keep up with it because it's our business to, but sometimes a Joe- or Jill-average visitor to our sites just wants to find out one bit of information. To some of them, even common elements such as a simple GIF can cause as many problems as bleeding-edge elements might for us. Perhaps they can't view it, or it wasn't saved in a K-saving way that allows for swift download. Other elements, however, cause problems for a variety of viewers, depending on who they are and how they are accessing the web.

Let me step back for a minute and explain that I know that there are many sites out there that are designed with the express purpose to entertain, visually stun, and technologically wow their visitors. A site that promotes high-end graphical or animation software, or is an online interactive game, obviously needs to utilize a great many of the preceding web features, such as frames and Shockwave. These become sticklers only when they potentially inhibit your target audience's experience. As long as you know that your audience has access to what they want, you're on the right track.

additional access advantages

Just as the closed-caption function of my mom's television served to enhance my use of the set, many enhancements to multimedia elements of a site, such as an inline QuickTime movie, serve to assist a lot of people in a lot of different situations. For example, you might consider adding a transcript as an alternative to sound files as a way for people who are hearing impaired, such as my mom, to access and understand what's going on. But there are other, some perhaps less obvious, situations in which the alternative may be appreciated.

"forced quiet" environments

Offering text alternatives to sound clips or captioned movies not only assists people who are hearing impaired, but avoids the annoyance (or trouble!) factor in places where people must work closely together (such as open offices) or where quietness is requested or enforced (such as libraries and classrooms).

slow modems or older equipment limitations

A sound, graphic, or movie file takes significantly more time to download than a text file. Offering text alternatives gives people with slow modems or older, less-powerful equipment a choice to spend the time waiting for a larger file to download or not.

timed access

Not everyone has unlimited access to the Internet at a flat rate. Although there are package deals available from some of the big online services (Prodigy and CompuServe) for example, there are still tons of people who end up paying an hourly rate after a certain number of "free" hours. For users who have to watch the clock, time is of the essense. Faster-loading pages and information in lower-K formats are more financially advantageous. If they remember your site among the throng of your competitors as the one that offers them a "faster" option, they'll probably be back.

how accessible do you have to be?

The web is an international forum for information exchange. To be considered a conscientious site designer, must you therefore create a version of your site in French, Dutch, Japanese, and Hebrew? What about Greek, or the multitude of Native American languages? Should you offer both an American English version and a British English version? Do you have to worry about making your site accessible at all? Well, there are no laws that say you have to, just as there's no law that says a grocery store has to sell more than one brand of food.

evaluating your audience

You or someone on your web site team is probably responsible for a marketing strategy to figure out how to best serve your viewership. This is just smart business, anyway. So only you, either by spending thousands of dollars on marketing surveys, or simply by gut instinct and reading the e-mail your site visitors send your way, know who your audience is and what they want and need. You may know that your audience is composed of people who have T1 lines and 21-inch, high-resolution monitors, with tons of memory and hard drive space, and suited up with the latest version of Internet Explorer.

But if you're not sure of your market, or have a wide-ranging audience (you sell books or clothing, or provide financial tips to customers), it's crucial to have a wide-ranging site. If you know that you have customers in France, it's wise to consider a French version of your site. If you know that school children may want to learn about the zoo animals you write about on your site, larger type, smaller paragraphs, and web pages that are viewable on a 9-inch Macintosh SE screen may be in order. The more you can do for the millions of potential viewers to your site, the better. This book will guide you through the necessary steps to point out potential access barriers, and enhance or change those areas to give your viewers the choices they deserve and, in turn, will give you the satisfaction of creating what you set out to in the first place: to provide information within an ever-growing medium in the most creative and beneficial way possible, and to reach as many people as possible with your message or product.

is this book for you?

Universal Web Design is for anyone—both the professional web designer and people new to the medium—who create and/or produce web sites, whether for business, educational institutions, entertainment, or other widespread information dissemination. If you're interested and concerned about reaching as many people in your market as possible *and* keeping them coming back, then we're on the same wavelength.

My goal in writing *Universal Web Design* is to help you enhance what you have to its fullest potential, as well as to create from a more universal outlook on the benefits these access options make in overall web design finesse. Even if you know everything about how to make GIF images as small as they can be in file size, you may not be aware of some of the barriers they cause for many people. At the same time, graphics can greatly enhance a web site's navigational and cognitive interpretation. This book aims to show you how to find a balance among elements that takes advantage of the technology, serves your viewers, and doesn't sacrifice design quality. Still with me?

what you need to know

The skill set necessary to take advantage of this book is minimal: it really helps if you know the basic concepts of HTML coding, and know how to edit a web page using whatever application you happen to prefer. Much of the software you need to experiment with and enhance your site is either on the accompanying CD-ROM or easily procurable online (and I'll tell you where as we go along)—or you may already have it.

Most important, I hope you possess the desire to make your site as accessible as possible using the principles and practices discussed in the book. I hope you like to experiment with different layouts and formats and technologies, even if you're not a techno-wizard.

how you'll benefit

There are numerous reasons I think learning about universal access design benefits you as a web designer:

■ You will be able to create accessible web sites suitable for reaching more people in your market.

■ You'll be a more well-rounded, marketable web site designer.

■ You'll be better prepared to comply with laws in relation to accessibility for employees with disabilities, or any sort of ADA or other legislation for fair accessibility to public information.

■ If nothing else, you'll be politically correct. (And we all know it's politically correct to be politically correct.)

■ If you're not sure how to measure your market or find out what kinds of browsers or modems viewers are using, you'll be able to cover your bases.

And

■ You may discover just how accessible your site already is.

what's in this book

chapter 1
elements of the web experience

> This chapter examines the three elements that determine the web site experience and the potential related problems. It also discusses your role as "educator" for your audience. How responsible are you for their experience?

chapter 2
navigational rules & options

> Here's where we talk guidelines about the navigational options to best enhance your visitor's trip inside your site, including using imagemaps, text links, design consistency, and icons.

chapter 3
graphic enhancements

> Besides discussing making graphics small and picking the right format, Chapter 3 talks about image tags, descriptions, thumbnails, captions, and other augmentations and proposed access standards.

chapter 4
page sizes

> How big is that browser in the window? Standard browser default window sizes vary, as do the monitor sizes of your audience. Chapter 4 shows how to make sure your layout is consistent through the variations and actually shows up on-screen.

chapter 5
text transformations

> Writing for the web may not be that different from paper, but its presentation must be edited uniquely for readability, navigation, and cognitive interpretation.

chapter 6
forms & functionality

Even though a lot of browsers support forms, alternatives are necessary for viewers to communicate easily with you.

chapter 7
putting it on the table

Chapter 7 discusses designing tables for faster loading and easy reading comprehension, as well as providing table alternatives.

chapter 8
frames

People love 'em, people hate 'em. Here's how to optimize your frames, provide helpful NOFRAMES information, and more.

chapter 9
sound bytes

Improve sound quality, provide the proper formats, and consider sound alternatives.

chapter 10
movin' & shakin'

Investigate the temptation and challenges of movie and motion formats, and how to make them work for you, instead of against your viewers.

chapter 11
color & contrast

If you can't read it, neither can they! Find out how to work with and without color, and test your site for readability.

chapter 12
the importance of html

HTML is an amazing "cross-platform" multi-accessible standard. How can you keep it that way?

chapter 13
the text-only option

"Text-only" doesn't have to mean boring. And it's not the "only" way to go for accessibility.

chapter 14
downloadables

Which are the most popular formats for particular files, and how can you provide the best mix?

chapter 15
accessibility review & resources

Take your site through a checklist of important accessibility issues.

chapter 16
WebTV

Is the future here? Learn about designing for WebTV and how designing for the WebTV viewer is different from designing for the Web.

chapter 17
assistive technology & legislation

Are you legally obligated to make your site accessible? You may not be now, but things may change.

appendix i
connections

Where do you turn to for more help? Check out this list of books, sites, organizations, statistical resources, tools, conferences, training, and more.

about the cd-rom

The accompanying CD-ROM is chock full of samples, software, browsers for testing your site, fonts, navigational buttons, plug-ins, and a lot of info for your library. Most notably it contains the text of this book, as well as the text of the Americans with Disabilities Act. It's cross-platform except, of course, there are some platform-specific applications, such as for Windows and the Mac.

the end is in site

Books, while cool to have on the coffee table, still take time to get there. Developments in this industry pop up nearly every day which, of course, means I'm going to miss some of them while this book is at the printer. For up-to-date information on accessibility issues, links to new software, and so on, please check out http://www.typo.com and follow the universal web design link. Don't forget to drop me a line at crystal@typo.com with your comments, ideas, and suggestions.

CHAPTER 1

> *"Beyond a critical point within a finite space, freedom diminishes as numbers increase... the human question is not how many can possibly survive within the system, but what kind of existence is possible for those who do survive."*
>
> — *Frank Herbert,* Dune

elements of the web experience

what you can and can't control

Just how do people experience the web? How do they get to and utilize the sites that they fall upon when they're browsing? As you may have guessed, there's no easy answer, given that there are currently tens of millions of web users and that the number of people accessing the net is growing every day. In order to best design your site for as many people as possible within your target market, you've got to examine the three major elements that determine the web site experience for a user:

- The access method by which the user connects to the web
- The person using the web
- The site itself

You also need to pay attention to potential problems relating to the web experience. As you'll notice, a lot of these elements overlap and affect each other, depending on the combination. Basically, we can sort of face this as a 10 million people = 10 million possible combinations.

Insight information

The three major elements that determine the web site experience for a user:

- The access method by which the user connects to the web

- The person using the web

- The site itself

Is your audience getting tired of being told what to do?

the access method

The first element that influences the web experience is *the way the web is accessed* by the user. The component that web designers seem most concerned with is the type of browser a person uses. You may have heard of that little company named Microsoft or that browser thing from Netscape. It's amazing that Microsoft's Internet Explorer and Netscape's Navigator have taken web browsing as far as they have. However, as entrenched as some of us can be in these ever-upgrading browsers and the "standards" that struggle to make it to the top of the designers' wish lists, there are lots of people out there who just aren't as eager to "download now!" the moment a new browser version is released. If you're like me, you don't like someone else telling you what to do, even if (or perhaps especially because) it's "for your own good," which translates to "do this my way, or get lost!" Although the percentage of people using graphical browsers is increasing, it's pretty well accepted that text-browser users will be around for a long time.

It's a pain to keep up with what Netscape and Microsoft and AOL and all the other browser companies are doing to stretch their browser's limitations and enhance their capabilities. And it's even more troublesome to have to worry about what your code is doing within the screen of each of their products, not to mention each version of their products. Netscape Navigator may show your images in the place you intended for them to show up, but AOL may stack all your images together on one side, one on top of the other, with all of the text underneath. The design factor of the site is all but rendered worthless. Other browsers, such as Microsoft Internet Explorer, interpret pages designed for Netscape Navigator almost to the exact pixel in some cases. Knowing what browser(s) your audience uses can determine the overall navigability, usefulness, and aesthetic value of your site.

the platform and configuration

The next factor in site design is the *platform* used. Even if everyone in your audience uses the latest version of Netscape, the Windows version makes some web pages look different from the Macintosh version. Default font sizes are different on-screen on different platforms, and monitors on the two platforms show colors differently (PCs tend to show colors darker than the Mac, for example). Unix or OS/2 machines running Netscape look

different, too. Default window sizes are also generally different in both width and height.

Which leads us to *the computer*. In this case, rather than talking platform, we're talking hardware—how much RAM, how much hard drive space, and how much data-crunching power your visitors have packed into their desktop or laptop computer. As a guideline, consider that Netscape recommends at least 8 MB of RAM for the Windows 3.1, 95, and NT versions of Navigator 3.0; 9 MB of RAM for the Macintosh version, and (gulp) 32 MB for the Unix version. The company has minimum requirements as well, but personally, I've never been able to run Netscape Navigator 3.0 with even the recommended amount of RAM with much success. Although the processor speeds seem a little more reasonable (386sx for the Windows platforms, 68020 for Mac), any of you who have ever tried to run this or many other new applications on your processors knows that you're in for some long waiting times, assuming you can get it to run in the first place. Educational facilities can't afford to replace all those text-based access terminals, or perhaps even the Mac SEs they bought 10 years ago. RAM, even at its lowest price, costs a bundle for multiple machines, and for some people, upgrading just their one machine is a serious investment. Is your audience likely to shell out for more techno-toys and power or to make do with the minimum?

Then of course, there are *plug-ins*, which also may demand a lot from a system. Plug-ins are the nifty add-on routines that have taken over the role of helper applications, jumping in to handle tasks that your browser can't do by itself, such as viewing QuickTime movies, playing certain animation formats, or playing sounds. Macromedia's Shockwave, one of the more popular plug-ins, will run on a 68k Macintosh and most PCs, according to the Macromedia technotes (http://www.macromedia.com/support/technotes/shockwave/browser/win/index.html). However, Shockwave requires that you have an FPU (floating point processor, otherwise known as a math coprocessor) in order to work. People with older computers may be left out because their system didn't include an FPU, or they haven't bothered to buy one.

These are only a few of the never-ending, always growing list of plug-ins that help us to view, hear, and play various web enhancements.

To keep up to date on all the latest plug-ins, keep an eye on BrowserWatch's Plug-In Plaza at http://browserwatch.iworld.com/plug-in.html.

monitors and displays

Monitor size and *bit depth* play an obvious part in how a site is seen and used. According to the GVU Sixth WWW User Survey[1] (http://www.cc.gatech.edu/gvu/user_surveys/), which had more than 15,000 respondents from Europe and the U.S., more than 99 percent of users have color monitors. According to the survey's analysis, 34.76 percent of those surveyed were unsure of their monitor's bit depth. Of those who did know, 38.16 percent reported 24-bit color, and 20.19 percent reported 16-bit color. If your color combination is such that it demands high-end monitors, then lots of detail, and possibly all the readability quotient, may be lost.

In the survey, 60.36 percent of web users reported that they owned normal sized monitors of 13 to 15 inches; 22.77 percent use monitors from 16 to 18 inches, and 6.20 percent of those who answered the survey browse the web using monitors from 19 to 21 inches. The survey goes on to say that European users owned more larger monitors than their American counterparts.

The ever-informative GVU WWW User Surveys can be found at http://www.cc.gatech.edu/gvu/user_surveys.

Again, default browser-window sizes differ, depending on the size of the screen. Even a one-inch difference can mean that a significant part of your page's content, navigational cues, or design is cut off. Resizing a window may seem relatively painless, but having to do it repeatedly is simply a pain.

The computer platform of choice affects the monitor's *display capability* as well because, for example, PC video cards and Mac video cards display at different gamma levels. At average settings, Mac monitors are "brighter" than their PC monitors counterparts. In other words, an image or color combination may look great on a Mac monitor, but dark, muddy, and unreadable on a PC.

speed and location

The most obvious determination of a person's ability to access the Internet is the *speed of connection*, whether by modem, ISDN, T1, or even faster than that. 28.8 Kbps modems lead the pack at 51.40 percent of the modem population in use, whereas 19.69 percent of users use 14.4 modems. Although 14.4 is now generally considered crawlingly slow, there's still a meager part of the population (just about half a percent) that use even slower modems.

Topping off the list of access methods is the *location* from which people are connecting. Depending on where in the world users are connecting from, they may have intermittent access time at best (whether they're in a country with bad phone service, subscribe to a too-busy ISP, or are accessing from a public facility, such as a college library). Their access time may also be limited by long-distance phone calls to the service provider. They could also be using someone else's system—the local library, a friend's computer, or one at school—and they have no control over what modem is used or how long they can stay online. The longer it takes for these users to download that 200k Shockwave file to their system, the less they are inclined to be happy with their visit to your site, especially if the Shockwave file is something they could really do without.

the person using the web

Ah… the people! The web audience is something else altogether. Every single person is different; every person has different abilities and levels of knowledge. Some people like frames or hate them; some people can tear their computer apart with one hand and put it back together blindfolded; others are petrified that touching the Delete key will wipe out their hard drive. In the web world, it may seem as though you can't please any of the people any of the time, let alone all of the people all of the time. In any case, here are some factors to consider when designing for your audience.

comfort levels

If your site demands a lot from your visitors—such as customizing their browsers to show specific fonts, downloading and installing plug-ins, changing monitor bit depth, you name it—you have to

consider your viewer's *familiarity* and *comfort level with technology*. If users don't know what "point and click" means or that they have to click inside a form box to type into it, they'll get easily frustrated. This doesn't mean that every site has to give people basic computing lessons; it just means that if you are gearing your site toward computer newbies, you better be prepared to guide them through any potential rough spots or avoid potential rough spots altogether.

language barriers

Because the web is available practically world wide, you may have to consider the language(s) that your visitors understand or may use as a *native language*. Obviously, if you're selling a product but your company doesn't ship to Portugal, you don't have to worry too much about translating all of your information into Portuguese. Or if you're designing a site for a U.S. university and all of the students must know a certain amount of English to attend the school, you probably don't have to make translating your information into every student's native language a priority. But translation is a consideration if you intend to market to a worldwide audience—even if it's accepted that English is a widely understood language. Considering the university example once again, you might consider translating introductory information explaining language requirements, topics of study, and online applications to other languages for potential students in other countries, for example.

Netscape Communications offers its site in 10 languages other than English. It presents access to these sites from its main home page at http://www.netscape.com.

International
Brazilian Portuguese Site
Danish Site
Dutch Site
French Site
German Site
Italian Site
Japanese Site
Korean Site
Spanish Site
Swedish Site

NAVIGATOR 3.01 NOW AVAILABLE IN JAPANESE, GERMAN, AND FRENCH
Get the world's most popular Internet client with high performance, ease of use, and advanced graphics capabilities. Netscape Navigator 3.0 introduces a number of exciting ways to communicate and share information over the Internet with a real-time phone and chat tool. The final Japanese, German, and French versions of Navigator 3.01 are now available. Purchase it today.

These headers are from Netscape's English, French, Dutch, Japanese, Korean, and Brazilian Portugese sites, respectively. For a company with such a widespread audience as Netscape Communications, these customized-to-the-customer sites aren't just a nice gesture, they are good business.

21

Yahoo! (http://www.yahoo.com) also creates sites for different cultures and languages, which are all accessible via its main screen. Note that even though these screen shots were all taken on the same day (before the U.S. holiday Valentine's day), the motif in each header is different depending on the country. Also note that the iconography within the headers are different depending on the country. These pages are for the U.S., France, Canada, and Germany sites, respectively.

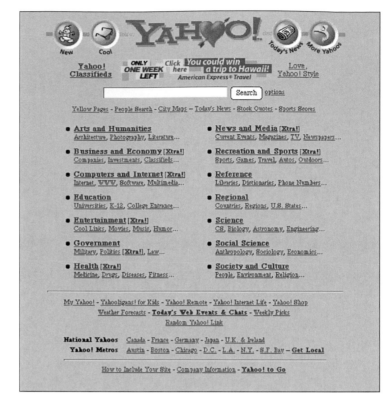

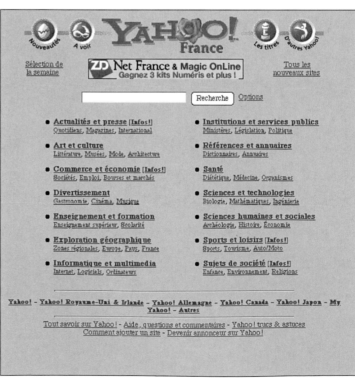

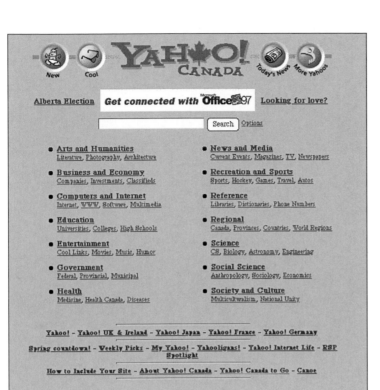

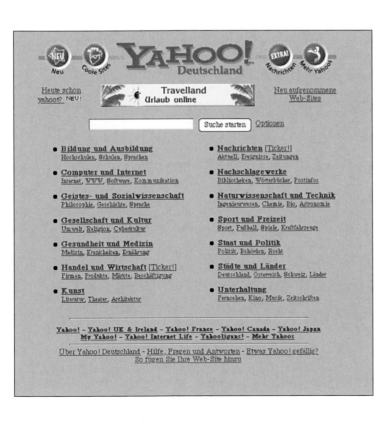

money matters

After realizing the hardware demands that some browsers require and that Internet access doesn't come cheap in some areas of the world (including many parts of the U.S.), you also have to consider the money your users have to spend for hardware. Although 28.8 modems are hitting the $100 mark nowadays, that's still a big chunk of change for some people, especially if they just bought a new computer that already has a 14.4 modem included. Hey, they just got one "for free;" who are we to ask them to lay out more cash? They just spent a couple hundred bucks on a 14.4 a year and a half ago, and they don't spend much time online, so spending more money on a modem doesn't make sense for them. They aren't as immersed in the net as those of us who thrive on it, and they're putting it off until they can justify the cost.

Then there's the whole issue of access time charges. Although most ISPs seem to charge around 20 bucks a month for unlimited access, there are still those who access the web through other online services, that, after a certain amount of free hours, start charging an hourly fee. And there are those people who have to dial in long-distance to their ISP, so the minimum they're paying for online access is about seven cents a minute, or about $4.20 an hour. This may not sound like much, but it adds up quickly. Because most people use the web 7 to 12 hours a week, this can add up to a $200+ phone bill before you know it.

time limits

The amount of money it costs to access the Internet for the user, of course, affects the amount of browsing time, along with other factors, such as where the web is accessed from (work, school, or home), how many other activities take priority over web browsing (family quality time, TV, studying, exercise, commuting, eating, sleeping, taking the dog for a walk), and so on. If users have web access from work only, they may have the pressure of a boss who thinks that "webbing" is a colossal waste of time constantly looking over their shoulder. Or at home, they may have a daughter who needs a bed-time story read to her, or a house that needs to be cleaned. All of these factors make time on the web of the essence. People want something or they need something, and they have limited time to get at it.

Another important consideration is the question of what information they're trying to get to. If the information is buried deep

within a site, in an area that's not too intuitive to get to, then they'll go to another site that offers the same, or similar, information. Some people like to casually browse around until they find something interesting that catches their eye; others log on for a specific fact and want to find it right away.

dislikes

Oh yeah, and then there are *people who* don't like frames; people who don't like imagemaps; people who prefer text browsers to high-falutin' graphical browsers. User preferences are hard to determine and difficult to fulfill. Some people are impressed with Shockwave and JavaScripts and unique GIF animations; others just want info, info, info.

disabilities

Another part of the audience that is often overlooked are *people with disabilities*, such as people with visual, hearing, cognitive, or physical impairments. The web and the net as a whole represent a world of information that is otherwise difficult to access. But as one person who wrote to me once said, "My friend who is blind says that trying to access information on some sites is like being blind all over again."

A person who is blind can't navigate a site that is dependent on graphics for navigational cues (unless there is proper use of <ALT> tags and other descriptions; more on that in chapter 3, "graphic enhancements"). A person with dyslexia may not be able to read long pages of text comfortably, or perhaps with comprehension at all, and may find graphical navigational cues much more preferable and usable than text cues. The definition of "disability" is far ranging indeed, but with 49 million people in the U.S. alone (that's one in five, if you're curious) with a legally defined disability, it should be enough to prompt most designers to consider alternate access to their site's information.

your site—the only factor you can control

Finally we're on to the one factor that you do have control over: your site. As a designer, whether you simply have a personal web page or you're a subcontracted freelancer or are on staff at a major business, you're ultimately responsible for how your site looks,

Note | **25**

Legally, as defined by the Americans with Disabilities Act (ADA), examples of physical or mental impairments include, but are not limited to, such contagious and noncontagious diseases and conditions as orthopedic, visual, speech, and hearing impairments; cerebral palsy, epilepsy, muscular dystrophy, multiple sclerosis, cancer, heart disease, diabetes, mental retardation, emotional illness, specific learning disabilities, HIV disease (whether symptomatic or asymptomatic), tuberculosis, drug addiction, and alcoholism. Read more about this in chapter 17, "assistive technology & legislation."

functions, navigates, and communicates to your audience. While taking into account the factors mentioned previously, the design and accessibility of your site—and what you can do to enhance, fix, and change it—is what this entire book is about.

The *amount of content* is important when determining how to split it up into digestible portions of information. Your decision about how much text and how many graphics to put on one page, for example, determines download time no matter what the speed of access.

How the content is presented in your design is crucial to a user's experience. If the design overwhelms the content, it comes across as gratuitous and doesn't serve the user efficiently. If design elements, such as large tables, Shockwave files, frames, animated GIFs, scrolling JavaScript messages in the status bar, huge imagemaps, or other large graphics disrupt navigation or don't serve to enhance an experience, then a site is not serving its audience wisely.

The *number of graphics* on a page, the size of graphics, and the type of graphics chosen by the designer greatly determine the overall downloading time of a page, the look of a page, and the interpretation of the site's information in some cases. The more graphics you have, the longer it takes for the information to download. The bigger the graphic, the longer it takes to appear.

Graphic descriptions, whether via <ALT> tags or other image description methods (such as "D" tagging, explained in chapter 3, "graphic enhancements"), can play a huge part in the understanding and navigability of your site to those who choose not to load images or who are incapable of loading them, whether it's because of browser choice (for example, a text browser such as Lynx) or because they can't use them (such as a person who is visually impaired in some way). Generally, text descriptions don't interfere with the design of a page, and their possible assistance to those people unable or unwilling to view graphics can mean a difference of whether they get to your site's information.

I'm very impressed with *web gizmos* such as Java and the growing number of plug-in dependent features that push browsers to their limits. But the kind of, and amount of, gee-whizzers you add to your site greatly affects the user—namely because the user has to usually download something to get your whiz-bang techno-wow-ism to work. Limiting these kinds of elements in your site gives your viewers less to deal with when they want to get at the guts of your information. If you know, for example, that most of your visitors don't use browsers that can view frames or other nonstandard nifties, then including such elements does not serve your customers in the most efficient or business-savvy way.

On the net, access is always under construction.

The National Center for Accessible Media, or NCAM, (http://www.boston.com/wgbh/pages/ncam/ncamhome.html) uses <ALT> tags to describe the images on its home page.

On the net, access is always under construction.

In addition to <ALT> tags, NCAM also provides image descriptions via D-tags for those who wish further text descriptions of an image.

Image Description:
Fading, blue-colored, block letters spell out: "N C A M." Words above and below it read: "The CPB/WGBH National Center for Accessible Media."
Return

Image Description:
Around the outside of a ring, the words "NII Awards" appear in a mirror image. The words "National Information Infrastructure Awards" are printed in a light band around the inner circumference of the ring, with heavy vertical lines filling the center space.
Return

Clicking on the D link takes the user to a separate page that includes image descriptions. Note that there is a link back to the page from which the description is linked.

Navigational cues and how people respond to them have been the subject of many a study. Although everyone is different, there are certain logical placements of navigational cues (such as stop signs) as well as recognizable icons (such as disk icons that represent downloadable files) or logical ways of handling unique graphical iconic intimations (for example, your home page is always represented by a picture of a blue dog) that make for an easily navigational site. If you put "back" and "next" arrows at the bottom on one page, for example, keep these same arrows on the bottom of all other pages. Most people can quickly acclimate to a certain cueing procedure, but they'll get flustered if you change icons or link placements. Consistency is key. If you have text links along the top of 12 screens, but screen 13 has the link on the bottom, you've just introduced an element of possible confusion and frustration.

The Britannica Guide to Black History (http://blackhistory.eb.com/) utilizes an effective mouse-over technique to show users where they are and where they are going.

When users pass the cursor over a date, the date changes color to a light blue. This notifies the users of the place they will go if they choose to click on the highlighted text.

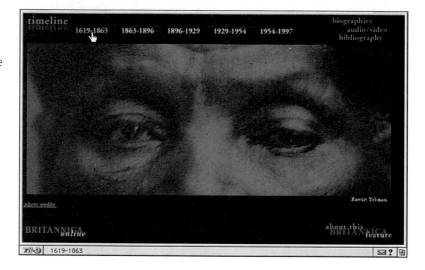

Note also that the information in the bottom status bar also shows the possible destination. Additional navigational clues such as this can only assist users in better navigating the site and knowing where they are and where they are going.

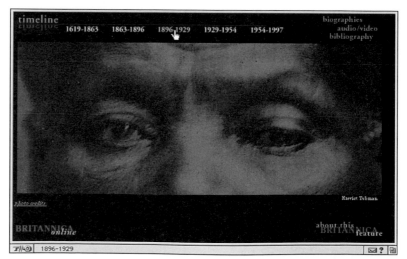

Once users have chosen what part of the timeline to enter, a golden marker shows them where they are, and the dates again highlight in blue to show where the click will take them.

the web designer as educator

How responsible are you for your viewer's experience? Some designers would say "completely!" and others would say "if they don't use what I want them to use to see my site, or if they can't find their way around, then forget 'em." Of course, these are the two extremes.

The only "right" answer for your site has to come from you. Think about your target market—or better yet, ask your target market what they think of your site. A site geared toward professional web designers probably doesn't have to spend a great deal of time explaining how to use the browser's "back" and "forward" buttons. However, a site that targets techo-beginners or those with a number of levels of computer savviness, such as c|net, does well to include a hefty "help" section, including its "navigation help" area (http://www.cnet.com/Help/navhelp.html), how to troubleshoot a browser (http://www.cnet.com/Help/browser-help.html), and general all-encompassing, getting-around-the-web info (http://www.cnet.com/Help/web.html).

30

c|net's navigational help area at http://www.cnet.com/Help/navhelp.html gives its visitors basic lessons in how to find their way around the c|net site. (Reprinted with permission from c|net: The Computer Network, ©1995-7; www.cnet.com.)

---

c|net

CNET.COM
home

Join now for FREE

Menu
NEWS
Radio

REVIEWS
Hot list
Just in
All comparisons
CD-ROM central
Best of the Web

FEATURES
Techno
How to
Digital life
Events

GAMECENTER

PERSONALITIES
Christopher Barr
Rafe Needleman
Mark Glaser
Don Steinberg
Movers & shakers

CNET TV
The shows
The hosts
Air times
Live studio cam

COMMUNITY
About CNET
Feedback
Member services
Posting
Today's poll
CNET jobs

RESOURCES
Software central
Glossary
Product finder

HELP

CNET Services
NEWS.COM
GAMECENTER.COM
SEARCH.COM
DOWNLOAD.COM
SHAREWARE.COM
MEDIADOME.COM

Marketplace
BUYDIRECT.COM
CNET store
Sponsors

back to top
CNET.COM

---

help   navigation help

navigation help

If you are a regular visitor to CNET.COM, you will notice a new navigation menu on every page. The graphical toolbars at the top and bottom are gone, but the content and the sections of the site are exactly the same. If you are new, maybe you aren't quite sure how to get around. Either way, we're here to explain how CNET.COM is organized and to offer tips for better surfing!

Surfing CNET.COM is easy. There are three kinds of links: text links, image links, and location bars.

In general, colored text indicates a link to the page suggested by that text. Click on the colored text, and you will be taken to another page. A blue link is one you have not yet visited; a green link is one you have.

Also, many images in CNET.COM are links as well. For the most part, images that are links will have a beveled edge (these example images are not linked, of course, so don't bother clicking on them):

This is a beveled bar:

about CNET

This is a nonbeveled bar:

about CNET

the index bar

As shown in the yellow index bar on the left, CNET.COM is divided into ten main sections:

News
Reviews
Features
Gamecenter
Personalities
CNET TV
Community
Resources
Help
Marketplace

You can use the yellow index bar to quickly link to any section, as well as to specific areas within each section.

Once you are in a section, you will see a bar that indicates exactly where you are in that section.

features   digital life

The yellow bar above tells you that you are reading a story in the *digital life* section of *features*. You can click on the *features* bar to go to the top-level page of *features*, or you can click on the *digital life* bar to go to a complete list of all of the *digital life* stories. Linking to sections works the same way throughout the site.

And when you want to go home--to the CNET.COM front door, that is--simply click on the CNET logo in the upper-left corner of every page.

If after reading this you have additional questions about how to surf CNET.COM, please send email to support@cnet.com.

Welcome, good luck, and have fun!

CNET.COM
home

Join now for FREE

Menu

NEWS
Radio

REVIEWS
Hot list
Just in
All comparisons
CD-ROM central
Best of the Web

FEATURES
Techno
How to
Digital life
Events

GAMECENTER

PERSONALITIES
Christopher Barr
Rafe Needleman
Mark Glaser
Don Steinberg
Movers & shakers

CNET TV
The shows
The hosts
Air times
Live studio cam

COMMUNITY
About CNET
Feedback
Member services
Posting
Today's poll
CNET jobs

RESOURCES
Software central
Glossary
Product finder

HELP

CNET Services

NEWS.COM
GAMECENTER.COM
SEARCH.COM
DOWNLOAD.COM
SHAREWARE.COM
MEDIADOME.COM

Marketplace
BUYDIRECT.COM
CNET store
Sponsors

back to top
CNET.COM

---

help :: browser troubleshooting

browser troubleshooting

What do I do if my images don't display?

Check the preferences setting in your browser to make sure that images are set to load automatically. If you get a generic icon for each image, auto-load is not set. You can click on these icons to manually load images.

If images still won't display after auto-load is set, there may be an error with the server or your connection. Try reloading the page or quitting the application and relaunching your session. You may need to restart your machine as well, especially if your browser app crashed earlier.

What if I'm not using a graphical browser?

Text-only browsers will get you through CNET, assuming that they are forms-capable. Lynx is forms-capable; other text-only browsers may not be. Try to pick up a nicer browser if you can.

How can I change text size, styles, and colors?

Go to the type styles dialog box in your browser (sometimes found in the preferences setting) to change style tags. During a session of browsing the Web, your browser will change the color of any text or graphical links you have already visited. (This will not work on image maps.)

Why won't movies/sounds play on my computer?

You must have an extension and a movie player application (such as Simple Player or Movie Player on the Macintosh; Windows comes with Media Player) or, for sounds, a sound player application installed on your machine. Some browsers ship players with their software; others are available from public ftp sites (visit our survival kit for helper software). Once you've installed a player, go into the preferences file in your browser, and tell it which application to use to view movies and/or play sound files.

If the player application won't launch, you can still download movies and sound files and manually play them outside of the browser. If the browser won't launch because there isn't enough memory, try quitting other applications and then downloading the files again. If the player still won't work, it may be corrupted, and you'll want to reinstall it or switch to a different application.

Some movie and sound files are quite large and may take a long time to download, depending on the speed of your connection. Some browsers allow you to interrupt and cancel a download (see the help section of your browser for details).

Back to CNET's front door.

c|net's browser help area at http://www.cnet.com/Help/browser-help.html assists visitors in how to best utilize and set up their browsers. (Reprinted with permission from c|net: The Computer Network, ©1995-7; www.cnet.com.)

c|net's basic web help page (http://www.cnet.com/Help/web.html) is a primer in the concept of the web, and leads visitors to outside informational resources on the basics of hyperlinked documents and the history of the web. (Reprinted with permission from c|net: The Computer Network, ©1995-7; www.cnet.com.)

---

help | the World Wide Web

the World Wide Web

The World Wide Web (W3) is a large-scale, networked, hypertext information system started by CERN, the European Laboratory for Particle Physics in Geneva, Switzerland.

The official World Wide Web home page is now run by the World Wide Web Consortium.

how the Web works--Hypertext Markup Language

All W3 documents are written using a structural language called HTML, which stands for Hypertext Markup Language. It's not a really complicated, geeky computer nerd kind of programming language, but a series of commands you put in your writing to make a Web browser (Mosaic, Netscape, and so on) display it with headlines, the pictures in the right place, and the links set properly.

Links are the underlined and/or colored text you see on Web pages. When you click on a link, it sends you to the URL (address) of the new page that was specified by the person who wrote the HTML. Pictures can serve as links, and links can call up sound, video or pictures, as well as new pages.

The W3 Consortium has good advice on how to make and post your own Web pages. NCSA also has a good beginner's guide to HTML, as well as all kinds of Web-related tutorials.

where to go on the Web

While the Web is now incredibly huge, it's not impossible to find things you're interested in. One place to start is the WWW Virtual Library. Dewey Decimal eat your heart out.

Another way to get started is by doing a search. Head over to SEARCH.COM to use the most powerful search tools available on the Web.

Back to CNET's front door.

c|net

CNET.COM
home

Join now for FREE

Menu

NEWS
Radio

REVIEWS
Hot list
Just in
All comparisons
CD-ROM central
Best of the Web

FEATURES
Techno
How to
Digital life
Events

GAMECENTER

PERSONALITIES
Christopher Barr
Rafe Needleman
Mark Glaser
Don Steinberg
Movers & shakers

CNET TV
The shows
The hosts
Air times
Live studio cam

COMMUNITY
About CNET
Feedback
Member services
Posting
Today's poll
CNET jobs

RESOURCES
Software central
Glossary
Product finder

HELP

CNET Services
NEWS.COM
GAMECENTER.COM
SEARCH.COM
DOWNLOAD.COM
SHAREWARE.COM
MEDIADOME.COM

Marketplace
BUYDIRECT.COM
CNET store
Sponsors

back to top
CNET.COM

How much do you have to teach your visitors? Do you have to teach them how to use a web browser? How to use your site? How to look at an image? Part of c|net's mission, of course, is to teach people about technology, so it's easy to see how the preceding help files are applicable to the audience.

Obviously, if your site has a lot of elements as well as a number of unique navigational and informational cues (custom icons, plug-ins, special password-protected areas, and so on), even an experienced web user could probably use a bit of assistance at first. You don't need to include extensive help files on every page, but it wouldn't hurt to have "help" a click away in another dedicated page or section.

Note 33

Remember to provide alternative support if you think a part of your audience uses browsers that don't support forms, or they can't access forms for one reason or another. Read more about this in chapter 6, "forms & functionality."

the web designer as student—listening to your audience

How do you figure out how to serve your audience? The most crucial way is to *listen*. This means either surveying your proposed audience beforehand or including feedback mechanisms in your site once it's up and running. These can be as simple as MAILTO: tags that are directed to the appropriate person on your web team or feedback forms that ask specific questions about specific topics. And it doesn't hurt, if you're able to handle it, to include phone numbers or your snail-mail address as well, especially if you design for a commercial site.

You don't have to act on every single person's wishes when they contact you, but it's sure to give you some food for thought. For example, when a good chunk of visitors to my site complained that one of my pages just took too long to load (it was in a really long table), I split the information into two pages. It didn't hurt the design, and it added functionality for all visitors. On the other hand, I've received only one negative letter regarding the color scheme of my site (they didn't like the light text on the black background).

It wouldn't have been prudent to change my entire site just for this one person. Instead, I wrote back and suggested that if they were interested in the site's contents, they could change their browser preferences—and then I explained how to do it.

Another method for gathering information about your audience and its views on your site is to organize focus groups. Focus groups, whether informal or done by a professional focus group organization, can give you valuable feedback. Depending on the format, you can watch people of various interests and skill levels interact with your site, listen to suggestions, ask questions, and learn from their experience.

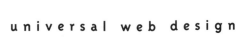
34 Digital Dreams (http://www.
surftalk.com/) offers both a
simple form…

Guest Book & Mailing List

If you would like to be notified of updates to this site, such as new software and demos, enter your full name and e-mail address in the fields below and press the "send" button. We will then notify you of any significant changes to this area via e-mail.

Please let us know how you found this site and any additional comments you may have.

Full Name:

E-mail address:

Comments

[send]   [clear]

DREAMS ▪ SHOWCASE ▪ HOT LINKS ▪ SOFTWARE ▪ CREDITS

Copyright © *Digital Dreams*, 1995. All rights reserved worldwide.

…and a MAILTO: link for visitors to
send comments and questions.

dreams@surftalk.com

| Send Now | Quote | Attach | Address | Stop | Crystal W <crystal@typo.com> |

Subject:

▽ **Addressing**   **Attachments**

Mail To: dreams@surftalk.com

Cc:

You could try writing to newsgroups or mailing lists that have members belonging to your target market and asking them to check out your site. Remember, however, that commercial posts, or posts that sound like sales pitches of any sort, are highly discouraged and could give you a nasty reputation before you even launch the site. It's a good idea to spend a lot of time lurking on a list and be sure to read the list FAQ (if there is one available) before you make a post. To find out about mailing lists that are relevant to your target market, try a few searches at the Liszt Directory of E-Mail Discussion Groups (http://www.liszt.com/). For USENET newsgroups, try out DejaNews (http://www. dejanews.com/), a searchable database of groups and archived postings.

Note   35

Focus groups are generally like blind taste tests. The participants don't know who is sponsoring the test. Instead they see products, or in this case sites, from a number of companies and compare them.

The Liszt Directory of E-Mail Discussion Groups (http://www. liszt.com/) hosts a searchable database of more than 65,000 e-mail groups worldwide.

36 DejaNews (http://www.dejanews. com/) gives you access to archived USENET postings and information about thousands of newsgroups.

Surveys are another way to gather info. It never hurts to ask your site's visitors what they think of any given layout, idea, or the quality of your site's content. Just keep in mind that asking lots of personal questions—especially given the hesitancy that most people have about the security of transmissions over the net—can be a pretty big turn off. Ask only what you really need to know and explain why you need to know it.

market research resources

If you'd rather leave the research to the experts than do your own, you have plenty of reports from which to choose. It seems that there are countless numbers of organizations that do studies on the web and its users—from marketing firms to Internet magazines to those companies doing business on the web.

Unfortunately, some of the reports cost some big bucks, and the rest are hard to find results from—not to mention that no one seems to be able to agree just how many people are using the Internet or just how to reach them. If you work for a corporation whose web presence is of significant marketing or product distribution value, then these elusive reports may be worth the price. Don't be surprised, however, if the numbers don't match up among the surveys. Each organization gathers its research in a different way, bases numbers on different procedures or projections, and some are highly sophisticated whereas others are informal.

One of the popular freebies available includes the one I've mentioned throughout this chapter, the *GVU WWW User Survey* (http://www.cc.gatech.edu/gvu/user_surveys/). This survey covers such areas as web and Internet usage habits, consumer preferences and behaviors, attitudes and opinions on politics, privacy, webmastering, Java and HTML authoring of HTML and Java, and web service providers, among others. I like this one because it's voluntary—people fill it out if they like, and fill out only those sections that are of interest. And GVU's survey sample is usually a pretty healthy turnout (more than 10,000 responses).

A few statistical details can be found at the *CommerceNet/Nielsen Internet Demographic Study* site (http://www.commerce.net/work/pilot/nielsen_96/position.html), or you can go the Nielsen Media Research page directly (http://www.nielsenmedia.com/). There's a lot of stuff to wade through to actually find numbers (such as lots of statistical terminology about how the surveys were taken and their information compiled), but eventually you'll get to the numbers that might interest you, such as Internet users' age groups, viewing time, geographical info, and other basic stats.

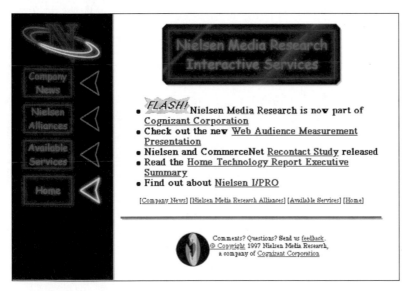

Nielsen Media Research is well known for its demographic information gathering.

BrowserWatch (http://www.browserwatch.com), a site from iWorld, compiles and provides the browser statistics of its own site, as well as provides news and rumors about the industry, and a fairly up-to-date catalog of plug-ins and the wide world of browsers.

An interesting—and perhaps cynical—look at the web population game is the *Inter-NOT: Online & Internet Reality Check* by Bruce

Note

The *Inter-NOT: Online & Internet Reality Check* (http://www.newnetworks.com/) provides much information in its survey executive summary. Obviously, no matter what the statistical informational-gathering process is for each analysis and no matter what the result, the industry should at least be able to agree that no one really knows just how many people are out there using the Internet and the web.

Kushnick of New Networks Institute (http://www.newnetworks.com/). Kushnick's report claims that there never were 25 million U.S. computer users online, which has been the generally accepted number of online users thrown about the industry, and that there aren't 25 million people online today. Kushnick's analysis comes up with a maximum of 15 million U.S. computer users online, which is about 10 percent of U.S. households and 6 percent of the total population. At press time, this report had a cover price of $495.

summary

I know this isn't a comforting chapter at all—there are just so many elements that affect your site's layout, perception, design, navigation, and overall usability that it's always going to be a challenge to meet the needs of your audience. Not to mention the fact that there are very likely some audience members who have no idea what it is that they want from you and your site! It's always a good idea to offer a line of communication to your audience and to encourage the use of any sort of feedback mechanism you can employ. And listen to these folks. Chances are you'll get some unreasonable demands, or notes from people who rag on you because you chose the color blue for your background. Don't let this stop you from listening to the good suggestions.

And remember, you can't control two of the three major categories of factors that affect the web site "experience"—the access method and the people themselves. It doesn't hurt to ask your audience to use Netscape Navigator 3.0 if that's the best way to view and navigate through your site, but it can be annoying if a significant percentage of your target audience doesn't have the capabilities to use it. Demanding compliance of high-end gizmos just for the sake of techno-wowdom doesn't communicate a professional image. Instead, design with and for your audience, and you'll find that you'll get much better results. On with the show.

CHAPTER 2

> *"The first principle of human interface design, whether for a doorknob or a computer, is to keep in mind the human being who wants to use it. The technology is subservient to that goal."* [1]
>
> — *Donald Norman*

navigational rules & options

guidelines for getting around

A major concern of many of the computer industry's research and development teams is human–computer interface interaction. These teams pursue the designs of applications that are most effective, which in turn make users more comfortable and productive with an application. If a person can't figure out how to operate, navigate, or even launch a software product (let alone turn on a monitor), then they aren't likely to be very productive—or happy, for that matter. Technophobia is a real condition that many people who are new computers must deal with in our lovely technotronic society.

But these people aren't alone in their struggles. Even highly experienced computer and net users can have difficulty navigating a new application or web site. Having used a number of applications, experienced users come to prefer certain applications over others for their ease of use and functionality, and they develop certain expectations when using other techno-products. This doesn't necessarily mean that "you can't teach an old geek new tricks," but what it does mean is that if the old geek can't get anything from site in a manner that is intuitive or productive, you've lost a viewer.

---

[1] *This opening quote is by Donald Norman, author of* The Psychology of Everyday Things, *in his interview for* The Art of Human-Computer Interface Design, *which was edited by Brenda Laurel, ©1990 Apple Computer. Interview by Howard Rheingold. Addison Wesley, ISBN 0-201-51797-3.* The Design of Everyday Things, *formerly published as* The Psychology of Everyday Things *by Donald Norman, ©1988 Donald Norman. Doubleday/Currency, ISBN 0-385-26774-6.*

Note

There are four key elements to designing for effective navigation—whether via iconography, terminology (the way directions are worded), imagemaps, or you name it.

- **Familiarity:** How acquainted is your audience with this picture, action, or structure?

- **Consistency:** Is there cohesion among your elements? Do the images work well together, and do they mean the same thing in the same areas?

- **Simplicity:** Is your message distinct, clear, and uncomplicated?

- **Clarity:** Is it clear what your icons and other navigational aids represent? Or do you have to explain them at length?

Typical application or desktop icons include those shown here which represent a calculator application, an inserted disk, a notepad, and a Rolodex-like information accessory.

As I said in my first book, *Web Concept & Design*, someone who is comfortable getting around your site will probably spend more time there and enjoy the experience that much more. I used the following example.

Although web design and implementation isn't the same as developing, say, an ergonomic toaster, the same basic human-thing interface rules apply. Namely, no matter how innovative, beautiful, or zippy your site or appliance is, if it doesn't serve the person using it, it's no good. And yes, we are at the mercy of whatever browser our viewers happen to be using. This we can't help, but we can make the information we present accessible in a familiar—yet unique—method. Nearly every part of your navigational structure—icons, symbols, imagemaps, and overall design—will base its success on four key elements: familiarity, consistency, simplicity, and clarity.

icons & metaphor

Since the advent of graphical user interfaces for both computer operating systems and the applications that run on them, computer users have been clicking on icons to start or complete a task that was previously accomplished by keystrokes. As you may have noticed, if you look at your computer's desktop right now, you probably have a few icons up there that represent a number of different kinds of actions, files, and storage mechanisms. Most standard icons are metaphorically based on the physical product they represent. Text documents are represented by pieces of "paper" that you can place in a garbage can when you want to delete them, for example, and the CD-ROM you have in your drive is pictorially represented as a shiny, round disc or a CD-ROM drive image—which differentiates it from the floppy disk icons, icons of various removable media icons, and so on.

In general, iconography (a pictorial representation of the action to be performed) usually aids and reinforces a user's comprehension. Sometimes we get in trouble when we use an icon that might, in fact, perfectly mimic its tangible counterpart, but the user isn't familiar with the actual physical product or action represented.

For example, a common icon used to represent either "click here to receive mail" or "click here to send mail" is the loaf-of-bread-shaped, metal, North American mailbox on a post with its little red flag sticking up. Another North American symbol used is the blue, four-legged, rounded-top mail receptacle found on street corners

The typical U.S. mailbox icon would be modeled after the blue, four-legged mailbox found on many street corners, or the rounded-top metal canister with a red flag.

and in front of U.S. post offices. But, hey, what do mailboxes look like in the U.K.? For one thing, they are red, have a flat top, no legs, and are cylindrical. In Japan, mailboxes are also cylindrical but instead have a rounded top. Some mailboxes are even shaped like animals. If someone isn't familiar with the shape and color of an item, then a simple picture won't describe what it needs to.

Note

The definition of "metaphor" is: a figure of speech in which the context demands that the word or phrase not be taken literally, such as *the sun is smiling*; a comparison that doesn't use the words *like* or *as*.

Common sayings such as "I have butterflies in my stomach" are metaphors. "Life is like a box of chocolates" is a simile because it compares one thing to another using the word *like*. If the saying were "life *is* a box of chocolates," it would be metaphor.

Mailboxes around the world come in different shapes and colors. Using an icon based on one from one country may not communicate the right message to your audience.

Tip

When designing, you may be tempted to create an icon for every single link choice. However, this can get you into trouble if you need to create icons that aren't easy to represent with graphics. Links such as "Search" and "Help," for example, lend themselves to understandable icons, but an item such as "January Sales Newsletter" is more difficult to represent visually. If you need too much explanatory text with an icon, you may just be better off to skip the fancy icon and simply use text!

So when faced with the challenge of finding icons that represent the same thing to all people, what can we do? First of all, don't rip your hair out in a frenzy. It probably can't be done—there are just too many different cultures, languages, and preferences among the human population.

It's very likely your market doesn't need to have a series of mailbox icons from around the world. A simple remedy is to use an envelope icon because most mail sent is placed in an envelope before mailing. Ideally, with the help of explanatory text, your

42 Using a worldwide icon, such as an envelope for "mail," communicates the right message to as many people as possible.

icons will be representative enough to illustrate what you want them to, as well as explain enough to make the audience curious enough to click on them.

symbols & symbolism

Symbols are different from icons. They usually need to be learned or explained in more detail than icons do. Symbols are generally more abstract than an icon, and they may represent something intangible. A good example of this is the symbol for radiation.

This symbol, or variations of this pattern, indicates "radiation."

Because radiation is impossible to see, there are two options to choose from when forming its representation: the word *radiation* itself or the symbol that has become the standard to represent the presence of radiation.

Another common universal symbol is the circle with a diagonal line across its interior, often placed over a word or other symbol, meaning either "don't do what's in this circle" or "no *xxx* allowed."

Some symbols have become universal. Many countries and cultures have adopted certain symbols to represent certain items, places, or situations. Others, although widespread, could mean one thing to one person, and another to someone else.

So how do we "teach" people to recognize a symbol that represents what we've intended it to represent? People become familiar with certain concepts in these ways:

It's commonly recognized that this symbol means "don't do this" or "whatever is inside this crossed circle is not allowed," such as "no dogs allowed" or "no smoking."

analogy: a symbol on the icon represents something we are familiar with, so we assume it means something similar to what we know

trial and error: we click on something to see what it represents, does, or where it takes us, and we assume that it will do that in the future

example: we learn by being told what something is, by someone who knows

To teach someone via analogy, your icons must be based on something your viewers are more than likely to be familiar with. For example, many people would recognize a musical note or another symbol related to music, and probably would assume that any links or pages represented by these symbols have something to do with music. Using these symbols, or combining them with others, would probably lead the viewer to assume that the new symbols are also associated with music. Of course, in order for someone to have learned what the initial symbol represents, they would have had to learn by example.

A helpful layman's guide to symbols, as both a reference and historical tool, is the *Dictionary of Symbols* by Carl G. Liungman (©1991, ABC-CLIO, ISBN 0-87436-610-0). Whether you're looking for ideas to create buttons for your site or a logo that represents your site's mission, chances are, in the past 20,000 years or so, someone has come up with a symbol or two that already represents the idea you're shooting for.

Using either one of these symbols would most likely lead your viewers to assume that the associated link would be related to music in some way.

Trial and error is just that: viewers who are curious enough will click on anything to see where it goes or what it does. As long as the symbol is used consistently throughout the site and as long as what viewers "receive" when they arrive at a page is clear—and also assuming that your viewers are curious—the trial-and-error lesson should work. Trouble can occur, however, if a number of unfamiliar symbols are used or if the symbols look too much alike.

Learning by example is a lot easier for me; I like to be told what something represents, even if I go to a site repeatedly. This doesn't mean you need to include lengthy explanations next to each symbol or icon in every instance it appears. You can add a couple of words to the initial screen in which the symbol first appears, or add information to a "help" or "about this site" area.

At some point in our lives, most of us learned that the gold rounded-top *M* symbol represented the McDonald's restaurant chain. But first, someone had to teach this to us. In this case, it was probably the word "McDonald's" on each sign, or in each television commercial. However, if you see the symbol by itself, you probably think "McDonald's" (what the M represents) and not "Hey, there's a gold, rounded-top M."

These atypical icons are labeled with text to aid the user in navigation.

navigation bars

Navigation bars are usually thin, graphical imagemaps that give the user the option to click to another area of the site. Navigation bars that are unobtrusive not only help people get around, but they assist in orientation, reminding users where they happen to be in the entire scheme of things. Many designers change the appearance of the button in cases in which it appears in the areas it represents. Its color appears either "grayed out," "pressed" (recessed), or its color has been changed ("You are here!").

An important factor in the success of your navigation bar is to use consistent placement. If it's at the top of the page in one area and then the bottom of the page in another area, you're demanding unnecessary "work" from your viewers.

Personal Finance

| AT HOME | CREDIT CARDS & LOANS | CHECKING |
| SAVINGS & INVESTMENTS | HOMEBANKING | STUDENT UNION |

This navigation bar from the Bank of America site (http://www.bankamerica. com/) always appears at the top of the page within its relative section.

Also, buttons on the navigation bar should be placed in the same order on every page. Can you imagine using a program that randomly moved its buttons and commands around?

the imagemap conundrum

Imagemaps, if done well, can be highly effective navigational aids. They not only give you the opportunity to design a page to your liking, but they also allow you to forego the limitations of default font choices given to us by the medium.

Obviously, a person who is blind (or who has images turned off or who uses a text browser) can't use images to navigate a page. This is why I've always advocated including text navigation bars. However, client-side imagemaps allow for ALT tags to be included in link descriptions of a given AREA. These ALT tags (which appear as text) can be read by a text browser or a "speaking" browser or other screen reader. If you really don't want to include a text navigation bar, this is a helpful navigational alternative.

It's also important to create imagemaps that make sense. Just as in the other options mentioned here, such as icons, the active places on your imagemap—unless you're doing a treasure-hunt sort of site—should represent where the click will take your visitors, graphically or via text. Placement of clickable areas shouldn't be so close together, or so small, as to make it difficult for the areas to be accessed. In other words, make the areas discernible from one another so that a not-so-well-aimed mouse click will take your visitors to the proper area.

text navigation

Again, we can fall back on good old text as a navigational alternative to reach the largest number of people. The text option is an ideal companion to imagemaps and is usually unobtrusive to the page design. Generally, the text option includes the exact same links that are in the imagemap, and placed in the same order that they are in the map, *if* there is a logical order to the layout of the imagemap.

clicking required

You can arrange "click on me" text links in a number of ways.

■ Separate them with "bars":

About our company | Product Information | Sales Information | Contact Us

■ Separate them with graphics (but keep in mind that those who can't see the images will have the [IMAGE] filler show up unless you provide an ALT tag such as ALT=" " or ALT="o"):

About our company • Product Information • Sales Information • Contact Us

■ List them on separate lines:

About our company

Product Information

Sales Information

Contact Us

[FamilyFinder Index | Genealogy Mall | Genealogy How-To | Genealogy Classifieds]
[World Family Tree Project | Home Pages | Genealogy Message Boards | About Broderbund]
[Home | Guest Book | Credits | Download a Free Demo | Tech Support | Help | Search]

Family Tree Maker (http://www.familytreemaker.com/) offers a text navigation option at the bottom of each page.

when clicking isn't an option

Most of the navigational systems on web sites are designed around
the assumption that the viewer is able to use a mouse to click on
certain icons. However, there are people who are unable to use a
mouse to navigate a page. This category of users includes people
with physical disabilities that prevent or restrict their arm or hand
movement, people who are visually impaired to a point at which
they are unable to see the screen, and people who don't use a
graphical browser. Viewers who can see the screen using a graphical browser yet are unable to use a mouse appreciate the availability of keyboard equivalents to mouse actions. Common examples
of this type of page navigation are pressing the arrow keys to
move a pointer and certain key combinations that activate the
desired action.

Although Windows 95, the Macintosh, and the two most popular
browsers (Netscape Navigator and Microsoft Internet Explorer)
provide a number of accessibility functions via keyboard commands, your web site basically functions as an application *within*
an application. Even though some people may be able to navigate
your site via a voice recognition system or via keyboard commands, most are still dependent on the simple logical and
descriptive structure of your text links.

For example, Microsoft Internet Explorer 3.0 has a number of
accessibility features. Pressing the Tab key, or the Tab key with
other keys (such as Ctrl), for example, gives the user access to text-
based links, image-based links, forms elements, client-side
imagemap links, and movement among frames. Movement among
frames is dependent on the FRAME tag's positions in the HTML
document—an order for which you are responsible. And although
Explorer lets the user view and access areas via ALT tags, if your
ALT tags don't make sense, neither will the navigation of your site.

If you'd like to test your site using keyboard commands, drop by the Microsoft Accessibility Support page at http://www.microsoft.com/windows/enable/default.htm and learn more about the commands it supports.

summary

Logic plays a key role in creating a well-designed navigational system for your site. It doesn't need be complicated; as a matter of fact, the simpler, the better. Remember your own experiences with applications and even noncomputer examples, such as street signs, road maps, and VCR instructions. What makes sense? What makes you react with the thought "What the hell were they thinking when they did *this*?"

To anyone who wants to get anything from your site, simple navigation is essential. If you don't know what you want to head toward, you won't know how to get there. If you know what you want, but don't know how to get there, you're just as sunk.

You can probably assume that most of the people new to the web have at least had a bit of experience pointing and clicking. Eventually, they might learn by association that when they click on an underlined word, they will probably be led somewhere. They may also learn by association that the little pointing hand that appears over a link may take them somewhere. This is much easier to assume because it is the general standard among graphical browsers and other applications. The more people do something, the more they—in theory—become familiar with it.

Using unique iconography and symbols is very cool, but if you've chosen a symbol that could possibly be out of the realm of your market's knowledge, be sure to provide an explanation in some area of your site—either on the top level in which the icons or symbols first appear or in a separate help section. And make sure there's a clear path to the "help" page.

Overall, your design will be most successful with a balance of familiarity, consistency, simplicity, and clarity.

Accessibility Support

Microsoft's Accessibility Support page offers a number of resources, including how to set up Windows for people with disabilities and how to create specific keyboard commands for navigating Internet Explorer.

CHAPTER 3

> *"I am always doing that which I can not do, in order that I may learn how to do it."*
> — *Pablo Picasso*

graphic enhancements

making a picture-perfect web site

Can you imagine what the web would look like without graphics? It would be far less visually stimulating with long, dense pages of straight text. Graphics are great for leading the eye to places, or through places, as well as for illustrating product features, story elements, or simply the skill and creativity of the artist who created them. They can be staid pointers to information, beautiful story illustrations, or entertaining eye candy. They are also being more widely used in place of text for navigation and for more design control over how type appears and page elements fall. Luckily, there are a few standard graphic formats that most web browsers support. The most common are GIFs and JPEGs.

Unfortunately, graphics foster many common troubles as well. The problems surface in two circumstances: when the graphics are too large for visitors to patiently wait for them to load (whether the graphics are large by web measures or the person trying to view them has a slow connection), and when graphics can't be viewed by the user (either because they use a text browser, choose not to load graphics, or they are visually impaired to a degree that they are unable to see the graphics). As you can imagine, pages that are composed of many graphics—especially if your site relies on them for visitor navigation—could potentially render the site useless.

Your page runs the risk of unbelievable boredom without graphics, but it would possibly be awkward or slow with them. So what's a designer to do? Relax. A few simple enhancements to your graphics and coding, as well as some text alternatives, could be the balancing factors between having an attractive and accessible site.

use the right graphic format

Although GIF and JPEG are both excellent graphics compression formats, you shouldn't use them interchangeably because each has slightly different merits.

gif

GIF (Graphics Interchange Format) is a type of image compression file format that has been used for many years to make bit-mapped images smaller for more efficient online transfer and viewing. Its compression scheme is effective, especially in images that use a lot of flat colors (which means images that aren't photographs or that have a lot of dithering) because it bases its compression on the number of times pixel colors change along the horizontal axis of an image. The more colors, the bigger the GIF. Because GIFs are indexed images, however, they can hold no more than 256 colors. Although this limits file sizes somewhat, it means GIF isn't the best format for photographs or images that originally have more than 256 colors.

The top wow! image was saved as a GIF; the bottom as a JPEG. GIFs work best for flat art, such as this, because saving flat art as a JPEG can cause color "warping."

A close-up shows that the JPEG version (shown on the right) of the flat art is relatively mottled, especially near the edges of the various color shapes.

GIFs come in two different flavors: GIF87a and GIF89a. The smaller of these is GIF89a. When you save an indexed image as a CompuServe GIF (one of Photoshop's file formats), you're saving it as a GIF87a. To save it as a GIF89a, which is necessary if you want to make your image transparent or interlaced, you'll need an application that will either translate your image (such as Transparency for the Mac or LView Pro for Windows), or you'll need a plug-in that will save as GIF89a (such as Boxtop Software's PhotoGif plug-in for Photoshop.)

Interlaced 89a GIFs appear on the screen as a whole, in lower resolution blocks that rev up to full resolution as the file loads. Although this may be preferable to watching an 87a GIF draw downward from the top of the image to the bottom as it loads, some designers think the effect is ugly when interlaced images do their chunky thing. It does, however, help viewers determine whether they're in the right place or whether they want to wait for the rest of the image to download. By the way, interlaced images don't load any faster than their regular counterparts; they just load differently.

An interlaced GIF draws itself in "chunks" as the image loads, rather than from top to bottom.

jpeg

JPEGs are generally best used on images with lots of subtle changes in colors, such as photographs. The format's compression method is lossy—it cuts out colors and approximates them with colors that are within the palette. The good thing about JPEGs is that you can save images in 24-bit, and when they are decompressed on someone's screen that happens to have their monitor set to that specific resolution, they'll be able to appreciate the greater resolution.

The top knife-and-tomato photograph was saved as a GIF; the bottom was saved in JPEG format. JPEGS are better for photographs than GIFs because GIFs tend to dither the many colors in a photographic image.

A close-up of the tomato (GIF on the left; JPEG on the right), shows the blockiness, or dithering, of the colors when a photograph is saved in GIF format.

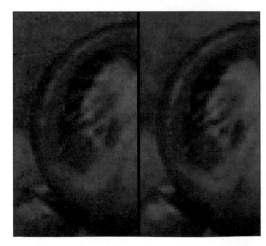

A JPEG can save even more space in an image file than GIF, but can take more time to decompress. So if your image file is about the same size when saved in JPEG or GIF (and it looks acceptable as a GIF), save it in GIF format. If you do, then those people with slower modems will receive the data bit more quickly.

think smaller

Making images smaller in file size encourages their downloading and viewing, whereas very large images can take way too long to load up and check out. If you're like me, patience is not only a rare virtue, it's most scarce when you're cruising around with a browser trying to get at some important information quickly.

check your colors

One guaranteed way to make your images smaller is to use the 216-color, browser-safe color palette. Available from http://www.lynda.com/hex.html, the browser-safe palette can be downloaded and opened in the graphics application of your choice. You're able to use the eyedropper tool to select colors from the palette as you need them.

The benefit of using browser-safe colors is that they don't dither on-screen. Dithering, or spotty, rough colors, is what happens when a color is not available in the browser's palette and the browser tries to compensate by combining pixels of other similar colors to make up for the missing color, possibly making colors look splotchy and uneven. At press time, 216 colors are all the most popular browsers can handle, so having any more than 216 in an image wastes bandwidth. When your image is strewn with dithers, it will also probably add some significant and unnecessary kilobytes to your image.

Your image may look great in Photoshop or other graphics programs, but check it out in whatever browser you're using before you put it on your site. In most browsers that will view GIFs or JPEGs, for example, you can go to your File menu and choose Open Local File or Open File to view a GIF or JPEG that's on your hard drive. Remember to also set your monitor to 256 colors; if its resolution is higher, you won't get an accurate representation of what your image will look like on others' screens.

54

physical image size

Unless you're right-on with every photograph you take, chances are you will have to crop some of it, or cut off the edges, in order to make it a more potent image.

Numerous ways exist to crop an image to help make it more relevant to the story, as well as cut down on the physical file size of the image. Cropping is also good for creating thumbnails for large images, which is discussed further on.

Here's the original image, before cropping.

By cropping out some of the background of the image, we can better focus on the main point of the photo, as well as cut down on total file size.

Although you can simply cut out a part of the image to use as your cropped image, it's a good idea to pay attention to the area of the image you are calling attention to. First of all, how crucial is the background to the overall purpose of the picture? Is the subject's head the main point you need to get across in the image or is it what the subject is holding that's important?

save images as 72 dpi

If you use a digital camera or scanner to bring your artwork or photos into your computer, or you use artwork that has appeared in print, you easily can reduce file size significantly by changing the image resolution to 72 dots per inch. Although saving an image at a higher resolution does make an image look better on paper and on high-resolution screens, it doesn't hold true for web pages. Web screens show us images at a whopping 72 dpi, and that's it. If you're going to be manipulating an image, working with a larger file is okay. It almost always looks better to shrink an image than to enlarge it.

Here are examples of how the dots per inch of an image determine its byte size.

Obviously, you can keep on cutting away at a photograph or image to further save in file size, but make sure that you're keeping enough of what you want the photo to show.

This 3 by 4.4 inch (798×1164 pixels) photograph of my sister Lois was scanned in at 266 dots per inch. Its file size when saved in JPEG format is a whopping 689k.

When the image resolution is cut down to 133 dots per inch, the file size is now 77k.

At 72 dots per inch, this JPEG takes up only 17k. Because computer monitors are limited to viewing images at 72dpi, then there's no reason to keep images at their higher resolution, unless you are offering them for download for other purposes (such as for a photo and image library from which you offer images that others can use in printed documents).

It's true that, for example, a 45k image isn't all that big of a file to begin with, but chances are you have more than one image on your page—and all of these images add up, resulting in long download times. You also have to factor in the file size of the accompanying text file. Think of it as using a credit card: All those "little" charges can add up to a whopping bill.

make images smaller

Besides cutting down in dots per inch, the dimensions of an image significantly determine its file size. This example shows an image at various sizes, and its resulting JPEG file size.

a.) The original image of Winona, at 4.5 inches wide by 7.4 inches tall, is a 42k JPEG.

b.) At 4 inches wide, the image falls to 38k.

c.) When we hit 3.5 inches wide, the image size is 33k.

d.) At 3 inches wide, the image is 29k.

a.)

b.)

c.)

d.)

e.)

f.)

g.)

h.)

e.) 2.5 by 4.2 inches (180×304 pixels), results in a file size of 24k.

f.) At a width of 2 inches, there's a file size of 21k.

g.) At a width of 1.5 inches, we're down to 18k.

h.) Even though Winona weighs in at only 15k at one inch wide, it's starting to get a bit difficult to see any detail in the image.

thumbnails

A time-saving solution that works well for such highly graphical sites as galleries, photo albums, or catalogs is a menu of thumbnail graphics as an entry point to view larger versions of the images. Offering the choice of images a person can download is a nice touch, especially if there are a lot to choose from.

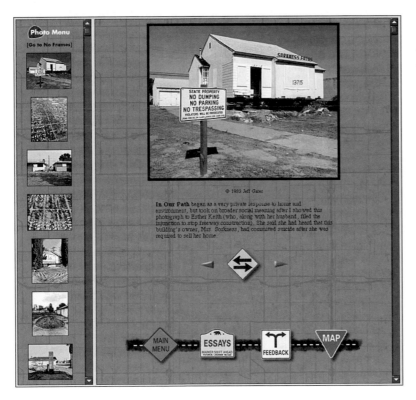

Photo-dependent sites, such as Jeff Gate's In Our Path (http://www.tmn.com/iop/index.html), show thumbnails—shrunken replicas of each of the photographs—of each available image in a section in one frame of the page. The frame on the right shows whichever image has been selected.

In my site's gallery and other areas where there are many possible images to view, I generally create thumbnails of each image and let the viewer know how big the full-size image is. Users can then decide whether they want to continue on. In the example figure, the K sizes are next to each respective image. Note that users are given a line of directions—"Click on a thumbnail below to view a larger image"—just in case they haven't encountered this kind of layout before.

Each image in this gallery page is a thumbnail—a shrunken-down version—of the actual image. Next to each thumbnail is the size of each respective file.

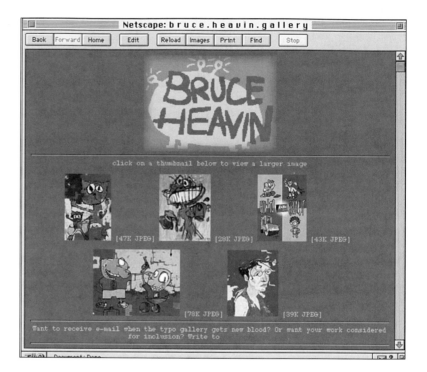

An alternative to simply shrinking images to make thumbnails is to crop a certain part of the image to give a teaser of the total image. If it's a photograph, check out the previous section about cropped images. If it's a piece of digitized or computer-generated artwork, ideally with clearly identifiable details, there are more creative ways to use cropping as an effective tease into the full image.

Here's the full scale image that we want to tease people into viewing.

Teasing viewers into a page using sections of a piece of artwork can be beneficial in a number of ways. First of all, you're saving valuable K size on a page, which is the obvious reason. Second, it allows for the detail of the image to show up, if only a small part of it—see the difference between a smaller-sized image and the cropped version. Last, it allows you to make thumbnails a consistent size, which makes for an easier design that incorporates a number of differently shaped or sized images.

When providing links or thumbnail images that lead to larger images, consider providing size, format, and time warnings, such as "20K JPEG; 30 seconds at 14.4." If you're not sure of the time it takes to download a particular size image, check the chart in chapter 14, "downloadables."

specify image size

By specifying the image height and width in your tag, browsers such as Netscape will keep placeholders for those images while the rest of the page loads, which gives the page the appearance of loading faster. In addition, the textual part of the site maintains its layout if the user opts never to load the graphics. To add the height and width attributes of an image, use the following:

```
<IMG SRC="sam.gif" WIDTH=215 HEIGHT=285>
```

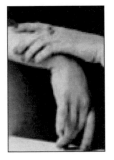

The numbers refer to the size of the image in pixels. If you're not sure of an image's size, open it up in your graphics application and change your unit of measurement to pixels. If you have Netscape Navigator, open up the image file. With either version,

you choose Open File from the File menu. Mac users then hold down the mouse button on the image and choose View this Image, whereas Windows users click on the image with the right mouse button and choose View this Image. When the image comes up in Navigator, its dimensions will appear in the title bar, height by width in pixels.

be descriptive

As the web has grown, so has the number of graphically oriented sites—as well as the dependence upon graphics for navigational and content comprehension cues. The most serious problem that has popped up because of this has been the barrier to those people who are blind or visually impaired. Not only is it impossible for them to see a page or access its information if it's solely graphical, but certain color combinations, such as those with low contrast, also make viewing particular pages difficult for those with colorblindness (see chapter 11, "color & contrast," for more on color combinations in relation to visual impairments).

Pages that are text-based are usually accessible to people who are blind because the text usually can be read aloud by a screen reader—a piece of software that scans the text on-screen and reads it aloud—if the user's computer supports sound. However, keep in mind that the HTML coding structure that you've used can make or break a visually impaired user's experience. This is discussed in greater detail in chapter 12, "the importance of html."

The best compromise between an all-text, but accessible site and a graphics-intensive site is to offer descriptions of your graphics. You have several options for doing so.

providing ALTernatives

Nowadays web designers often include <ALT> tags with their images, although there are plenty of sites out there that still don't include them. The <ALT> tag inserts a line of text in the place of a graphic if the graphic doesn't load (whether images are turned off or the user's browser doesn't support graphics).

When you include <ALT> tags, it's extremely important that they make sense. Simply including the name of the graphic, such as buzz.gif, or something as generic as "click me," doesn't

Note

The Archimedes Project at Stanford University (http://kanpai.stanford.edu/arch/arch.html), in conjunction with the Western Blind Rehabilitation Center (http://wwwcsli.stanford.edu/arch/GUI/wbrc.html), and the TRACE R & D Center (http:// www.trace.wisc.edu), are hosts to the WEB ACCESS 97 conference, which will be held as a part of the Sixth International World Wide Web Conference. (If by the time this book gets into your hands, the conference is over, look for it next year! Find info at http://wwwcsli.stanford.edu/arch/GUI/.) While past conferences have concentrated on graphical user interfaces (GUIs) in general, WEB ACCESS 97 focuses its attention on the world wide web and its GUI.

The GUI access conferences were inspired by the fact that while GUI interfaces such as the Mac and Windows, and all of their subsequently developed applications, have helped many people get over the hurdle of technophobia (by using pretty icons instead of having to type arcane commands), the growing impulse to make everything graphical also increases the barriers to those people who are blind or visually impaired.

communicate anything useful. Basically, your <ALT> tag should describe the function of the graphic, especially if it is a link, rather than describe the graphic visually.

Here are some <ALT> tag suggestions for common graphical elements:

element	do	don't
bullets	<IMG SRC="bullet.gif" ALT="*"> <IMG SRC="bullet.gif" ALT="o">	<IMG SRC="bullet.gif" ALT="This is a round red bullet">
horizonal rules	<IMG SRC="rule.gif" ALT="--">	<IMG SRC="rule.gif" ALT="section separator"> <IMG SRC="rule.gif" ALT="this is a three-inch wide horizontal rule">
company logo	<IMG SRC="logo.gif" ALT="Typo company logo">	<IMG SRC="logo.gif" ALT="says typo.com in large blue courier font on black background">
graphical counters	<IMG SRC="counter.cgi" ALT="visitor count">	n/a
drop caps	<IMG SRC="C.gif" ALT="C">	<IMG SRC="C.gif" ALT="this is the capital letter C">
GIF "spacers" (invisible GIFs used for precise placement of text & graphics images as links)	<IMG SRC="space.gif" ALT=" "> (just insert a blank space between the ALT quotemarks)	<IMG SRC="space.gif" ALT="this is a gif spacer">
	<A HREF="aboutus.html"><IMG SRC="about.gif" ALT="read about us">	<A HREF="aboutus.html"><IMG SRC="about.gif"> (this returns simply [LINK] to a text browser, which tells a viewer nothing) <A HREF="aboutus.html"><IMG SRC="about.gif" ALT="click here to read all about the people at our company">
large images	<IMG SRC="picture.gif" ALT="employee group photo - 42KB GIF">	<IMG SRC="picture.gif" ALT="5 inch color photo of our employees">

proposed D tag standard

D tagged, or described, images use the letter D as a link to a page that contains a textual description of an image. Ideally, there should be a link back to the graphic from the end of the image description. Proposed (and utilized) by The National Center for Accessible Media (http://www.boston.com/wgbh/ncam) as an enhancement to <ALT> tags, D tags are implemented in a few sites.

I've run across some arguments against D tags—namely that a description of an image for someone who is unable to see images really does them no good. This argument has some basis to it I suppose. For example, if I've never been able to see the sky and you tell me that your graphic is "sky blue," what good does that do for me?

My response is to write useful descriptions—those that convey the purpose of the image, as well as descriptions of the actual image. Unlike <ALT> tags, D tags can be as long as you like, affording you the opportunity to describe an image and its purpose as fully as necessary.

Describing the look of a company logo may be of little value to someone who can't see it, but highly descriptive text is valuable in the case of those images that either assist in navigation, or complement a story.

Make sure you are thorough and specific in your descriptions. Consider the figure on the next page as an example. The image by itself does have some obvious elements—six people are sitting on some steps; the temperature is probably kind of cool because they are wearing relatively warm clothes. But what kind of help is this description? In theory, you're not going to include random photographs or images that simply state "here are six people sitting on some steps." Perhaps it's an illustration for a story about teenage girls and their feelings of not belonging (note the girl to the left is not paying particular attention to the camera). Perhaps it's a documentary about families that lived on farms in Vermont in the 1960s while the hippies did their thing. Maybe it's a close family, maybe it's not. Your story line, and what the graphic has to do with it, plays a large part in how the image is described textually.

captions

Photo and image captions should be written with the same slant as image descriptions—with a clear purpose. If the viewer can see the image, it is not necessary to describe the content of the image if it is obvious just by looking at it ("This is a tree next to a river."). Use the D tag format to describe a picture visually, and use a caption to describe an image contextually.

JPEG images are capable of including comments in their files that are readable by text browsers. Include these comments when you can. Some image editors, such as GifConverter for the Mac, allow you type in JPEG image comments in a pop-up dialog window, and some text-only browsers permit viewing of these comments.

What this image says to you may be different from what the web designer intends. A detailed description would clear the confusion.

imagemaps

Obviously, a person who is blind, has images turned off, or uses a text browser, can't use images to navigate a page; for this reason I've always advocated including text navigation bars. However, client-side imagemaps allow <ALT> tags to be included in link descriptions of a given area, and <ALT> tags (which appear as text) can be read by a text browser, a "speaking" browser, or other screen reader. If you really don't want to include a text navigation

bar, the following code may be a helpful navigational alternative. Each AREA SHAPE reference refers to an area on an imagemap that has been selected to link to a particular page, and each one of these references can include an <ALT> tag.

```
<MAP NAME="XYZ_CO">
  <AREA SHAPE="shape1" COORDS="x,y,..." HREF=
  ➡"./about.html" ALT="about XYZ Company">
  <AREA SHAPE="shape2" COORDS="x,y,..." HREF=
  ➡"./clients.html" ALT="XYZ client list">
  <AREA SHAPE="default" NOHREF>
</MAP>
```

Unfortunately, server-side imagemaps don't provide this option so other navigational options must be provided, such as a navigational bar below the image (see chapter 2, "navigational rules & options," for more information on creating a navigational bar).

summary

You don't have to sacrifice graphics to make them work to their fullest potential as navigational and contextual accents to your site, or even if they are the pinnacle element of your site. Adding <ALT> tags is the bare minimum you should strive to accomplish. Those images that need more of an explanation can be handled with D tags or captions.

The most crucial element of the images themselves is their file size. Cut down on file size as much as possible to avoid adding unnecessary downloading hassles for your viewers.

CHAPTER 4

page sizes

if it don't fit, fix it

Browser window sizes are, quite simply, a pain in the butt. As a designer, you can hope that your audience will resize their windows to the width and height you want them to, but because you have no power over another person's monitor or preferences, you've just got to spend a lot of time praying.

If you're not the praying type, try planning. Although default browser window sizes vary, there are "typical" sizes that you can design for and test on to see whether your design works within a certain constraint.

smallest common denominator

Probably the smallest screens you have to work with are certain notebook or PowerBook screens (or perhaps those on all-in-one compact Macintoshes, such as the Plus, SE, and Classic). Notebook screens generally run in the 9- to 12-inch diagonal range. Consult the table on the next page for a sampling of notebook monitor sizes.

Screen Dimensions of Portable Computers

Brand Name	Model	Diagonal Size
Apple	PowerBook 190	9.5"
Apple	PowerBook 190cs	10.4"
Apple	PowerBook 1400	11.3"
Apple	PowerBook 5300 series	10.4"
Compaq	Armada Series	10.4", 11.3", 11.8"
Compaq	LTE Series	10.4", 11.3", 12.1"
IBM	ThinkPad 365ED Series	10.4"
IBM	ThinkPad 560 & 760 Series	11.3" or 12.1"
Toshiba	Satellite Series	11.3"
Toshiba	Tecra Series	12.1"

Will a huge part of your audience be accessing the web via portable computers? If you're hosting a site that is business, travel, or sales oriented, that could be the case. Students and magazine editors who bring their work home with them on portable machines are also large parts of the small-monitor crowd. I've been writing a lot of this book on a grayscale Mac PowerBook with a 9.5" screen.

Here's what my home page looks like on my PowerBook at the default screen size. Its content is cut off both horizontally and vertically.

Even if the browser is expanded to full size on the PowerBook screen, we have only 8.625×5.25 inches (621×380 pixels) in which to work. The window size is made smaller if there are any scroll bars present.

What can you do with a small screen like that? The following table lists the maximum sizes you can design to fit in the default screens on my little PowerBook 190. Keep in mind that if you have more content vertically or horizontally, scroll bars will eat up some screen space.

Small-Screen Specs

Browser	Pixels (W×H)	Inches (W×H)
Microsoft Internet Explorer	497×324	6.903×4.5
NCSA Mosaic	512×377	7.111×5.236
Netscape Navigator	490×337	6.806×4.681

Not much to work with, huh? Especially if you're used to working in paper design, where you've got complete control of the end result.

popular screen sizes

If your audience isn't largely made up of portable users, chances are you'll have another four or five inches of screen to work with. The standard 14-inch monitor still seems to be the monitor of choice for most web users, although generally (judging by walks through mainstream computer and electronics stores, and browses

through computer catalogs) the new systems usually include 15 inch monitors. The most affordable large-sized screen is the 17-inch monitor, although the desktop design crowd prefers 20- to 21-inch monitors.

Unfortunately, if your background is in graphic design, chances are you're currently working on one of the larger screens. By now you may have guessed that your resulting design, if designed for the default browser screen that appears on your window, won't fit properly on smaller monitors.

If your market is wide-ranging and consumer-oriented, the safest bet is to create your pages for a 14-inch monitor. Your approximate page default size in this case would be 7 inches wide and 3.66 inches deep (504×264 pixels).

With a design space possibly limited to 7 inches × 3.66 inches, be prepared to make a splash with the amount of space you have available.

this is all the room you (may) have...

so you better make the best of it.

However, if you follow the stats—which claim that most people use PCs (versus other platforms) and that most people still use Netscape Navigator—it may be safe to base your design size on basic Netscape default window sizes.

According to *Web Developer* magazine (http://www.webdeveloper.com/), the stats in the following table are default Netscape Navigator browser window sizes (in pixels) according to resolution.

Default Netscape Window Sizes

Screen Resolution	Macintosh Window	PC Window
640×480	470×300	580×300
800×600	470×430	580×430
1024×768	470×600	580×600

paper versus screen

Any size of screen you design will force you to deal with the differences of designing for a screen instead of paper. Typical paper design is taller than it is wide, and computer screens are the other way—wider instead of taller. The key to design is not the size of the page, but the balance of the page's elements. The same sort of design guidelines that are used in print publications, such as using grids or columns, also work with web page design.

Controlling the layout of a web page is a *bit* more difficult than a paper layout because of the limits imposed by the medium, as well as the viewer's choice of monitor and browser.

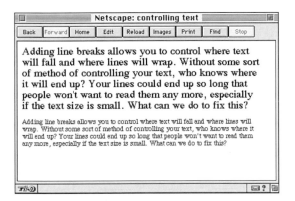

At different window widths, uncontrolled text is manipulated by the window size alone. Depending on the width of the window, that's where the text will wrap.

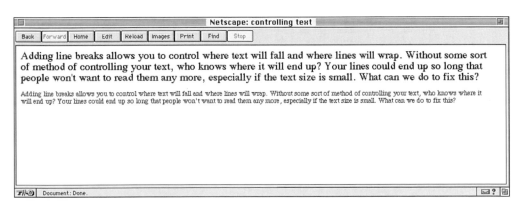

If there are no tags inserted that control where text will break, the text will flow and wrap at whatever width the viewer happens to have his window sized to. Tables (more on these in chapter 7, "putting it on the table") and frames (chapter 8, "frames") can help, as well as adding line break codes, <BR>, or paragraph breaks, <P>, to break your text consistently no matter what the window size.

70 Using a table with a set pixel width (in these examples, WIDTH=504, WIDTH=252, and WIDTH=171, respectively) to control the width of your text guarantees that no matter what the size of the browser window, the text will appear at the width you specify.

```
<TABLE WIDTH=504 BORDER=1 BGCOLOR=ECECFF>
<TR>
<TD>
<FONT SIZE=+2>
Adding line breaks allows you to control where text will
fall and where lines will wrap. Without some sort of
method of controlling your text, who knows where it will
end up? Your lines could end up so long that people won't
want to read them any more, especially if the text size is
small. What can we do to fix this?
</FONT>
<P>
Adding line breaks allows you to control where text will
fall and where lines will wrap. Without some sort of
method of controlling your text, who knows where it will
end up? Your lines could end up so long that people won't
want to read them any more, especially if the text size is
small. What can we do to fix this?
<P>
</TD>
</TR>
</TABLE>
```

However, if you use a table with a set pixel width and the window is made smaller (or its default size is smaller) than the table WIDTH specification, text is cut off from readers unless they are able to make their browser window larger.

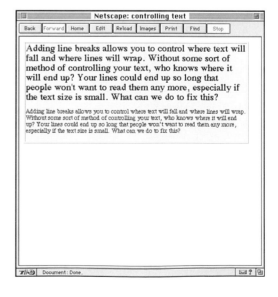

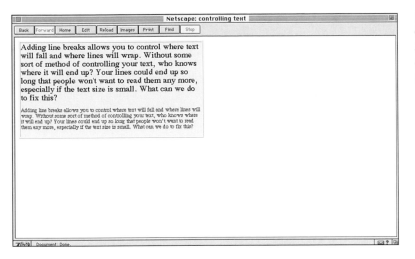

Using proportional-width tables (shown here with WIDTH=100% and WIDTH=50% respectively) ensures that text blocks will not be cut off when the window is resized.

Because proportional-width tables readjust their width as a window is resized, text lines start wrapping at different points again. Depending on the size of your text, this could make text lines difficult to read.

Using the line break tag (<BR>), your lines become single-spaced and break where the tag is entered.

```
Adding line breaks
<BR>
allows you to control
<BR>
where text will fall
<BR>
and where lines will
<BR>
wrap.
```

> Adding line breaks allows you to control where text will fall and where lines will wrap.

Paragraph breaks (<P>) at the end of each line make your text appear double-spaced.

```
Without some sort of method
<P>
of controlling your text,
<P>
who knows where it will end up?
<P>
```

> Without some sort of method
>
> of controlling your text,
>
> who knows where it will end up?

Single-pixel transparent GIFs are growing in popularity to assist designers in controlling specific line spacing and text placement. In this case, adjusting the image HEIGHT puts specific space among the lines of text. By adjusting image placement and WIDTH specifications, the single-pixel GIF could be used for indents and other text placement tricks.

```
Your lines could end up
<IMG SRC="1pixel.gif" ALT=" " HEIGHT="5"><BR CLEAR=ALL>
so long that people won't
<IMG SRC="1pixel.gif" ALT=" " HEIGHT="15"><BR CLEAR=ALL>
want to read them any more,
<IMG SRC="1pixel.gif" ALT=" " HEIGHT="25"><BR CLEAR=ALL>
especially if the text size
<IMG SRC="1pixel.gif" ALT=" " HEIGHT="35"><BR CLEAR=ALL>
is small. What can we do
<IMG SRC="1pixel.gif" ALT=" " HEIGHT="45"><BR CLEAR=ALL>
to fix this?
<IMG SRC="1pixel.gif" ALT=" " HEIGHT="55"><BR CLEAR=ALL>
```

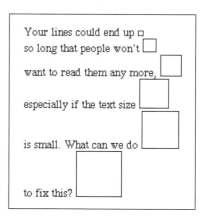

using javascript to resize browser screens to your specifications

If your users' browsers support JavaScript, you can determine the size the browser window appears on-screen. For example, if you want your window to fit within a 14-inch screen at a size other than the default of 504×264 pixels, you can specify the window size using the window.open command's width and height parameters. For example, if you design for a 640×480-pixel screen, you can set the window size to be 640×480, thereby filling the screen. If you design for a bigger screen, you can still set the 640×480 window but your viewers will have to scroll to see the entire page.

In the following JavaScript, I've set up a button that opens my home page, http://www.typo.com/, within a specified window size of 504×420 pixels.

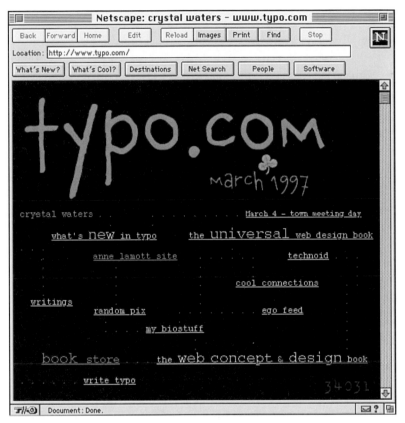

The resulting custom window using JavaScript to size it to 504×420 pixels.

```
<HTML>
<HEAD>
<TITLE>Creating a custom-sized Window</TITLE>

<SCRIPT LANGUAGE="JavaScript">
function makeNewWindow()
{
var newWinObj =
window.open('http://www.typo.com/','newWin','toolbar=1,
➡location=1,directories=1,status=1,menubar=0,scrollbars=1,
➡resizable=0,copyhistory=0,width=504,height=420')
newWinObj = window.open('http://www.typo.com','newWin')

</SCRIPT>
</HEAD>
<BODY>
```

```
<FORM>
<INPUT TYPE=button value="Testing Custom Window Size"
onClick="makeNewWindow()">
</FORM>

</BODY>
</HTML>
```

Another method of setting a specific window size is to include the following script with the splash page that contains your site's initial URL. The script opens a new page with a height of 422 pixels and a width of 633 pixels.

```
<HTML>
<HEAD>
    <TITLE>Opening a Custom-Sized Window Automatically
    ➥</title>

<SCRIPT LANGUAGE="JavaScript">
var doubledip = true
function makeNewWindow() {
        var newWindow =
window.open("http://www.typo.com/welcome.html",
➥"TypoMainPage","status,height=422,width=633")
        if (doubledip) {
                doubledip = false
                makeNewWindow()
        }
        doubledip = true
}
</SCRIPT>
</HEAD>

<BODY onLoad="makeNewWindow()">

</BODY>
</HTML>
```

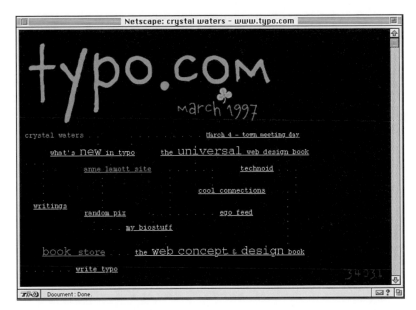

The resulting custom window, using JavaScript to size it to 633×422 pixels.

monitor tests without the monitor

You can't be sure of how your design will look on a given monitor until you test it at that size. No, this doesn't mean you have
to buy a fleet of monitors. If you have access to multiple monitors, great. If you don't, try creating an HTML file with the following JavaScripts to mimic the various sizes. Notice that the
width and height numbers change according to the size I happen
to be testing. Simply click on each button and enter the URL
you'd like to check.

```
<HTML>
<HEAD>
<TITLE>Creating a custom-sized Window</TITLE>

<SCRIPT LANGUAGE="JavaScript">
function makeNewWindow()
{
var newWinObj =
window.open('http://www.typo.com/','newWin','toolbar=1,
➥location=0,directories=1,status=0,menubar=0,scrollbars=0,
➥resizable=0,copyhistory=0,width=504,height=420')
newWinObj = window.open('http://www.typo.com','newWin')

</SCRIPT>
</HEAD>
<BODY>
```

```
<FORM>
<INPUT TYPE=BUTTON VALUE="Testing for 497 by 324"
onClick="window.open('http://www.typo.com/','497x324',
➥'toolbar=no,directories=no,menubar=no,width=497,
➥height=324')">
</form>

<FORM>
<INPUT TYPE=BUTTON VALUE="Testing for 640 by 480"
onClick="window.open('http://www.typo.com/','640x480',
➥'toolbar=yes,status=yes,scrollbars=yes,location=yes,
➥menubar=yes,directories=yes,width=640,height=480')">
</FORM>

<FORM>
<INPUT TYPE=BUTTON VALUE="Testing for 800 by 600"
onClick="window.open
('http://www.typo.com/','800x600','toolbar=yes,status=yes,
➥scrollbars=yes,location=yes,menubar=yes,directories=yes,
➥width=800,height=600')">
</FORM>

</BODY>
</HTML>
```

Using this JavaScript, you can create your own browser window test page. You decide what elements to turn on and off (such as the browser status bar, the location buttons, or toolbar), enter the page you want to test (replacing my "http://www.typo.com"), and the size window you'd like to try out, and you've got a tool in which to test various monitor sizes without having to buy a bunch of monitors.

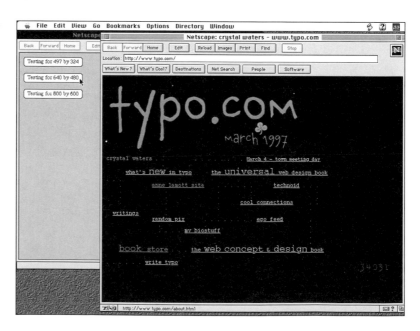

what's inside

Monitor size also affects what you are able to include in your window. Planning ahead, however, can help you avoid some common trouble spots when working with text, background images, and navigational cues.

text and page size

Times Roman is the default proportional typeface that is commonly used on the web and is the default font for most browsers. For Netscape Navigator, Times Roman's default size is 12 points. For Microsoft's Internet Explorer, the default size is "medium," or 14 points. The default monospace typeface tends to be 12-point Courier, and default monospace type in forms or input boxes tends to be 10-point Courier.

In most browsers, the user can change his default typefaces to suit his fancy. This can wreak havoc on your intended design, of course. You can request users to use certain typefaces, as well, but if users have to change their typefaces every time they come to your site, or if they don't have the typefaces you require, they might be "inspired" to move on.

There's not a lot you can do to help those who need to increase your type size to be able to read it more easily. Test your site's text at various sizes; see how well it reads, and how graphics interact with the text. If you've used forced line breaks to make text wrap with <BR> or <P> tags at certain points, reading might become extremely awkward due to the text being larger because the tags have been moved.

You can make all text part of graphics files for ultimate control over text appearance, but that starts up a whole new ball of wax. The problems include risking large file sizes and longer download times for users, as well as yet another barrier to those who are visually impaired. For tips on making images more accessible, see chapter 3, "graphic enhancements."

navigational and organizational cues for oversized pages

If you insist on making pages that are larger than standard default browser windows, don't forget the navigational elements (see chapter 2, "navigational rules & options"). This is especially crucial on framed sites. Even though scroll bars might look ugly, they are imperative for proper page navigation when there is a possibility that the design might not fit on a person's screen.

summary

There's no easy way to make every page fit every monitor. Surveying your market and finding out what size and quality of monitor the people in it are using, as well as their browser of choice, is your best bet. If you're not sure what equipment they are using, go with the smallest common denominator your design can afford.

CHAPTER 5

> *"If I had more time, I would write a shorter story."*
> — *Samuel Clemens*

text transformations

the words have it

Although you might not expect it to be, text on your web site can cause a problem for parts of your audience. The presence of text is not the problem; rather it is the appearance of the text. Huge chunks of text are sometimes jumbled together on one page with no apparent breaks. People with text-comprehensive impairments such as ADD (Attention Deficit Disorder) and dyslexia can have a rough time getting through a poorly organized site. Other people may get annoyed because they are forced to scroll, scroll, scroll to reach the information they want. As the designer, you can improve a site's content and organization, making it more comprehensible for all your visitors, and you can find inspiration in the old-fashioned printed page.

There's a reason that printed products—namely books and magazines—are printed on standard sizes of paper. These standard sizes occur because of the way paper is made and printing presses are manufactured. It's easier to read text in blocks that are limited by standard page sizes (not to mention that it's a lot easier to carry an 8-by-10-inch book than it is to carry, say, one that is 2-by-5 feet wide). These "blocks" we affectionately call "pages" also serve another purpose: navigation. We can look up a topic, or remember a place where we left off reading, if the pages have numbers on them.

I know that it's pretty rare to find page numbers on web pages (because it's more of a three-dimensionally laid out format), but you can use the standard page length rules—or at least limit the amount of pages worth of text on one web page. Not only is scrolling through vast fields of text annoying, but such pages take a lot longer to load, resulting in your users having to wait longer to get the info they want. Also, various platforms, browsers, and

processor speeds create numerous variations of how fast the user can navigate or move through a document. What you think of as a slightly lengthy block of text may seem like a monologue of epic proportions to a user with a slow system and simplistic browser.

It's pretty rare to find page numbers on web pages, which is one reason why it can be hard for a viewer to find his way around a site.

```
01                                 .  introduction intro  . . . . . . . . . . . . .
   02                           .  non-web examples                               .
      03             . . . . .  . accessible by mistake
         04              . . .    will design be sacrificed?
            05        . . . . .   image access enhancement example
          ⌐∿06       . . . . . . common problem site elements                     .
             07   . . . . . . . . additional access advantages                    .
               08  . . . . . . .  how accessible do you have to be?               .
            . .09 . . . . . . .   is this book for you?                           .
          . . . .10 . . . . .     what you need to know                          .
        . . . . . .11  . . .      how you'll benefit                             .
      . . . . . . . .12     . .   what'll be in the book
    . . . . . . . . . .13  . .  . access design links                     you
  . . . . . . . . . . . . .14   web access survey                         are
  . . . . . . . . . . . .15 write to me                                   here
```

Unlike a book or magazine, which is read linearly, web site structures are generally organized in a more tree-like fashion. This is one of the beauties of hypertext; one page can refer to another and to another and then back again in relevant areas. However, all that jumping around can leave a user feeling quite lost if there is no visual indication of where he is or where he is going in the scheme of things.

Don't assume it's fine to use long text passages because you include <A NAME="placeonthepage"> tags that lead a user to a particular area on a page when they click on a <A HREF= "#placeonthepage">go here!</A> link. These tags can result in their own navigation problems, even if there's a "back to the top

General Rules of Thumb for Text Length

Long pages of text are difficult to navigate and read. To make it easier on your audience, try the following tips.

- Limit the amount of text on each web page to the amount that fits on two basic screens, or one click-scroll down.

- For a standard 14- to 15-inch screen, one "page," or screenful, of text at default

browser type size is approximately 250 to 275 words. (This accounts for the variation of type size among platforms and browsers, most of which are 12-point Times Roman.)

- When in doubt, break up your document into multiple pages that are easily accessible from one another.

of the page" link that takes users back to the menu. Why? For one thing, if it's a very long page and the browser hasn't had a chance to load the <A NAME="n"> target area, nothing happens, and possibly, the page stops loading.

Another reason not to use long text passages is in cases in which your visitor has navigated around your page using the <A HREF="#n">go here!</A> links. If the user starts pressing his browser's Back button hoping to leave the page, he'll be led backward through each link in order of appearance. Only if the user's browser has a "history" feature, such as Netscape Navigator's Go menu provides (and the user knows how to use it), or if the user remembers the URL he wants to go to and types it, will he be able to back out in a non-bothersome fashion.

reading and writing

Just as you don't want to let the length of text passages run unchecked, you shouldn't let the length of each line of text get out of hand. Sixty characters is the standard number of characters per line that is considered the maximum for comfortable reading. Most word processors or text-based HTML editors enable you to count selected characters if you don't feel like counting by hand.

Why is 60 characters or less easiest to read? Because when you're done reading one line, your eye searches for the beginning of the next line. When your lines are any longer than 60 characters, your reader is forced to do extra work to "find" the beginning of the next line. Just wrestle with the following paragraph to see what I mean.

> As you can see, when type is small and it doesn't break here, after about 60 characters, it's much more difficult to read. It's even harder to read if the type is this small! Imagine how tired your readers would get if they had to read page after page of type that spread far, far across pages without anyplace for their eyes to rest. It's more difficult for our eyes to find the beginning of the next sentence if text spreads too far without breaking, as well.

Our eyes and our brains need guidance. Think of line breaks as a form of punctuation. My favorite example of this is to say that it's sort of like if we didn't have punctuation or capital letters at the beginning of sentences we would never stop reading or know when to pause then we end up spending more time trying to figure out when to stop than reading and enjoying ourselves if you know what i mean and i think you do by now

speaking of punctuation...

Punctuation, as you can see from the preceding example, is crucial for reading comprehension. How else do you know when to stop reading? Punctuation communicates to the reader where to pause (such as after the comma coming up or within these parentheses) and portrays levels of importance, mood, and context. What does a question mark do? It portrays to readers that a question is being asked of them, whether literal or rhetorical. Periods stop us. Exclamation points (used sparingly, please!) communicate a mood of excitement or demand attention for the words they follow. The colon: It is a tool that leads us to an explanation; semicolons break up a sentence into relative, yet separate entities.

When a site visitor is using a screen reader, or another type of text-to-speech application, punctuation "tells" the software how to "read" the text out loud, just as someone might read a speech out loud for the first time. We depend on the punctuation to inflect certain words or depict certain states of communication.

break up text

Columns help to break up long lines of text into more readable segments. Here's the same page of text in a one-column, two-column, three-column, and four-column layout. The table width is set at 466 pixels, about the width of a default browser screen. Although the two-column layout definitely is easier to read than the one-column layout…

Classifieds

Old Fairgrounds Tack Shop

1/9/97. In Vermont-**For Sale-Gorgeous AQHA gelding**, foaled June 3, 1983. 15.3 hands. Doc Tom's Peppy has done cross country, and loves to go. Chestnut with star, two flashy white socks. Bloodlines include Doc Bar, Peppy, Jameen Tivio. Tommy has been exposed to many elements, including cattle, pigs, chickens, turkeys, dogs, cats, tractors and other farm equipment, gymkhanas, fairs, shows, and has even brought home the Christmas tree! Asking $3500, negotiable, or let's talk trade for a ranch horse. E-mail tackshop@together.net, or snail mail to Katie Deberville, PO Box 756, Washington, VT 05675, or call 802-883-2290.

1/9/97. In VT-**Dressage Saddle Package**, Silver Fox rarely used, 16", black, doesn't fit my Arab. With cutback head, deeper seat, long slightly padded flaps. Girth, snaffle bridle, irons, leathers. Asking $200. E-mail tackshop@together.net, or snail mail to Liza Deberville, same address and phone as above.

1/9/97-in VT-**AQHA mare**, Ima Son Dee Honey, age 14, 15.2 hands, excellent conformation and muscle. Chrome chestnut, perfect diamond. Bloodlines include Son Dee Bar, Blondys Dude, King Bars. Proven Broodmare. Western, English, shown successfully locally.

Round pen training & professional training. Been exposed to same elements as Tommy, above. Sell, or trade for AQHA stallion, gelding or mare of equal value. E-mail tackshop@together.net, or snail mail to Liza Deberville, address and phone above.

Please send your classifieds to me, and I'll post them in exchange for a link from you to me. I'll also link to your picture(s) on your site. I do not take responsibility for any selling or buying anyone does through these classifieds. Contact each other directly!

...it isn't until the page is transformed into three columns that the lines of text start hitting the desired character-per-line length of about 30 characters.

Classifieds

Old Fairgrounds Tack Shop

1/9/97. In Vermont-**For Sale-Gorgeous AQHA gelding**, foaled June 3, 1983. 15.3 hands. Doc Tom's Peppy has done cross country, and loves to go. Chestnut with star, two flashy white socks. Bloodlines include Doc Bar, Peppy, Jameen Tivio. Tommy has been exposed to many elements, including cattle, pigs, chickens, turkeys, dogs, cats, tractors and other farm equipment, gymkhanas, fairs, shows, and has even brought home the Christmas tree!

Asking $3500, negotiable, or let's talk trade for a ranch horse. E-mail tackshop@together.net, or snail mail to Katie Deberville, PO Box 756, Washington, VT 05675, or call 802-883-2290.

1/9/97. In VT-**Dressage Saddle Package**, Silver Fox rarely used, 16", black, doesn't fit my Arab. With cutback head, deeper seat, long slightly padded flaps. Girth, snaffle bridle, irons, leathers. Asking $200. E-mail tackshop@together.net, or snail mail to Liza

Deberville, same address and phone as above.

1/9/97-in VT-**AQHA mare**, Ima Son Dee Honey, age 14, 15.2 hands, excellent conformation and muscle. Chrome chestnut, perfect diamond. Bloodlines include Son Dee Bar, Blondys Dude, King Bars. Proven Broodmare. Western, English, shown successfully locally. Round pen training & professional training. Been exposed to same elements as Tommy, above. Sell,

or trade for AQHA stallion, gelding or mare of equal value. E-mail tackshop@together.net, or snail mail to Liza Deberville, address and phone above.

Please send your classifieds to me, and I'll post them in exchange for a link from you to me. I'll also link to your picture(s) on your site. I do not take responsibility for any selling or buying anyone does through these classifieds. Contact each other directly!

The advent of tables and table-supporting browsers made columns of text possible. As any newspaper or magazine page proves, columns definitely make text easier to read because they break up large chunks of text into shorter lines of comprehensible text. Because of the general size limits of a web browser screen, however, you can have too much of a good thing—too many columns can cause more problems with reading comprehension because the lines become too short. Ideally, columns should be at least five or six words wide, or about 30 characters. Any longer than that, and you risk running your text off the page; any shorter, and you're again creating a reading challenge for those visiting your page.

Columns should be spaced evenly and have enough space between each other to make one decipherable from the next. A quarter of an inch or so is a good minimum, although the larger your text is, the larger the space between columns should be.

86

Here's the original three-column layout of the Old Fairgrounds Tack Shop page. Table width is 466 pixels, and column widths are 155 pixels, or 466 divided by 3 (I dropped the fraction). The code for each column is <TD WIDTH=155 ALIGN=LEFT VALIGN=TOP>. Unfortunately, this very basic coding leaves little space between each column, which also makes readability low.

Here's the original three-column layout, except I added a BORDER=2 to the TABLE definition so that you can better see where the column edges fall. Note how the text goes right up to the edge of the border.

Classifieds

Old Fairgrounds Tack Shop

1/9/97. In Vermont-**For Sale-Gorgeous AQHA gelding**, foaled June 3, 1983. 15.3 hands. Doc Tom's Peppy has done cross country, and loves to go. Chestnut with star, two flashy white socks. Bloodlines include Doc Bar, Peppy, Jameen Tivio. Tommy has been exposed to many elements, including cattle, pigs, chickens, turkeys, dogs, cats, tractors and other farm equipment, gymkhanas, fairs, shows, and has even brought home the Christmas tree! Asking $3500, negotiable, or let's talk trade for a ranch horse. E-mail tackshop@together.net, or snail mail to Katie Deberville, PO Box 756, Washington, VT 05675, or call 802-883-2290.

1/9/97. In VT-**Dressage Saddle Package**, Silver Fox rarely used, 16", black, doesn't fit my Arab. With cutback head, deeper seat, long slightly padded flaps. Girth, snaffle bridle, irons, leathers. Asking $200. E-mail tackshop@together.net, or snail mail to Liza Deberville, same address and phone as above.

1/9/97-in VT-**AQHA mare**, Ima Son Dee Honey, age 14, 15.2 hands, excellent conformation and muscle. Chrome chestnut, perfect diamond. Bloodlines include Son Dee Bar, Blondys Dude, King Bars. Proven Broodmare. Western, English, shown successfully locally.

Round pen training & professional training. Been exposed to same elements as Tommy, above. Sell, or trade for AQHA stallion, gelding or mare of equal value. E-mail tackshop@together.net, or snail mail to Liza Deberville, address and phone above.

Please send your classifieds to me, and I'll post them in exchange for a link from you to me. I'll also link to your picture(s) on your site. I do not take responsibility for any selling or buying anyone does through these classifieds. Contact each other directly!

Using cellspacing (<TABLE WIDTH=466 CELLSPACING=10>; shown here with borders off and on, respectively) puts a nice amount of space between the columns, significantly increasing the columns' readability. However, cellspacing also indents the columns on the outside margins, so if you want your table width to appear the same, this method won't work.

Classifieds

Old Fairgrounds Tack Shop

1/9/97. In Vermont-**For Sale-Gorgeous AQHA gelding**, foaled June 3, 1983. 15.3 hands. Doc Tom's Peppy has done cross country, and loves to go. Chestnut with star, two flashy white socks. Bloodlines include Doc Bar, Peppy, Jameen Tivio. Tommy has been exposed to many elements, including cattle, pigs, chickens, turkeys, dogs, cats, tractors and other farm equipment, gymkhanas, fairs, shows, and has even brought home the Christmas tree! Asking $3500, negotiable, or let's talk trade for a ranch horse. E-mail tackshop@together.net, or snail mail to Katie Deberville, PO Box 756, Washington, VT 05675, or call 802-883-2290.

1/9/97. In VT-**Dressage Saddle Package**, Silver Fox rarely used, 16", black, doesn't fit my Arab. With cutback head, deeper seat, long slightly padded flaps. Girth, snaffle bridle, irons, leathers. Asking $200. E-mail tackshop@together.net, or snail mail to Liza Deberville, same address and phone as above.

1/9/97-in VT-**AQHA mare**, Ima Son Dee Honey, age 14, 15.2 hands, excellent conformation and muscle. Chrome chestnut, perfect diamond. Bloodlines include Son Dee Bar, Blondys Dude, King Bars. Proven Broodmare. Western, English, shown successfully locally.

Round pen training & professional training. Been exposed to same elements as Tommy, above. Sell, or trade for AQHA stallion, gelding or mare of equal value. E-mail tackshop@together.net, or snail mail to Liza Deberville, address and phone above.

Please send your classifieds to me, and I'll post them in exchange for a link from you to me. I'll also link to your picture(s) on your site. I do not take responsibility for any selling or buying anyone does through these classifieds. Contact each other directly!

This example appears to still have three columns when, in fact, it now has five. The two gutters between the columns are also coded columns of 10 pixels each, using <TD WIDTH=10></TD> between the text-filled columns. The text-filled column codes now read <TD WIDTH=148 ALIGN=LEFT VALIGN=TOP>. I filled in the blank columns with colors so that you could see their placement between the columns.

Classifieds

Old Fairgrounds Tack Shop

1/9/97. In Vermont-**For Sale-Gorgeous AQHA gelding**, foaled June 3, 1983. 15.3 hands. Doc Tom's Peppy has done cross country, and loves to go. Chestnut with star, two flashy white socks. Bloodlines include Doc Bar, Peppy, Jameen Tivio. Tommy has been exposed to many elements, including cattle, pigs, chickens, turkeys, dogs, cats, tractors and other farm equipment, gymkhanas, fairs, shows, and has even brought home the Christmas tree! Asking $3500, negotiable, or let's talk trade for a ranch horse. E-mail tackshop@together.net, or snail mail to Katie Deberville, PO Box 756, Washington, VT 05675, or call 802-883-2290.

1/9/97. In VT-**Dressage Saddle Package**, Silver Fox rarely used, 16", black, doesn't fit my Arab. With cutback head, deeper seat, long slightly padded flaps. Girth, snaffle bridle, irons, leathers. Asking $200. E-mail tackshop@together.net, or snail mail to Liza Deberville, same address and phone as above.

1/9/97-in VT-**AQHA mare**, Ima Son Dee Honey, age 14, 15.2 hands, excellent conformation and muscle. Chrome chestnut, perfect diamond. Bloodlines include Son Dee Bar, Blondys Dude, King Bars. Proven Broodmare. Western, English, shown successfully locally.

Round pen training & professional training. Been exposed to same elements as Tommy, above. Sell, or trade for AQHA stallion, gelding or mare of equal value. E-mail tackshop@together.net, or snail mail to Liza Deberville, address and phone above.

Please send your classifieds to me, and I'll post them in exchange for a link from you to me. I'll also link to your picture(s) on your site. I do not take responsibility for any selling or buying anyone does through these classifieds. Contact each other directly!

Classifieds

Old Fairgrounds Tack Shop

1/9/97. In Vermont-**For Sale-Gorgeous AQHA gelding**, foaled June 3, 1983. 15.3 hands. Doc Tom's Peppy has done cross country, and loves to go. Chestnut with star, two flashy white socks. Bloodlines include Doc Bar, Peppy, Jameen Tivio. Tommy has been exposed to many elements, including cattle, pigs, chickens, turkeys, dogs, cats, tractors and other farm equipment, gymkhanas, fairs, shows, and has even brought home the Christmas tree! Asking $3500, negotiable, or let's talk trade for a ranch horse. E-mail tackshop@together.net, or snail mail to Katie Deberville, PO Box 756, Washington, VT 05675, or call 802-883-2290.

1/9/97. In VT-**Dressage Saddle Package**, Silver Fox rarely used, 16", black, doesn't fit my Arab. With cutback head, deeper seat, long slightly padded flaps. Girth, snaffle bridle, irons, leathers. Asking $200. E-mail tackshop@together.net, or snail mail to Liza Deberville, same address and phone as above.

1/9/97-in VT-**AQHA mare**, Ima Son Dee Honey, age 14, 15.2 hands, excellent conformation and muscle. Chrome chestnut, perfect diamond. Bloodlines include Son Dee Bar, Blondys Dude, King Bars. Proven Broodmare. Western, English, shown successfully locally.

Round pen training & professional training. Been exposed to same elements as Tommy, above. Sell, or trade for AQHA stallion, gelding or mare of equal value. E-mail tackshop@together.net, or snail mail to Liza Deberville, address and phone above.

Please send your classifieds to me, and I'll post them in exchange for a link from you to me. I'll also link to your picture(s) on your site. I do not take responsibility for any selling or buying anyone does through these classifieds. Contact each other directly!

Classifieds

Old Fairgrounds Tack Shop

1/9/97. In Vermont-**For Sale-Gorgeous AQHA gelding**, foaled June 3, 1983. 15.3 hands. Doc Tom's Peppy has done cross country, and loves to go. Chestnut with star, two flashy white socks. Bloodlines include Doc Bar, Peppy, Jameen Tivio. Tommy has been exposed to many elements, including cattle, pigs, chickens, turkeys, dogs, cats, tractors and other farm equipment, gymkhanas, fairs, shows, and has even brought home the Christmas tree! Asking $3500, negotiable, or let's talk trade for a ranch horse. E-mail tackshop@together.net, or snail mail to Katie Deberville, PO Box 756, Washington, VT 05675, or call 802-883-2290.

1/9/97. In VT-**Dressage Saddle Package**, Silver Fox rarely used, 16", black, doesn't fit my Arab. With cutback head, deeper seat, long slightly padded flaps. Girth, snaffle bridle, irons, leathers. Asking $200. E-mail tackshop@together.net, or snail mail to Liza Deberville, same address and phone as above.

1/9/97-in VT-**AQHA mare**, Ima Son Dee Honey, age 14, 15.2 hands, excellent conformation and muscle. Chrome chestnut, perfect diamond. Bloodlines include Son Dee Bar, Blondys Dude, King Bars. Proven Broodmare. Western, English, shown successfully locally.

Round pen training & professional training. Been exposed to same elements as Tommy, above. Sell, or trade for AQHA stallion, gelding or mare of equal value. E-mail tackshop@together.net, or snail mail to Liza Deberville, address and phone above.

Please send your classifieds to me, and I'll post them in exchange for a link from you to me. I'll also link to your picture(s) on your site. I do not take responsibility for any selling or buying anyone does through these classifieds. Contact each other directly!

Keep in mind that type size will affect your column's length and width, at least as far as readability. Whether you or your viewer determines what size the type will be viewed, there's always the risk that making the type bigger (which is easier to read) will also break lines into too-short segments.

A multicolumn page on which a viewer is forced to scroll down to finish a column, only to have to scroll back up to start a new column, also diminishes the navigability and readability of the page.

On a web page, however, even if your columns are spaced nicely, your viewers may have to scroll down a long way to read one column and then have to scroll back up the page to jump to the next. This makes their chances of getting lost within your web page much higher. For example, try to remember a time when you've tried reading a full-sized newspaper on the subway train or in a small space in which you've had to fold your paper to keep from giving your neighbor a paper cut. When you got to the end of one column, you had to unfold the paper and search for the next column. And what happened by the time you found the new column? Had you gotten lost? Did you forget what you were reading about? You can see how searching and jumping around like this makes it easy to lose your place, so if you do decide to table your text in columns, keep the columns as short as possible.

Note

Columns and tables can also cause problems for those who use screen readers. Because screen readers generally read straight across the page, the screen reader reads the first line of each column, then the second line of each column, and so on. A column or table read this way is totally incomprehensible to the visitor.

The fact is that any time our eyes have to do more work, the text is more difficult to read.

IT'S MORE WORK TO READ LARGE BODIES OF TEXT IN ALL CAPS BECAUSE IT'S HARDER FOR OUR EYES TO DIFFERENTIATE AMONG THE LETTERS. LOOKING AT A LARGE AMOUNT OF ALL CAPS TEXT ALSO MAKES THE WHOLE PARAGRAPH OR PAGE VISUALLY BLEND INTO A BLOB.

It's difficult to read a large body of
centered text—especially if the lines are of significantly different sizes—because,
again, the reader's eye has to search
for the beginning of the next line. Each line
starts in a different place, and it's hard for a person's eyes to find
the beginning of the line following the one they just finished reading.

Text that is aligned on the right is
harder to read than text that is aligned
to the left for the same reason.

Columns may make reading easier, but if
they
are too
thin, or
if there
are man-
y hyphen-
ated
words,
it puts
too many
"pauses"
in the
sentence, a-
gain ob-
structing
reading ease.

Capital letters may seem important—and they are—but using them in excess will deem your page one hard-reading mess.

Classifieds Old Fairgrounds Tack Shop

1/9/97. IN VERMONT-**FOR SALE-GORGEOUS AQHA GELDING,** FOALED JUNE 3, 1983. 15.3 HANDS. DOC TOM'S PEPPY HAS DONE CROSS COUNTRY, AND LOVES TO GO. CHESTNUT WITH STAR, TWO FLASHY WHITE SOCKS. BLOODLINES INCLUDE DOC BAR, PEPPY, JAMEEN TIVIO. TOMMY HAS BEEN EXPOSED TO MANY ELEMENTS, INCLUDING CATTLE, PIGS, CHICKENS, TURKEYS, DOGS, CATS, TRACTORS AND OTHER FARM EQUIPMENT, GYMKHANAS, FAIRS, SHOWS, AND HAS EVEN BROUGHT HOME THE CHRISTMAS TREE! ASKING $3500, NEGOTIABLE, OR LET'S TALK TRADE FOR A RANCH HORSE. E-MAIL TACKSHOP@TOGETHER.NET, OR SNAIL MAIL TO KATIE DEBERVILLE, PO BOX 756, WASHINGTON, VT 05675, OR CALL 802-883-2290.

1/9/97. IN VT-**DRESSAGE SADDLE PACKAGE,** SILVER FOX RARELY USED, 16", BLACK, DOESN'T FIT MY ARAB. WITH CUTBACK HEAD, DEEPER SEAT, LONG SLIGHTLY PADDED FLAPS. GIRTH, SNAFFLE BRIDLE, IRONS, LEATHERS. ASKING $200. E-MAIL TACKSHOP@TOGETHER.NET OR SNAIL MAIL TO LIZA DEBERVILLE, SAME ADDRESS AND PHONE AS ABOVE.

1/9/97-IN VT-**AQHA MARE,** IMA SON DEE HONEY, AGE 14, 15.2 HANDS, EXCELLENT CONFORMATION AND MUSCLE. CHROME CHESTNUT, PERFECT DIAMOND. BLOODLINES INCLUDE SON DEE BAR, BLONDYS DUDE, KING BARS. PROVEN BROODMARE. WESTERN, ENGLISH, SHOWN SUCCESSFULLY LOCALLY.

ROUND PEN TRAINING & PROFESSIONAL TRAINING. BEEN EXPOSED TO SAME ELEMENTS AS TOMMY, ABOVE. SELL, OR TRADE FOR AQHA STALLION, GELDING OR MARE OF EQUAL VALUE. E-MAIL TACKSHOP@TOGETHER.NET, OR SNAIL MAIL TO LIZA DEBERVILLE, ADDRESS AND PHONE ABOVE.

PLEASE SEND YOUR CLASSIFIEDS TO ME, AND I'LL POST THEM IN EXCHANGE FOR A LINK FROM YOU TO ME. I'LL ALSO LINK TO YOUR PICTURE(S) ON YOUR SITE. I DO NOT TAKE RESPONSIBILITY FOR ANY SELLING OR BUYING ANYONE DOES THROUGH THESE CLASSIFIEDS. CONTACT EACH OTHER DIRECTLY!

Italics are useful to stress certain words or phrases, but too many also make the page harder to read. On-screen italicized letters, unless pretty large, are usually too jaggedy to be very readable.

Classifieds Old Fairgrounds Tack Shop

*1/9/97. In Vermont-**For Sale-Gorgeous AQHA gelding**, foaled June 3, 1983. 15.3 hands. Doc Tom's Peppy has done cross country, and loves to go. Chestnut with star, two flashy white socks. Bloodlines include Doc Bar, Peppy, Jameen Tivio. Tommy has been exposed to many elements, including cattle, pigs, chickens, turkeys, dogs, cats, tractors and other farm equipment, gymkhanas, fairs, shows, and has even brought home the Christmas tree! Asking $3500, negotiable, or let's talk trade for a ranch horse. E-mail tackshop@together.net, or snail mail to Katie Deberville, PO Box 756, Washington, VT 05675, or call 802-883-2290.*

*1/9/97. In VT-**Dressage Saddle Package**, Silver Fox rarely used, 16", black, doesn't fit my Arab. With cutback head, deeper seat, long slightly padded flaps. Girth, snaffle bridle, irons, leathers. Asking $200. E-mail tackshop@together.net, or snail mail to Liza Deberville, same address and phone as above.*

*1/9/97-in VT-**AQHA mare**, Ima Son Dee Honey, age 14, 15.2 hands, excellent conformation and muscle. Chrome chestnut, perfect diamond. Bloodlines include Son Dee Bar, Blondys Dude, King Bars. Proven Broodmare. Western, English, shown successfully locally.*

Round pen training & professional training. Been exposed to same elements as Tommy, above. Sell, or trade for AQHA stallion, gelding or mare of equal value. E-mail tackshop@together.net, or snail mail to Liza Deberville, address and phone above.

Please send your classifieds to me, and I'll post them in exchange for a link from you to me. I'll also link to your picture(s) on your site. I do not take responsibility for any selling or buying anyone does through these classifieds. Contact each other directly!

When in doubt, a one-column format works quite nicely. Adding a <BLOCKQUOTE> tag or two indents your margins by about an inch on either side. This can also be achieved using the <DL></DL> tags, which indent from the left-hand column at

approximately half–inch intervals, depending on how many you insert. Another way to align a one-column layout is to use a multicolumn table (with no borders) but only include text in one of the columns. Using the table in this way gives you the option to provide specific pixel widths of columns, and placement of the columns, on your page.

This image again shows the Classifieds page as one block of text in its original width.

Classifieds   Old Fairgrounds Tack Shop

1/9/97. In Vermont-**For Sale-Gorgeous AQHA gelding**, foaled June 3, 1983. 15.3 hands. Doc Tom's Peppy has done cross country, and loves to go. Chestnut with star, two flashy white socks. Bloodlines include Doc Bar, Peppy, Jameen Tivio. Tommy has been exposed to many elements, including cattle, pigs, chickens, turkeys, dogs, cats, tractors and other farm equipment, gymkhanas, fairs, shows, and has even brought home the Christmas tree! Asking $3500, negotiable, or let's talk trade for a ranch horse. E-mail tackshop@together.net, or snail mail to Katie Deberville, PO Box 756, Washington, VT 05675, or call 802-883-2290.

1/9/97. In VT-**Dressage Saddle Package**, Silver Fox rarely used, 16", black, doesn't fit my Arab. With cutback head, deeper seat, long slightly padded flaps. Girth, snaffle bridle, irons, leathers. Asking $200. E-mail tackshop@together.net, or snail mail to Liza Deberville, same address and phone as above.

1/9/97-in VT-**AQHA mare**, Ima Son Dee Honey, age 14, 15.2 hands, excellent conformation and muscle. Chrome chestnut, perfect diamond. Bloodlines include Son Dee Bar, Blondys Dude, King Bars. Proven Broodmare. Western, English, shown successfully locally. Round pen training & professional training. Been exposed to same elements as Tommy, above. Sell, or trade for AQHA stallion, gelding or mare of equal value. E-mail tackshop@together.net, or snail mail to Liza Deberville, address and phone above.

Please send your classifieds to me, and I'll post them in exchange for a link from you to me. I'll also link to your picture(s) on your site. I do not take responsibility for any selling or buying anyone does through these classifieds. Contact each other directly!

Inserting a <BLOCKQUOTE> tag around the text indents it about one inch on either side. To use the <BLOCKQUOTE> tag, put <BLOCK-QUOTE> at the beginning and </BLOCKQUOTE> at the end of the text you want to indent.

Classifieds   Old Fairgrounds Tack Shop

1/9/97. In Vermont-**For Sale-Gorgeous AQHA gelding**, foaled June 3, 1983. 15.3 hands. Doc Tom's Peppy has done cross country, and loves to go. Chestnut with star, two flashy white socks. Bloodlines include Doc Bar, Peppy, Jameen Tivio. Tommy has been exposed to many elements, including cattle, pigs, chickens, turkeys, dogs, cats, tractors and other farm equipment, gymkhanas, fairs, shows, and has even brought home the Christmas tree! Asking $3500, negotiable, or let's talk trade for a ranch horse. E-mail tackshop@together.net, or snail mail to Katie Deberville, PO Box 756, Washington, VT 05675, or call 802-883-2290.

1/9/97. In VT-**Dressage Saddle Package**, Silver Fox rarely used, 16", black, doesn't fit my Arab. With cutback head, deeper seat, long slightly padded flaps. Girth, snaffle bridle, irons, leathers. Asking $200. E-mail tackshop@together.net, or snail mail to Liza Deberville, same address and phone as above.

1/9/97-in VT-**AQHA mare**, Ima Son Dee Honey, age 14, 15.2 hands, excellent conformation and muscle. Chrome chestnut, perfect diamond. Bloodlines include Son Dee Bar, Blondys Dude, King Bars. Proven Broodmare. Western, English, shown successfully locally. Round pen training & professional training. Been exposed to same elements as Tommy, above. Sell, or trade for AQHA stallion, gelding or mare of equal value. E-mail tackshop@together.net, or snail mail to Liza Deberville, address and phone above.

Please send your classifieds to me, and I'll post them in exchange for a link from you to me. I'll also link to your picture(s) on your site. I do not take responsibility for any selling or buying anyone does through these classifieds. Contact each other directly!

Classifieds
Old Fairgrounds Tack Shop

1/9/97. In Vermont-**For Sale–Gorgeous AQHA gelding**, foaled June 3, 1983. 15.3 hands. Doc Tom's Peppy has done cross country, and loves to go. Chestnut with star, two flashy white socks. Bloodlines include Doc Bar, Peppy, Jameen Tivio. Tommy has been exposed to many elements, including cattle, pigs, chickens, turkeys, dogs, cats, tractors and other farm equipment, gymkhanas, fairs, shows, and has even brought home the Christmas tree! Asking $3500, negotiable, or let's talk trade for a ranch horse. E-mail tackshop@together.net, or snail mail to Katie Deberville, PO Box 756, Washington, VT 05675, or call 802-883-2290.

1/9/97. In VT-**Dressage Saddle Package**, Silver Fox rarely used, 16", black, doesn't fit my Arab. With cutback head, deeper seat, long slightly padded flaps. Girth, snaffle bridle, irons, leathers. Asking $200. E-mail tackshop@together.net, or snail mail to Liza Deberville, same address and phone as above.

1/9/97-in VT-**AQHA mare**, Ima Son Dee Honey, age 14, 15.2 hands, excellent conformation and muscle. Chrome chestnut, perfect diamond. Bloodlines include Son Dee Bar, Blondys Dude, King Bars. Proven Broodmare. Western, English, shown successfully locally. Round pen training & professional training. Been exposed to same elements as Tommy, above. Sell, or trade for AQHA stallion, gelding or mare of equal value. E-mail tackshop@together.net, or snail mail to Liza Deberville, address and phone above.

Please send your classifieds to me, and I'll post them in exchange for a link from you to me. I'll also link to your picture(s) on your site. I do not take responsibility for any selling or buying anyone does through these classifieds. Contact each other directly!

Inserting two <BLOCKQUOTE> tags widens the margins even further.

Classifieds
Old Fairgrounds Tack Shop

1/9/97. In Vermont-**For Sale–Gorgeous AQHA gelding**, foaled June 3, 1983. 15.3 hands. Doc Tom's Peppy has done cross country, and loves to go. Chestnut with star, two flashy white socks. Bloodlines include Doc Bar, Peppy, Jameen Tivio. Tommy has been exposed to many elements, including cattle, pigs, chickens, turkeys, dogs, cats, tractors and other farm equipment, gymkhanas, fairs, shows, and has even brought home the Christmas tree! Asking $3500, negotiable, or let's talk trade for a ranch horse. E-mail tackshop@together.net, or snail mail to Katie Deberville, PO Box 756, Washington, VT 05675, or call 802-883-2290.

1/9/97. In VT-**Dressage Saddle Package**, Silver Fox rarely used, 16", black, doesn't fit my Arab. With cutback head, deeper seat, long slightly padded flaps. Girth, snaffle bridle, irons, leathers. Asking $200. E-mail tackshop@together.net, or snail mail to Liza Deberville, same address and phone as above.

1/9/97-in VT-**AQHA mare**, Ima Son Dee Honey, age 14, 15.2 hands, excellent conformation and muscle. Chrome chestnut, perfect diamond. Bloodlines include Son Dee Bar, Blondys Dude, King Bars. Proven Broodmare. Western, English, shown successfully locally. Round pen training & professional training. Been exposed to same elements as Tommy, above. Sell, or trade for AQHA stallion, gelding or mare of equal value. E-mail tackshop@together.net, or snail mail to Liza Deberville, address and phone above.

Please send your classifieds to me, and I'll post them in exchange for a link from you to me. I'll also link to your picture(s) on your site. I do not take responsibility for any selling or buying anyone does through these classifieds. Contact each other directly!

Creating a table but filling only one column with text is a way to control the width of your text and add white space where desired—either on the left or the right, or even both sides.

94

By using the table format to control your one-column width, it's also easier to insert images and additional text in the adjoining column at a later time.

Classifieds

Old Fairgrounds Tack Shop

1/9/97. In Vermont-**For Sale-Gorgeous AQHA gelding**, foaled June 3, 1983. 15.3 hands. Doc Tom's Peppy has done cross country, and loves to go. Chestnut with star, two flashy white socks. Bloodlines include Doc Bar, Peppy, Jameen Tivio. Tommy has been exposed to many elements, including cattle, pigs, chickens, turkeys, dogs, cats, tractors and other farm equipment, gymkhanas, fairs, shows, and has even brought home the Christmas tree! Asking $3500, negotiable, or let's talk trade for a ranch horse. E-mail tackshop@together.net, or snail mail to Katie Deberville, PO Box 756, Washington, VT 05675, or call 802-883-2290.

1/9/97. In VT-**Dressage Saddle Package**, Silver Fox rarely used, 16", black, doesn't fit my Arab. With cutback head, deeper seat, long slightly padded flaps. Girth, snaffle bridle, irons, leathers. Asking $200. E-mail tackshop@together.net, or snail mail to Liza Deberville, same address and phone as above.

1/9/97-in VT-**AQHA mare**, Ima Son Dee Honey, age 14, 15.2 hands, excellent conformation and muscle. Chrome chestnut, perfect diamond. Bloodlines include Son Dee Bar, Blondys Dude, King Bars. Proven Broodmare. Western, English, shown successfully locally. Round pen training & professional training. Been exposed to same elements as Tommy, above. Sell, or trade for AQHA stallion, gelding or mare of equal value. E-mail tackshop@together.net, or snail mail to Liza Deberville, address and phone above.

Please send your classifieds to me, and I'll post them in exchange for a link from you to me. I'll also link to your picture(s) on your site. I do not take responsibility for any selling or buying anyone does through these classifieds. Contact each other directly!

Katie riding
Doc Tom's Peppy

Liza riding
Ima Son Dee Honey

use headlines and subheads

Traditional print layouts can teach you other tricks as well. For example, you can mimic their use of effective headlines, subheads, and other "block" breakers for better comprehension and navigation through large amounts of text.

Breaking text into logical parts and pieces, headlines, and subheads not only assists in "announcing" the following text's contents, they also give a visual break for the eye. Good subheads and headlines are large enough to be easily distinguishable from the body text but not so large that they totally distract the reader from the body of text content. Just as I use subheads throughout these chapters, you can also use subheads in your text-heavy web pages to show, both visually and contextually, that "hey, a new section starts here."

Subheads are also used by readers to get an overall contextual understanding of the content of an article or book. Chances are that when you first picked up this book, you didn't simply start reading it from page one; you probably looked through the table of contents and flipped through the pages to see if something would catch your eye. Subheads, like graphics, give readers hints about what is in the meat of the surrounding text—they inform and invite.

RAMA'S LAST RIDE, by Lois Deberville, as printed in The World,1991.

Last summer, I met a woman named Patty, who came to my tack shop. We talked for quite a while about horses and different horse-related experiences. Patty has three horses she wanted to sell as soon as possible. One that I was interested in for my daughter, Liza, was a white gelding. The term 'aged' that Patty used didn't daunt me, for our favorite equines are "aged", yet are as spunky as young ones. What bothered me was that this horse, Rama, had been badly abused by the person from whom Patty rescued him Patty had heard about this horse, and while she had no room or reason to take him, she bought him just to save him from certain death of starvation. I admire her greatly.

We went to look at Rama one evening. We got lost, of course, so the whole trip had to be done over the next morning. We were shocked to see this large friendly animal. He was a mass of bones. His legs were so thin, we wondered how he held himself up. His gentle eyes weren't wary of us, which would have been expected after the horrible neglect he had apparently suffered.

Liza and her father saddled Rama up, and rode him up and down the road by the pasture. It seemed as though Rama's spirit just rose a mile when someone was on his back. We had worried about his rideability, yet Patty had assured us that she had been riding him a little bit each day to try to build up his strength.

While being ridden, Rama's eyes were lit up, his head arched forward, and his step was high and quick. He was proud, and loved being wanted. It was love at first sight for all of us.

We trailered Rama home a few days later. Liza cornered off a parcel of land where Rama would be away from the other horses, and also in our sight at all time. We began him on a diet of 14 percent protein grain mixed with Enhancer, which contained yeast for easier digestion. We didn't want to overprotein him suddenly in his poor condition. Liza showered him with lice powder, and we dewormed him.

My Uncle Art from Virginia, whom I'd just met for the first time, was visiting my mom next door, and Rama became his pet as well. He'd go out by the fence and talk to him. They were both older, and not feeling too well.

Liza rode Rama a few minutes each day. How he loved it! The pre-ride grooming, the nuzzling of noses, the treat she'd invariably have for him. We never really knew how old Rama was, our guess was 20. His back was sagging, his coat was scrungy and sparse, but his eyes were alive, and she never had any trouble with him.

On Aug. 15, just 16 days after Rama came home with us, I looked out in the morning to see him, as the first one up always did. He was gone. For the first time, Rama had gotten out of the one strand electric fence surrounding him. Then I saw him. He had come to the front yard, laid down exactly in front of Liza's bedroom window, and quietly died.

The impact of Rama's death was great. It was not only where he died, somehow being led to to window of someone who thought he was the most special thing on earth. It was the fact that somewhere out there, the person who allowed this tragedy to happen is not being punished. Rama was the case scenario that you read about in all the magazines, yet never think it happens near you. He was a lesson I wish my family never had to be part of. But, he was also worth knowing, albeit for such a brief time. My daughter will be involved with horses forever, but Rama will remain the White Knight in her dreams. My Uncle Art died shortly after, upon returning to his home. I would like to think he and Rama are sharing an apple somewhere.

Leona Schultz Waters and Otto Arthur Schultz, 1990. A wonderful reunion after 15 years apart. They laughed and laughed, and sounded just like children. Uncle Art gave me his 'lucky' horseshoe ring. He was a professional baker, and demonstrated his technique by mixing Russell's birthday cake batter with his hands! He died about six weeks later, upon returning to his home.

A page full of solid text, even with the occasional line break, not only *looks* intimidating, it *is* intimidating. Trying to read long passages like this, with no place for your eyes to start or rest, can be more trouble than it's worth, no matter how good the content.

Even after adding paragraph breaks, the page is still dull and lifeless.

RAMA'S LAST RIDE, by Lois Deberville, as printed in The World, 1991.

Last summer, I met a woman named Patty, who came to my tack shop. We talked for quite a while about horses and different horse-related experiences. Patty has three horses she wanted to sell as soon as possible. One that I was interested in for my daughter, Liza, was a white gelding. The term 'aged' that Patty used didn't daunt me, for our favorite equines are "aged", yet are as spunky as young ones. What bothered me was that this horse, Rama, had been badly abused by the person from whom Patty rescued him. Patty had heard about this horse, and while she had no room or reason to take him, she bought him just to save him from certain death of starvation. I admire her greatly.

We went to look at Rama one evening. We got lost, of course, so the whole trip had to be done over the next morning. We were shocked to see this large friendly animal. He was a mass of bones. His legs were so thin, we wondered how he held himself up. His gentle eyes weren't wary of us, which would have been expected after the horrible neglect he had apparently suffered.

Liza and her father saddled Rama up, and rode him up and down the road by the pasture. It seemed as though Rama's spirit just rose a mile when someone was on his back. We had worried about his rideability, yet Patty had assured us that she had been riding him a little bit each day to try to build up his strength.

While being ridden, Rama's eyes were lit up, his head arched forward, and his step was high and quick. He was proud, and loved being wanted. It was love at first sight for all of us.

We trailered Rama home a few days later. Liza cornered off a parcel of land where Rama would be away from the other horses, and also in our sight at all time. We began him on a diet of 14 percent protein grain mixed with Enhancer, which contained yeast for easier digestion. We didn't want to overprotein him suddenly in his poor condition. Liza showered him with lice powder, and we dewormed him.

My Uncle Art from Virginia, whom I'd just met for the first time, was visiting my mom next door, and Rama became his pet as well. He'd go out by the fence and talk to him. They were both older, and not feeling too well.

Liza rode Rama a few minutes each day. How he loved it! The pre-ride grooming, the nuzzling of noses, the treat she'd invariably have for him. We never really knew how old Rama was, our guess was 20. His back was sagging, his coat was scrungy and sparse, but his eyes were alive, and she never had any trouble with him.

On Aug. 15, just 16 days after Rama came home with us, I looked out in the morning to see him, as the first one up always did. He was gone. For the first time, Rama had gotten out of the one strand electric fence surrounding him. Then I saw him. He had come to the front yard, laid down exactly in front of Liza's bedroom window, and quietly died.

The impact of Rama's death was great. It was not only where he died, somehow being led to to window of someone who thought he was the most special thing on earth. It was the fact that somewhere out there, the person who allowed this tragedy to happen is not being punished. Rama was the case scenario that you read about in all the magazines, yet never think it happens near you. He was a lesson I wish my family never had to be part of. But, he was also worth knowing, albeit for such a brief time. My daughter will be involved with horses forever, but Rama will remain the White Knight in her dreams.

My Uncle Art died shortly after, upon returning to his home. I would like to think he and Rama are sharing an apple somewhere.

Leona Schultz Waters and Otto Arthur Schultz, 1990. A wonderful reunion after 15 years apart. They laughed and laughed, and sounded just like children. Uncle Art gave me his 'lucky' horseshoe ring. He was a professional baker, and demonstrated his technique by mixing Russell's birthday cake batter with his hands! He died about six weeks later, upon returning to his home.

RAMA'S LAST RIDE

by Lois Deberville

as printed in The World, 1991.

> Last summer, I met a woman named Patty, who came to my tack shop. We talked for quite a while about horses and different horse-related experiences. Patty has three horses she wanted to sell as soon as possible. One that I was interested in for my daughter, Liza, was a white gelding. The term 'aged' that Patty used didn't daunt me, for our favorite equines are "aged," yet are as spunky as young ones. What bothered me was that this horse, Rama, had been badly abused by the person from whom Patty rescued him. Patty had heard about this horse, and while she had no room or reason to take him, she bought him just to save him from certain death of starvation. I admire her greatly.

Meeting Rama

> We went to look at Rama one evening. We got lost, of course, so the whole trip had to be done over the next morning. We were shocked to see this large friendly animal. He was a mass of bones. His legs were so thin, we wondered how he held himself up. His gentle eyes weren't wary of us, which would have been expected after the horrible neglect he had apparently suffered.
>
> Liza and her father saddled Rama up, and rode him up and down the road by the pasture. It seemed as though Rama's spirit just rose a mile when someone was on his back. We had worried about his rideability, yet Patty had assured us that she had been riding him a little bit each day to try to build up his strength.
>
> While being ridden, Rama's eyes were lit up, his head arched forward, and his step was high and quick. He was proud, and loved being wanted. It was love at first sight for all of us.

Bringing Rama Home

> We trailered Rama home a few days later. Liza cornered off a parcel of land where Rama would be away from the other horses, and also in our sight at all time. We began him on a diet of 14 percent protein grain mixed with Enhancer, which contained yeast for easier digestion. We didn't want to overprotein him suddenly in his poor condition. Liza showered him with lice powder, and we dewormed him.

Sharing Apples with Uncle Art

> My Uncle Art from Virginia, whom I'd just met for the first time, was visiting my mom next door, and Rama became his pet as well. He'd go out by the fence and talk to him. They were both older, and not feeling too well.
>
> Liza rode Rama a few minutes each day. How he loved it! The pre-ride grooming, the nuzzling of noses, the treat she'd invariably have for him. We never really knew how old Rama was, our guess was 20. His back was sagging, his coat was scrungy and sparse, but his eyes were alive, and she never had any trouble with him.

Going Home

> On Aug. 15, just 16 days after Rama came home with us, I looked out in the morning to see him, as the first one up always did. He was gone. For the first time, Rama had gotten out of the one strand electric fence surrounding him. Then I saw him. He had come to the front yard, laid down exactly in front of Liza's bedroom window, and quietly died.
>
> The impact of Rama's death was great. It was not only where he died, somehow being led to to window of someone who thought he was the most special thing on earth. It was the fact that somewhere out there, the person who allowed this tragedy to happen is not being punished. Rama was the case scenario that you read about in all the magazines, yet never think it happens near you. He was a lesson I wish my family never had to be part of. But, he was also worth knowing, albeit for such a brief time. My daughter will be involved with horses forever, but Rama will remain the White Knight in her dreams.

Heavenly Friends

> My Uncle Art died shortly after, upon returning to his home. I would like to think he and Rama are sharing an apple somewhere.
>
> Leona Schultz Waters and Otto Arthur Schultz, 1990. A wonderful reunion after 15 years apart. They laughed and laughed, and sounded just like children. Uncle Art gave me his 'lucky' horseshoe ring. He was a professional baker, and demonstrated his technique by mixing Russell's birthday cake batter with his hands! He died about six weeks later, upon returning to his home.

With just a few code additions, the page is significantly more inviting. The title of the story, Rama's Last Ride, is set with the <H1></H1> code, and the inserted subheads are <H3></H3>. The body text has been indented using <BLOCKQUOTE>.

keep it simple

You may have heard the acronym KISS: Keep It Simple, Stupid (or Silly; or Susan if that's your name). Writing doesn't mean you simply have to word everything on a "see Spot run" level; it means you don't need to rehash things over and over, or be redundant, or say the same thing repeatedly. A simple way to tell whether your text makes sense is to read it out loud or have someone else read it out loud to you. This also gives you an idea of how a screen reader will read your page out loud to your visitors who use them.

I'm a big believer in writing the way you talk. This don't mean you ain't gotta have proper grammar. (Personally, reading stuff, even "cultural" novels written in dialect, drives me nuts.) What it does mean is that your text should sound natural. If you wouldn't be comfortable using a two-dollar polysyllabic word in a conversation, why use it in your writing? Use the two-cent word instead. Unless you are dictating a formal business letter, how often in real life do you say "Thank you for your attention to this matter" or "The variables you cited in your correspondence are under fastidious consideration"?

If it's necessary to talk the Talk, as for a very formal business page, go for it. Obviously, it depends on your business, your market, and whether or not the people you're trying to reach actually understand the words you are using—not to mention, if they *expect* to hear a certain tone of voice or High-Business Lingo. If a lawyer, for example, never used legal-speak (therefores and heretofores and so on), you might wonder about his qualifications. Just like a medical web page that refers to skin cancer as "that yucky stuff" won't win the respect of its visitors.

On the other hand, if your site features creative writing—fiction, poetry, what-have-you—then, obviously, what you say and how you say it is at your discretion. Free expression is highly encouraged. The key is to make the language appropriate to the content. Even on an experimental poetry site, you should keep the information intended to familiarize the visitor with your mission, your navigation, and your content clear and concise.

icons and links

Many people with dyslexia, ADD (Attention Deficit Disorder), and such have difficulties reading large blocks of text and benefit highly from the use of graphics as enhancements to body text. Using subheads throughout the text, as well as captions with images, aids in overall comprehension for most people, even if they don't have difficulty reading large blocks of text.

Horse Tales Old Fairgrounds Tack Shop

Rama's Last Ride

by Lois Deberville
as printed in The World, 1991.

Last summer, I met a woman named Patty, who came to my tack shop. We talked for quite a while about horses and different horse-related experiences. Patty has three horses she wanted to sell as soon as possible. One that I was interested in for my daughter, Liza, was a white gelding. The term 'aged' that Patty used didn't daunt me, for our favorite equines are "aged," yet are as spunky as young ones. What bothered me was that this horse, Rama, had been badly abused by the person from whom Patty rescued him Patty had heard about this horse, and while she had no room or reason to take him, she bought him just to save him from certain death of starvation. I admire her greatly.

Meeting Rama

We went to look at Rama one evening. We got lost, of course, so the whole trip had to be done over the next morning. We were shocked to see this large friendly animal. He was a mass of bones. His legs were so thin, we wondered how he held himself up. His gentle eyes weren't wary of us, which would have been expected after the horrible neglect he had apparently suffered.

Liza and her father saddled Rama up, and rode him up and down the road by the pasture. It seemed as though Rama's spirit just rose a mile when someone was on his back. We had worried about his rideability, yet Patty had assured us that she had been riding him a little bit each day to try to build up his strength.

Rama – The gentle white knight.
Our wonderful new friend, Rama, at his new home, August 1990.

While being ridden, Rama's eyes were lit up, his head arched forward, and his step was high and quick. He was proud, and loved being wanted. It was love at first sight for all of us.

Bringing Rama Home

We trailered Rama home a few days later. Liza cornered off a parcel of land where Rama would be away from the other horses, and also in our sight at all time. We began him on a diet of 14 percent protein grain mixed with Enhancer, which contained yeast for easier digestion. We didn't want to overprotein him suddenly in his poor condition. Liza showered him with lice powder, and we dewormed him.

Sharing Apples with Uncle Art

My Uncle Art from Virginia, whom I'd just met for the first time, was visiting my mom next door, and Rama became his pet as well. He'd go out by the fence and talk to him. They were both older, and not feeling too well.

Liza rode Rama a few minutes each day. How he loved it! The pre-ride grooming, the nuzzling of noses, the treat she'd invariably have for him. We never really knew how old Rama was, our guess was 20. His back was sagging, his coat was scrungy and sparse, but his eyes were alive, and she never had any trouble with him.

Going Home

On Aug. 15, just 16 days after Rama came home with us, I looked out in the morning to see him, as the first one up always did. He was gone. For the first time, Rama had gotten out of the one strand electric fence surrounding him. Then I saw him. He had come to the front yard, laid down exactly in front of Liza's bedroom window, and quietly died.

The impact of Rama's death was great. It was not only where he died, somehow being led to to window of someone who thought he was the most special thing on earth. It was the fact that somewhere out there, the person who allowed this tragedy to happen is not being punished. Rama was the case scenario that you read about in all the magazines, yet never think it happens near you. He was a lesson I wish my family never had to be part of. But, he was also worth knowing, albeit for such a brief time. My daughter will be involved with horses forever, but Rama will remain the White Knight in her dreams.

Heavenly Friends

My Uncle Art died shortly after, upon returning to his home. I would like to think he and Rama are sharing an apple somewhere.

Leona Schultz Waters and Otto Arthur Schultz, 1990. A wonderful reunion after 15 years apart. They laughed and laughed, and sounded just like children. Uncle Art gave me his 'lucky' horseshoe ring. He was a professional baker, and demonstrated his technique by mixing Russell's birthday cake batter with his hands! He died about six weeks later, upon returning to his home.

Mom and Uncle Art – 1990
Leona Schultz Waters and Otto Arthur Schultz. A wonderful sibling reunion after 15 years apart.

Continuing with the previous example, there are a few graphic enhancements to guide (and visually entertain) the user through the site.

First of all, a banner that is consistent with the other banners in the site was added to the top of the page. This reminds visitors what section they are in, as well as what site they are visiting.

Next, photos were added, along with descriptive captions. Both photo and captions were added in one-cell tables; the top one is a right-aligned table, and the bottom is left aligned.

The headline and caption text color was changed to a purple to add a bit of visual impact and set it apart from the body text. This color was chosen because it separated the text enough from the black of the body copy but didn't contrast so much as to be distracting.

Long lists of suggested sites, such as posting your bookmarks file to your site, can also be difficult to read. Splitting site lists (or any sort of lists, for that matter) into specific categories aids in overall comprehension. I've even seen bookmark lists-of-links that have an accompanying icon for each link. If done properly and consistently, this can be of great help. But before you start snagging logos and graphics from those pages you link to and start making link-icons, write to the owners of the pages and ask permission.

multipage formats

An 8- by 10-inch book is preferable to a 2- by 4-foot one, but sometimes a 4- by 6-inch book is the best of all. Cut long pages of text into separate pages. This does take some more mouse-work on your part, but it can significantly decrease the perception of overall download waiting time. People still have to download the same amount of text, but each page loads significantly faster, giving them a shorter waiting before each "payoff."

If you opt for this approach, make sure your users have guideposts to navigate the pages. Including "back" and "next" links or buttons is crucial, and I highly suggest that you also include some sort of indication to readers about where they are in the whole series of pages. This can be in the form of a "you are here" notification, or a navigation bar at the top or bottom of the page that gives links to the previous and subsequent pages. Although page "numbers" can be helpful as well, just like in print, it can be difficult to remember just what "7" represents. You'll notice that most books, even though they use page numbers, also include the chapter name in a header or footer of each page, or at least on one of the pages in a two-page spread. This way, when a person opens a book, he knows at a glance which chapter he's in.

Adding some indication of where a viewer is in the site also gives him an idea of where he's going. In this case, the viewer can go back to the last story, on to the next, or choose among those areas listed in the text menu that are highlighted as links.

 Horse Tales Introduction | About the author
Rama's Last Ride | Finding the Filly | Teddy's Tantrum | On the Road with Red
Home to the Old Fairgrounds Tack Shop

back   next

There is a downer about this kind of format, however. If you encourage the printing or saving of your many pages of information to disk, viewers must go to each page to get all of the information, and go through the repetitive task of printing or saving. In

this case, adding page numbers would be beneficial, helping to keep unattached printed pages together and in the proper order. If you want your viewers to have less work to do, offer them an option to go to a page that has all of the information on one page or provide the file in a downloadable format that they can later open in a word processor and print.

Of course, if you *don't* want people to save and print your pages, the multipage format and all the work it takes to print the many pages could be a healthy way to discourage the infringement of your copyright.

links and readability

Generally, sentences are a lot easier to handle if you limit links to one per line. This is especially important when dealing with screen readers because they read the linked text, rather than the words that are linked.

Deciding what words in a sentence will represent the link is also important. Look around, and you'll see that lots of sites use phrases such as "click here" for something, or use the word "this" (or "click this"). The trouble with using these vague words to represent links is that they give no indication of what the link is all about as a standalone word or phrase. For example, the invitation:

"Click this for a picture of the building"

works much better as

"There's also a picture of this building available."

Likewise, you could improve

"Click here to go on to the next page"

by rephrasing (and restructuring the link) to

"Go to the next page"

The alternative links tell you exactly what you'll get as a result of choosing the link.

One other way of making sure that your links don't interfere with a page's readability is to place as many links as possible at the end of the story, or within a specified area on the page. If your page is too long, consider placing relevant links at the end of each paragraph or section.

links

Elderly horses
. care and feeding
. riding
. retirement

Rescuing Abused Horses
. Associations
. Legal action

Losing a Pet
. grieving your friend
. animal memorials

Human Tales
. Liza
. Mom
. Uncle Art

Instead of innundating your text with links, consider pulling them out in an easy-to-reach sidebar or placing them at the end of your story.

summary

Writing for reading comprehension is a challenge. Although you might not have a writing background, simple rules and tips, such as using subheads or graphics to break up text, can greatly assist your viewer's comprehension of your content.

For more assistance on writing in general, consider taking a look through the following:

- *On Writing Well—An Informal Guide to Writing Nonfiction,* by William Zinsser. 5th Edition, Harper Collins, ISBN: 0062733036.

- *Elements of Style,* by William Strunk & E. B. White. 3rd Edition, Allyn & Bacon, ISBN: 0205191584.

Both of these books are brief, excellent guides to writing and editing for clarity and understanding. Basic writing skills can make a big difference in the comprehension of a message.

As for the physical element of text on a page, keep in mind that lots of text can take just as long (and crash just as many browsers) as lots of graphics or other gizmo ornamentations can. Breaking up text into bite-sized chunks, with navigational and pictorial cues, assists in overall enjoyability and cognition of a web site.

Oh…and avoid using words like "cognition" unless you really have to.

CHAPTER 6

> *"The miracle is not that we do this work, but that we are happy to do it."*
> *— Mother Teresa*

forms & functionality

accessible forms & alternatives

Forms have been a cool addition to the interactivity quotient of the web at large. By using a few HTML tags and some handy CGI scripts, designers can create a graphical representation of a paper form, complete with clickable buttons, pull-down menus, pop-up lists, and the capability to feed the incoming data straight into your database, among other capabilities. Forms invite viewers to correspond with a site's designers, its webmeisters, the sales force, tech support, and others. They give visitors an easy way to place orders, fill out surveys, or specify search criteria to locate information within your site or others. Visitors fill out the form elements, the information is sent to the server and processed by a CGI script, and voilà—you get what you want, and hopefully, they get what they want (either a thank you, the information they searched for, or what have you).

Unfortunately, forms are not supported on all browsers. Although most of the online population use browsers that support forms, there are still potential problems or inconsistencies with design, alignment, and layout.

104

Here's a basic order form shown in both Netscape Navigator and Internet Explorer, respectively. There are only slight differences in some text alignment and location of form fields; other than that, the design is well-adjusted to both browsers.

Netscape: Green Tomato order form

greentomato.com

we're ripe for the pickin' !

please fill out the following, and hit the SEND button when you're ready to give us your order. **If your browser does not support forms**, you can cut and paste the text into an email document and send it to orders@greentomato.com.

if you prefer, feel free to **print out this page** and fax or mail it to us at: **greentomato.com** - attn: orders dept. - 100 Tomato Way - San Francisco, CA 94000 - fax: 415 555 1111

[those areas marked below with an asterisk (*) **must** be filled in for us to process your order.]

shipping information

first name*
last name*
street address 1*
street address 2*
city*   state*   zip*
phone*   fax:
email address

billing information

please charge my...
   visa ☐   mastercard ☐   american express ☐
credit card number
expiration date (mm/yy)
name on card (if other than above)

what can we get you?

item	stock number	quantity	price (each)	amount ($)
Evergreen tomato seeds	4126		$2.59	
GreenTomato.com Sauce (32 oz jar)	3264		$3.69	
our very own Green Tomato Cook Book	2854		$19.95	
fried green tomato batter mixins (8 oz bag)	1399		$3.99	
expert tomato growing kit	5586		$39.99	
			subtotal	
overnight $12			shipping & handing	
			sales tax	
			TOTAL	

comments, questions or special instructions

☐ YES, put me on your snail mail list to receive your quarterly catalog.
☐ YES, I'd like to receive email when GreenTomato.com adds new products.

send it on in!.... or clear the form and start over...

[send order to GreenTomato]   [clear form & start over]

Green Tomato order form

green tomato.com

we're ripe for the pickin' !

please fill out the following, and hit the SEND button when you're ready to give us your order. **If your browser does not support forms**, you can cut and paste the text into an email document and send it to <u>orders@greentomato.com</u>.

if you prefer, feel free to **print out this page** and fax or mail it to us at: **greentomato.com** - attn: orders dept. - 100 Tomato Way - San Francisco, CA 94000 - fax: 415 555 1111

[those areas marked below with an asterisk (*) **must** be filled in for us to process your order.]

shipping information

```
first name*          [                    ]
last name*           [                    ]
street address 1*    [                    ]
street address 2*    [                    ]
city*      [          ] state* [    ] zip* [      ]
phone*     [                ]  fax:  [          ]
email address        [                ]
```

billing information

```
please charge my...
         visa [ ]    mastercard [ ]    american express [ ]
credit card number        [                ]
expiration date (mm/yy)   [          ]
name on card (if other than above)
                          [                          ]
```

what can we get you?

item	stock number	quantity	price (each)	amout ($)
<u>Evergreen tomato seeds</u>	4126	[ ]	$2.59	[ ]
<u>GreenTomato.com Sauce</u> (32 oz jar)	3264	[ ]	$3.69	[ ]
our very own <u>Green Tomato Cook Book</u>	2854	[ ]	$19.95	[ ]
<u>fried green tomato batter mixins</u> (8 oz bag)	1399	[ ]	$3.99	[ ]
<u>expert tomato growing kit</u>	5586	[ ]	$39.99	[ ]
			subtotal	[ ]
	[overnight $12 ▼]	shipping & handing		[ ]
			sales tax	[ ]
			TOTAL	[ ]

comments, questions or special instructions

```
[                                              ]
[                                              ]
[                                              ]
[                                              ]
```

[ ] YES, put me on your snail mail list to receive your quarterly catalog.
[ ] YES, I'd like to receive email when GreenTomato.com adds new products.

send it on in!.... or clear the form and start over...

(send order to GreenTomato) (clear form & start over)

Note

If you choose to include a text-based form, help your viewers out—Netscape users can click a MAILTO: tag on the page that displays the form. When Netscape users click the Quote button, the form is copied into the Netscape mail. Then, all they need to do is check any relevant check marks, fill out any relevant lines of information, and send it off to the address you included in the mailto. Microsoft Internet Explorer folks have to cut and paste the old-fashioned way.

form alternatives

The best workaround for problem forms is to offer form alternatives. Create forms that can be downloaded for printing or faxing. If you have forms that you've created in QuarkXPress or another page layout program, consider making Adobe Acrobat files that visitors can download and print using Adobe Acrobat Reader (the reader is free, except for the trouble of downloading from http://www.adobe.com/acrobat/; Acrobat itself costs around $295). After your visitor downloads the form, he can print it, fill it out by hand, and then mail or fax it to you.

Of course, in this case, you have to include your snail-mail address and fax number so people can actually get the form to you. Also, include your phone number in case they have questions or prefer to skip the form entirely and place their orders directly. Because you're in business to make money and to provide good customer service, you already have this contact information on your site, right?

Text forms are also a good option because they can be printed out or saved to disk, and cut and pasted into an e-mail message. Text forms are also consequential alternatives for people who have visual impairments that prevent them from viewing the screen.

mousing around

After you complete your thorough, visually appealing form, you must ask *yourself* a question: Is the form widely accessible? Or in other words, can users see all their choices and fill out the form without a mouse?

Standard forms can be very difficult to fill out if you can't see the form boxes, and impossible to fill out completely if pull-down lists or other mouse-dependent choices, such as radio boxes or check boxes, are used. The quickest way to test your form is to try filling it out *without* using your mouse. Not easy, huh? If you can access your form elements using the Tab key, simply add instructions to the beginning of your form telling users to use the Tab key to navigate through the form.

```
▦▦≡▦▦▦≡ Message Composition ≡▦▦▦▦▦
│ SendNow │ Quote │ Attach │ Address │  │ Stop │      Crystal W <crystal@typo.com>
Subject: My order
▽ Addressing                              Attachments
    Mail To: orders@greentomato.com
         Cc:


http://www.greentomato.com/tomato.html> [Image]
>
> please fill out the following, and hit the SEND button when you're
> ready to give us your order. If your browser does not support forms,
> you can out and paste the text into an email document and send it to
> orders@greentomato.com.
>
> if you prefer, feel free to print out this page and fax or mail it to
> us at: greentomato.com - attn: orders dept. - 100 Tomato Way - San
> Francisco, CA 94000 - fax: 415 555 1111
>
> [those areas marked below with an asterisk (*) must be filled in for
> us to process your order.]
>
> shipping information
>
>          first name*
>          last name*
>          street address 1*
>          street address 2*
>          city* state* zip*
>          phone* fax:
>          email address
>
> billing information
>
>          please charge my...
>                 visa    mastercard   american express
>          credit card number
>          expiration date (mm/yy)
>          name on card (if other than above)
>
>
> what can we get you?
>
>  item                             stockquantitypriceamout
>                                   number        (each) ($)
>  Evergreen tomato seeds           4126          $2.59
>
>  GreenTomato.com Sauce (32 oz jar)  3264        $3.69
>
>  our very own Green Tomato Cook Book  2854      $19.95
>
>  fried green tomato batter mixins (8 oz bag) 1399  $3.99
>
>  expert tomato growing kit        5586          $39.99
>
>                                          subtotal
>
>                                 shipping & handing
>
>                                         sales tax
>
>                                            TOTAL
>
> comments, questions or special instructions
>
>          YES, put me on your snail mail list to receive
>             your quarterly catalog.
>          YES, I'd like to receive email when GreenTomato.com
>             adds new products.
>
> send it on in!.... or clear the form and start over...
>
>
|
```

In both Navigator and Internet Explorer, clicking a MAILTO link brings up a mail form. In Netscape Navigator, clicking the Quote button in the mail window menu bar copies and pastes the contents of the current web page into the mail window, as shown here. Internet Explorer mail requires the user to manually copy and paste the form information into the mail window.

Even forms with only fill-out boxes can be hard to fill out for someone who doesn't have the use of a mouse. Long forms require that a person using Netscape keeps pressing the Tab key throughout the entire form to get back to the top. Internet Explorer supports Shift+Tab to move backward through form fill-out boxes; however, if a person is unable to press multiple keys, then they have to do the one-key click-through.

form design

Forms, just like the rest of your site, must have the elements of consistent design and familiar cues. Avoid adding fancy gizmos to forms just to prove you know how. Match the form element to your visitors' needs, and respect their preconceived notions about form structures.

the right element for the content

Elements available in web forms now include text fields, lists, check buttons, pop-up menus, radio buttons, and other stuff that can be edited, chosen, or filled in by your visitors. The type of information you ask your visitors for helps to determine the type of form tag you need to use.

Forms that use check boxes let viewers select as many boxes as they like out of the ones you provide. Radio buttons, on the other hand, enable the viewer to pick only one out of all the choices. The list view of choices lets viewers select as many options as they like, whereas the pop-up menu enables only one option to be chosen from the list.

Which one would you use if you wanted someone to select all the people they had heard of in a list? Check boxes or a list view would do the trick, by giving them the opportunity to select more than one option. If you need to know a visitor's salary range, marital status, or another topic in which they can select only one answer, then radio buttons or pop-up menus are obviously the best options.

Also keep in mind that form elements, especially boxed lists with scroll boxes, can look different on different platforms. This is because, for example, the Mac and the PC use different default typefaces for the text within forms. Because boxed lists usually end up being as wide as the longest line within the list, those whose font of choice, or whose default font, is a larger monospaced typeface than what you designed for, have a messed-up looking page. This usually shows up in pages that happen to have form elements

checkboxes

☒ would you like this?
☒ and this?
☐ and/or this one, perhaps?

Checkboxes let viewers make as many choices as they want to out of those provided:

```
<INPUT TYPE="checkbox" NAME="choic-
es" VALUE="this">would you like
this? <BR>
<INPUT TYPE="checkbox" NAME="choic-
es" VALUE="andthis">and this?<BR>
<INPUT TYPE="checkbox" NAME="choic-
es" VALUE="thisone">and/or this one,
perhaps?
```

within tables; the larger form box appears over the information in the adjacent column. The best way to prevent this is to test the form on various platforms, or allow sufficient space around form elements so that there's no risk of overlapping other page contents.

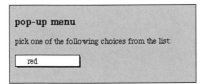

Radio buttons are a good way to offer a user a number of choices, but you need to request that they choose only one for their answer. For example, if you want to know someone's favorite junk food out of a number of specific choices, you would give each food its own radio button, but give each radio button the same NAME so that only one radio button can be chosen (if they click one and then click another, only the last radio button clicked will remain selected).

```
<INPUT TYPE="radio" VALUE="frenchfries" NAME="food">french fries<BR>
<INPUT TYPE="radio" VALUE="sundae" NAME="food">sundae<BR>
<INPUT TYPE="radio" VALUE="iccone" NAME="food">ice cream cone<BR>
<INPUT TYPE="radio" VALUE="nachos" NAME="food">nacho chips
```

Pop-up menus literally do pop up a list of choices when clicked. This is useful if you want to offer your audience a list of choices from which to choose an answer, but you don't want to take up a lot of space on the page. Keep in mind, however, that if you expect your viewers to print out and fill out your form, only the selected choice will show up on paper.

```
<SELECT NAME="color">
<OPTION SELECTED>red
<OPTION>orange
<OPTION>yellow
<OPTION>green
<OPTION>blue
<OPTION>purple
</SELECT>
```

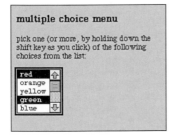

Multiple-choice menus offer a list of choices from which you can decide how much will show within the menu (in this case, SIZE="5", so five of the six options show on-screen). Clicking a choice deselects another choice by default; however, Shift+click lets a user choose multiple adjoining options, and Alt+Shift+click (Command+Shift+click on Mac) lets the user pick non-adjoining options, as shown here.

```
<SELECT SIZE="5" NAME="morecolor" MULTIPLE>
<OPTION SELECTED>red
<OPTION>orange
<OPTION>yellow
<OPTION>green
<OPTION>blue
<OPTION>purple
</SELECT>
```

text fields

name

address

phone

Text fields are ideal for that typed-in information that must be specifically separated into fields for data processing (such as in a mailing list application). Field SIZE can be set to a specific pixel width, and a MAXLENGTH tag limits the amount of text to the number of characters that are allowed within the field.

```
name <INPUT NAME="name" TYPE="text" SIZE="30"><BR>
address <INPUT NAME="address" TYPE="text" SIZE="59"><BR>
phone <INPUT NAME="phone" TYPE="text" SIZE="17" MAXLENGTH="17">
```

Text areas are generally free-for-all, let-'em-type-what-they-want areas, generally used for feedback forms or for comments and questions that aren't otherwise addressed in the form.

```
<TEXTAREA NAME="comments" ROWS="6"
COLS="50"></TEXTAREA>
```

text area

please let us know why you like to type in boxes:

Password fields are used for—well, you guessed it—passwords. Password fields are similar to text fields, but the information typed into the fields appears as bullets for the user's security (just in case someone's looking over her shoulder).

```
<INPUT NAME="pw" TYPE="password"
SIZE="10" MAXLENGTH="10">
```

password field

please enter your password:

●●●●●●●●●●

enter your password again for verification:

●●●●●●●●●●

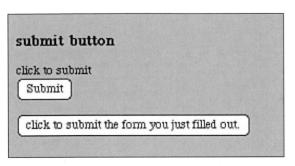

When your viewers are ready to send their information to you, all they have to do is click the Submit button. The Submit button text can simply say "Submit," or you can edit its text.

```
<INPUT NAME="action" TYPE="submit"
VALUE="Submit">
<INPUT NAME="action" TYPE="submit"
VALUE="click to submit the form you
just filled out.">
```

The Reset button simply clears all entered form information. The text you want to appear in the button is editable.

```
<INPUT NAME="name" TYPE="reset"
VALUE="Reset">
<INPUT NAME="name" TYPE="reset"
VALUE="Oh, darn, I put in all the
wrong information. I want to start
over.">
```

give direction

Whether you use standard forms or provide alternatives, it's important to include guidance to your viewers so they know what you want, or what they'll get.

[those areas marked below with an asterisk (*) **must** be filled in for us to process your order.]

shipping information

first name*
last name*
street address 1*
street address 2*
city* state* zip*
phone* fax:
email address

Make sure you label your form elements so that visitors know what you need in each box. It's also helpful to let them know which elements are optional or required for them to fill out.

This can be as simple as providing cues such as First Name: Last Name: Address: City: State:, and so on. Of course, if you're asking for more information, such as a multiple choice question of a food preference, then you have to explain both the purpose of the question and the action the visitor should take—for example, "What is your favorite kind of apple? Click one of the boxes next to your choice." If you're offering more than one choice, say so: "How many kinds of apples do you like? Click the box next to those kinds you like." In the case of offering multiple choices in a multiple choice list, provide directions on how to choose more than one item in the list: "To choose more than one item, use Alt+Shift+click (Command+Shift+click on Mac)."

Iowa
Kansas
Kentucky
Louisiana
Maine
Maryland
Massachusetts
Michigan
Minnesota
Mississippi
Missouri
Montana
Nebraska
Nevada
New Hampshire
New Jersey
New Mexico
New York
North Carolina
North Dakota
Ohio
✓ Oklahoma
Oregon
Pennsylvania
Rhode Island
South Carolina
South Dakota
Tennessee
Texas
Utah
Vermont
Virginia
Washington
West Virginia
Wisconsin
Wyoming
OTHER

Offering too many choices in an instance where it would be easier for a user to type a simple answer is more annoying than helpful. Putting all 50 states in a pop-up menu that scrolls off the page, rather than just giving users a two-character text field to type in a state abbreviation, is just a waste of both your coding time and their usage time.

consistency and logic

Remember how you have filled out forms. There are certain things that you expect to come in a certain order, and your form design should be a reflection of this, no matter how you decide to present it (either via standard web forms, text forms, or downloadable forms). Let's say all I want to know from you is your name and mailing address, but I ask for that information in the following order:

state:

last name:

apartment number:

zip code:

street address:

first name:

city:

I bet I wouldn't see you at my site again.

Offering too many choices in the name of convenience is also annoying to visitors. For example, if you make the "city" field a list of every town and city in the country instead of allowing viewers to type in their cities, they would have to scroll through thousands of choices before they found their hometown. Many sites do this with only the 50 states, and it's still a painful process. I'd rather type in the two letters myself than have to reach over to my mouse, click the pop-up, and scroll to my state. Simplicity is better than multiplicity.

problems with standard form printing

You might think it would be just as convenient for visitors to print your form from their browser (if they have the mad desire to fax or mail it) as it would be for them to use your Send or Submit button. However, Netscape Navigator is the only browser I've been able to get to print *both* the text within the forms *and* the form boxes and choices, regardless of the background color or text color. Microsoft Internet Explorer prints only the text that is not white or very light colored. NCSA Mosaic 3.0 prints only the text that happens to be links, and only a few of the applicable radio buttons. Unless you direct your users to change their text and background colors—or unless you provide an alternative form on a page with a white background with black text—they risk missing out on necessary text and form elements.

greentomato.com

we're ripe for the pickin' !

please fill out the following, and hit the SEND button when you're ready to give us your order. **If your browser does not support forms**, you can cut and paste the text into an email document and send it to orders@greentomato.com.

if you prefer, feel free to **print out this page** and fax or mail it to us at: **greentomato.com** - attn: orders dept. - 100 Tomato Way - San Francisco, CA 94000 - fax: 415 555 1111

[those areas marked below with an asterisk (*) **must** be filled in for us to process your order.]

shipping information

first name*
last name*
street address 1*
street address 2*
city*   state*   zip*
phone*   fax:
email address

billing information

please charge my...
visa ☐   mastercard ☐   american express ☐
credit card number
expiration date (mm/yy)
name on card (if other than above)

what can we get you?

item	stock number	quantity	price (each)	amout ($)
Evergreen tomato seeds	4126		$2.59	
GreenTomato.com Sauce (32 oz jar)	3264		$3.69	
our very own Green Tomato Cook Book	2854		$19.95	

The Green Tomato order form printed from Netscape Navigator and Internet Explorer, respectively. Navigator manages to print each form element except for two check boxes near the bottom of the page, and the Submit and Reset buttons (which aren't necessary in a printed form, so no big deal)…

fried green tomato batter mixins (8 oz bag)	1399		$3.99	
expert tomato growing kit	5586		$39.99	
			subtotal	
		overnight $12	shipping & handing	
			sales tax	
			TOTAL	

comments, questions or special instructions

YES, put me on your snail mail list to receive
your quarterly catalog.
YES, I'd like to receive email when GreenTomato.com
adds new products.

send it on in!.... or clear the form and start over...

114

...Explorer, however, caught every element. If you offer visitors the option to fax or mail in your form, don't forget to put fax and mail information on the form itself.

greentomato.com

we're ripe for the pickin'!

please fill out the following, and hit the SEND button when you're ready to give us your order. **If your browser does not support forms**, you can cut and paste the text into an email document and send it to **orders@greentomato.com.**

if you prefer, feel free to **print out this page** and fax or mail it to us at: **greentomato.com** - attn: orders dept. - 100 Tomato Way - San Francisco, CA 94000 - fax: 415 555 1111

[those areas marked below with an asterisk (*) **must** be filled in for us to process your order.]

shipping information

first name*
last name*
street address 1*
street address 2*
city*   state*   zip*
phone*   fax:
email address

billing information

please charge my...
      visa ☐   mastercard ☐   american express ☐
credit card number
expiration date (mm/yy)
name on card (if other than above)

what can we get you?

item	stock number	quantity	price (each)	amout ($)
Evergreen tomato seeds	4126	☐	$2.59	☐
GreenTomato corn Sauce (32 oz jar)	3264	☐	$3.69	☐
our very own Green Tomato Cook Book	2854	☐	$19.95	☐
fried green tomato batter mixins (8 oz bag)	1399	☐	$3.99	☐
expert tomato growing kit	5586	☐	$39.99	☐
			subtotal	☐
	overnight $12 ▼		shipping & handing	☐
			sales tax	☐
			TOTAL	☐

comments, questions or special instructions

☐ YES, put me on your snail mail list to receive your quarterly catalog.
☐ YES, I'd like to receive email when GreenTomato.com adds new products.

send it on in!.... or clear the form and start over...

[send order to GreenTomato] [clear form & start over]

Still, even if your visitors are using Navigator, they aren't able to print any form choices that happen to be in pop-up lists (except for the one that shows by default), or a complete list of whatever options appear in a list that has scroll bars.

summary

Whatever form your forms take, don't forget to explain things to your visitors along the way: what you want from your visitors and what they get from you.

Providing alternatives to forms not only aids people who are visually or physically impaired, but it also adds a level of convenience for people who prefer or are used to filling out forms the old-fashioned way. These forms can also be filled out when your visitors are offline—a nice touch if they happen to have an online account that is billed by the hour.

Consistency and logic are key; offering choices is good business.

CHAPTER 7

> *"There's an art to setting a beautiful table."*
> — *Martha Stewart*

putting it on the table

getting the place settings right

Tables were probably the first HTML tag set that made website designers jump up and down in glee. Suddenly, it became possible to divide text into columns, and separate blocks of text and graphics into either specified-pixel-width columns or relative percentage columns.

Today, more browsers are able to read or interpret tables in the manner in which designers want them to be shown, give or take a few pixels here and there. Netscape Navigator and Microsoft Internet Explorer show tables in practically the same manner; even NCSA Mosaic can handle most table setups, except for tables that use the <ALIGN> tag to place a table along the left or right margin.

how tables work

Tables work in a manner similar to a spreadsheet—information is set up and presented in columns or rows defined by the user. Each cross-section of a column and row is referred to as a *cell*.

118

A table is made up of cells much in the same way a spreadsheet is. Here's a basic three-column/two-row table, and the code that created it:

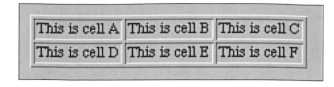

```
<TABLE BORDER>
    <TR>
<TD>This is cell A</TD> <TD>This is cell B</TD>
➥<TD>This is cell C</TD>
    </TR>
    <TR>
<TD>This is cell D</TD> <TD>This is cell E</TD>
➥<TD>This is cell F</TD>
    </TR>
</TABLE>
```

Certain definitions of rows and column widths and column heights can make for an interesting combination of cell shapes and sizes. However, if table rows and columns aren't set to appear at a specific or relative width, the table generally automatically sizes them to fit the content within the cell. Two cells next to each other expand or decrease in size depending on the width of the browser page and the amount of text or size of the image within the cell.

Without using additional tags, such as <CELLSPACING>, <CELLPADDING>, or <WIDTH>, the table follows its default of taking up as much space as it needs to, to show its content within. If you'd like columns and rows to be separated by a rule, you've got to specify the table's BORDER size (if you just include the word BORDER, and don't specify a size, you'll end up with the default border size of 1).

The <ROWSPAN> and <COLSPAN> tags direct cells to span more than one row or column. You can produce some really cool effects using these tags. The key thing to remember when you're designing your table is to design from the top right to the lower left. Odd combinations of <ROWSPAN> and <COLSPAN>, when rendered into straight text, can end up not making a whole lot of sense in the order it appears.

```
┌─────────── Netscape: Weird table layout demo ───────────┐
│                                                          │
│   ┌──────────────────────────────────────────────┐      │
│   │           I'm saving this row for a title.     │      │
│   │           It spans three column widths;        │      │
│   │           the first and fifth columns have     │      │
│   │           no contents.                         │      │
│   │                                                │      │
│   │  row 1,   row 1,    row 1,    row 1,           │      │
│   │  column 1 column    column 3  column          │      │
│   │           2                   4                │      │
│   │                                                │      │
│   │  row 2,   row 2, column 2.   row 2,  row 1, column 5. │
│   │  column 1 COLSPAN=2 makes    column  ROWSPAN=3       │
│   │           this column span   3       makes this 3 rows │
│   │           two column widths.         deep.           │
│   │                                                │      │
│   │  row 3,   row 3,             row 3,            │      │
│   │  column   column 2          column            │      │
│   │  1; two             row 3,  4                 │      │
│   │  rows     row 4,    column 3.                 │      │
│   │  deep.    column 1  Guess what                │      │
│   │                     made this                 │      │
│   │                     three     row 4, column 2. This cell uses │
│   │                     columns   COLSPAN=2 and   │      │
│   │  row 5,   row 5,    deep.     ROWSPAN=2.      │      │
│   │  column 1 column                              │      │
│   │           2                                   │      │
│   └──────────────────────────────────────────────┘      │
└──────────────────────────────────────────────────────────┘
```

If you're willing to play around with different widths and heights of columns and rows, tables can provide some pretty cool results. This relatively simple example shows how <ROWSPAN> and <COLSPAN> can be used for interesting text layout within a table.

Note that within this example we have yet to include any sizing controls (such as the exact width of columns and rows in pixels), except that we want the entire table to have a width of 80 percent of the screen (WIDTH=80%).

```
<TABLE BORDER=2 cellspacing=5 CELLPADDING=5 WIDTH=80%>

<TR> <TD> <TD COLSPAN=3 ALIGN="LEFT"><STRONG>I'm saving this
➥row for a title. It spans three column widths; the first and
➥fifth columns have no contents.</STRONG></TD> </TR>

<TR> <TD>row 1, column 1 <TD>row 1, column 2 <TD>row 1, column
➥3 <TD>row 1, column 4 <TD ROWSPAN=3>row 1, column 5.
➥ROWSPAN=3 makes this 3 rows deep. </TR>

<TR> <TD>row 2, column 1 <TD COLSPAN=2>row 2, column 2.
➥COLSPAN=2 makes this column span two column widths. <TD>row
➥2, column 3 </TR>

<TR> <TD ROWSPAN=2>row 3, column 1; two rows deep. <TD>row 3,
➥column 2 <TD ROWSPAN=3>row 3, column 3. Guess what made this
➥three columns deep. <TD>row 3, column 4 </TR>

<TR> <TD>row 4, column 1 <TD COLSPAN=2 ROWSPAN=2>row 4, column
➥2. This cell uses COLSPAN=2 and ROWSPAN=2. </TR>

<TR> <TD>row 5, column 1 <TD>row 5, column 2</TR>

</TABLE>
```

The <TR> tag defines a single row of a table. Within the tag you can include any relevant <ALIGN> (horizontal alignment) or <VALIGN> (vertical alignment) tags with the text within the row. Although some browsers are forgiving when you forget to include a </TR> at the end of each table row, some just assume the table row goes on.

```
<TABLE BORDER=2 WIDTH=50%>
<TR ALIGN="CENTER">  <TD>In this case, the row<BR> will be
➥center aligned.</TD> <TD>where am I?</TR>
<TR ALIGN="RIGHT">    <TD>This row will <BR>be right aligned
```

The <TR> tag is where you stick your alignment codes for each row. This example shows where text ends up when you add CENTER, RIGHT, TOP, and BOTTOM alignments via the <ALIGN> (for horizontal alignment) and <VALIGN> (for vertical alignment) tags.

In this case, the row will be center aligned.	where am I?
This row will be right aligned within the column.	Over here.
This row's text aligns with the top of the cell.	See?
This row's text aligns with the bottom of the cell.	I'm down here!
This row's text aligns right, and vertically aligns with the bottom of the cell.	Now, that's control.

```
➥<BR>within the column.</TD> <TD>Over here.</TR>
<TR VALIGN="TOP">     <TD>This row's text <BR>aligns with the
➥<BR>top of the cell.</TD> <TD>See?</TR>
<TR VALIGN="BOTTOM"> <TD>This row's text <BR>aligns with the
➥<BR>bottom of the cell.</TD> <TD>I'm down here!</TR>
<TR ALIGN="RIGHT" VALIGN="BOTTOM"> <TD>This row's text
➥<BR>aligns right, and <BR>vertically aligns with <BR>the
➥bottom of the cell.</TD> <TD>Now, that's control.</TR>
</TABLE>
```

tableless browsers

Most browsers that do not render tables on-screen simply run the information from each subsequent cell to the next. It's great that your viewers are able to get all of the information within a table, but unfortunately, if you don't throw in a few formatting tags, all of the text runs together in one long, long, long paragraph. Considering that the main reason to use a table is to create a page that is organized in a certain way, omitting a few simple extras can turn your page into a larger mess than it was without the tables.

Viewed in a browser that supports tables, this page looks as intended.

line breaks

Within each cell of text, include a
 (line break) tag at the end of its contents. This addition doesn't make a difference to someone viewing the table, nor does it change a table's layout and appearance. But for someone who can't see the table, it simply makes a normal line break that breaks the text at your specified spot, as opposed to a break made at the browser's whim.

In a non-table-supportive browser, this page looks rather gangly. Although it's no aesthetic masterpiece, the text is still readable and accessible. Note, however, that because there was no line break <BR> inserted at the bottom of the middle column, the third column (which begins with the graphic icon representing Wood Works) runs into the text.

You could, of course, make a page for those people who have browsers that don't support tables, but adding line breaks as safeguards to your table is a much quicker solution.

tack

saddles

gifts

book store

Thank you for stopping by and being part of our 'history'. We are a family-owned and operated tack and feed shop. We began this business in 1990, after an exhaustive search for inexpensive, yet safe, tack and equipment for our newly purchased palomino, Teddy. Having three children *and* a horse meant little money! (we still have the three children and little money, but have 8 pasture pals.)

The tack shop is housed in a small building at our home. The building was once part of the original Washington Agricultural Society. The Deberville homestead includes the original fair site, as well as the 1/2 mile race horse track.

So come on in and find that horsey thing you didn't even know you needed!

And please, give us your feedback!

Love and thanks to my sister, without whose support I would've said Neigh to this project. Visit her award winning site!

tack | saddles | gifts | bookstore
woodworks | linens | gear | links

wood works

linens

gear

links

Old Fairgrounds Tack Shop

Washington, VT

tack

saddles

gifts

book store

Thank you for stopping by and being part of our 'history'. We are a family-owned and operated tack and feed shop. We began this business in 1990, after an exhaustive search for inexpensive, yet safe, tack and equipment for our newly purchased palomino, Teddy. Having three children *and* a horse meant little money! (we still have the three children and little money, but have 8 pasture pals.)

The tack shop is housed in a small building at our home. The building was once part of the original Washington Agricultural Society. The Deberville homestead includes the original fair site, as well as the 1/2 mile race horse track.

So come on in and find that horsey thing you didn't even know you needed!

And please, give us your feedback!

Love and thanks to my sister, without whose support I would've said Neigh to this project. Visit her award winning site!

tack | saddles | gifts | bookstore

wood works

woodworks | linens | gear | links

linens

gear

links

Adding a line break tag <BR> moves the Wood Works icon down so that it at least aligns with the rest of the icons.

Looking at our oddly laid out table, it's easy to see how confusing a table's content can look when viewed in a browser that doesn't support tables (in this case, NSCA Mosaic 1.0.3).

Netscape: Weird table layout demo

I'm saving this row for a title. It spans three column widths; the first and fifth columns have no contents.

row 1, column 1	row 1, column 2	row 1, column 3	row 1, column 4	
row 2, column 1	row 2, column 2. COLSPAN=2 makes this column span two column widths.		row 2, column 3	row 1, column 5. ROWSPAN=3 makes this 3 rows deep.
row 3, column 1; two rows deep.	row 3, column 2	row 3, column 3. Guess what made this three columns deep.	row 3, column 4	
	row 4, column 1		row 4, column 2. This cell uses COLSPAN=2 and ROWSPAN=2.	
row 5, column 1	row 5, column 2			

Document: Done.

Adding <BR> tags after each cell's contents, however, at least puts each cell's contents on separate lines.

I'm saving this row for a title. It spans three column widths; the first and fifth columns have no contents. row 1, column 1 row 1, column 2 row 1, column 3 row 1, column 4 row 1, column 5. ROWSPAN=3 makes this 3 rows deep. row 2, column 1 row 2, column 2. COLSPAN=2 makes this column span two column widths. row 2, column 3 row 3, column 1; two rows deep. row 3, column 2 row 3, column 3. Guess what made this three columns deep. row 3, column 4 row 4, column 1 row 4, column 2. This cell uses COLSPAN=2 and ROWSPAN=2. row 5, column 1 row 5, column 2

I'm saving this row for a title. It spans three column widths; the first and fifth columns have no contents.
row 1, column 1
row 1, column 2
row 1, column 3
row 1, column 4
row 1, column 5. ROWSPAN=3 makes this 3 rows deep.
row 2, column 1
row 2, column 2. COLSPAN=2 makes this column span two column widths.
row 2, column 3
row 3, column 1; two rows deep.
row 3, column 2
row 3, column 3. Guess what made this three columns deep.
row 3, column 4
row 4, column 1
row 4, column 2. This cell uses COLSPAN=2 and ROWSPAN=2.
row 5, column 1
row 5, column 2

---

paragraph breaks

Adding a <P> tag at the end of a table cell's contents also results in the desired new paragraph for those who can't view your table. However, keep in mind that this may affect the appearance of your table, so if you want to have this much of a break between each cell's contents when it's viewed as text-only, be sure to account for its consequences within the table. It may not look all that bad if you use it consistently.

Note

If you're looking for yet another way to add captions to your images, take advantage of the TABLE attribute that adds a <CAPTION> tag to a table. This guarantees that the reader sees the text in relation to the image, as well as knowing that most browsers keep the relevant caption text with the image it's related to. Captions can be placed at the top or bottom of the table, depending on how you've set it up. You can get a similar result by making your table two cells—one for the image and one for the caption.

Mom and Uncle Art - 1990
Leona Schultz Waters and Otto Arthur
Schultz. A wonderful sibling reunion
after 15 years apart.

The first way to caption an image is to include both the picture and the text within the same box.

To include the text and the figure in the same block use the following code:

```
<TABLE BORDER=1 WIDTH=213
ALIGN=LEFT CELLPADDING=10
CELLSPACING=10>
    <TR>
    <TD>
        <FONT COLOR="#660033"
SIZE=4><IMG SRC="./momart.jpg"
ALT="Mom and Uncle Art"
WIDTH="193" HEIGHT="149" BOR-
DER="0">
        <BR CLEAR=ALL>
        <P>
        <STRONG>Mom and Uncle
Art - 1990</STRONG><BR>
        <FONT SIZE=3>Leona
Schultz Waters and Otto Arthur
Schultz.  A wonderful sibling
reunion after 15 years apart.
        <BR CLEAR=ALL>
    </TD>
    </TR>
</TABLE>
```

extra space

If you don't care whether all of your table cells' information runs together (if your table is small and has only a few lines of text in it to begin with), at least remember to add an extra space at the end of the last sentence in each cell. This way, when sentences run together, there's at least one space between them, rather than this:

End of sentence.Beginning of sentence.

Mom and Uncle Art - 1990
Leona Schultz Waters and Otto Arthur Schultz. A wonderful sibling reunion after 15 years apart.

Within a browser that doesn't support tables, this is how this would most likely appear.

You can also add a caption simply by adding another row, or a cell below the cell that holds the picture. Note that the <FONT> tag had to be moved in order for it to affect the text within the cell.

```
<TABLE BORDER=1 WIDTH=213 ALIGN=LEFT CELLPADDING=10 CELLSPAC-
ING=10>
    <TR>
    <TD>
        <IMG SRC="./momart.jpg" ALT="Mom and Uncle Art"
WIDTH="193" HEIGHT="149" BORDER="0"><BR>
    </TD>
    </TR>
    <TR>
    <TD>
        <FONT COLOR="#660033" SIZE=4><STRONG>Mom and Uncle Art -
1990</STRONG><BR>
        <FONT SIZE=3>Leona Schultz Waters and Otto Arthur
Schultz.  A wonderful sibling reunion after 15
years apart.<BR CLEAR=ALL>
    </TD>
    </TR>
</TABLE>
```

Mom and Uncle Art - 1990
Leona Schultz Waters and Otto Arthur
Schultz. A wonderful sibling reunion
after 15 years apart.

Here, the caption and figure are separated

Mom and Uncle Art - 1990
Leona Schultz Waters and Otto Arthur Schultz. A wonderful sibling reunion after 15 years apart.

Without table support, this case ends up similar to the first. Because I put a line break <BR> in the code, the text falls below the photograph at a distance of one line-space.

Using the <CAPTION> tag (in this case using ALIGN=BOTTOM to put the text below the image), we have the appearance of free-floating text outside of the table. However, in a browser that doesn't support tables, the text in the caption would appear just as it does in the previous non-table browser example.

To have your text appear as though it is floating outside of the table, use the following code:

Mom and Uncle Art - 1990
Leona Schultz Waters and Otto Arthur
Schultz. A wonderful sibling reunion
after 15 years apart.

```
<TABLE BORDER=1 WIDTH=213 ALIGN=LEFT CELLPADDING=10 CELLSPAC-
ING=10>
    <TR>
    <TD>
        <IMG SRC="./momart.jpg" ALT="Mom and Uncle Art"
WIDTH="193" HEIGHT="149" BORDER="0"><BR>

<CAPTION ALIGN=BOTTOM>
        <FONT COLOR="#660033" SIZE=4><STRONG>Mom and Uncle Art
- 1990</STRONG><BR>
        <FONT SIZE=3>Leona Schultz Waters and Otto Arthur
Schultz.  A wonderful sibling reunion after 15 years apart.
</CAPTION>
</TD
</TR>
</TABLE>
```

A long page using tables appears to load faster if you break up the information into multiple tables. In this example, each book gets its own table.

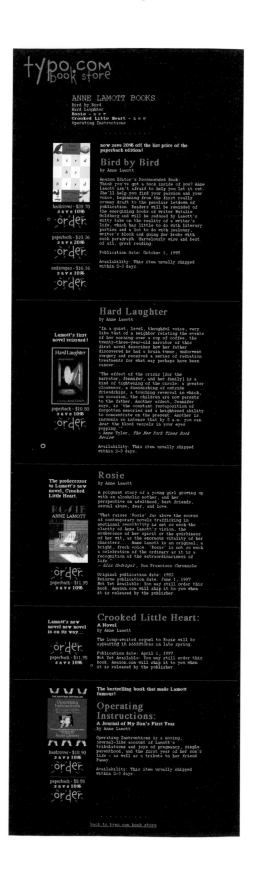

how tables load

Although the text in a table isn't any "bigger" in file size than text outside a table, large tables appear to slow down page loading, especially if they are longer than one screen page. This is because when a browser hits a <TABLE> tag, it generally waits to download all the enclosed information before it appears on-screen in its entirety.

To fix this, consider breaking long tables into multiple tables that are displayed either on the same page or on subsequent pages. Keep in mind that people don't usually like mega-long pages of anything, so if your table is humongous, breaking the information into digestible chunks is desirable anyway.

"table-like" pages for text browsers

If you think most of your audience will be using text browsers that can't handle tables, you can use the <PRE>, or <TT>, tag to set up a mock table. The same is true if you're dealing only with text elements in your pages. Using the <PRE> tag (or the <TT> tag if you prefer; its results are generally the same), your text happily follows the exact format of each letter and manual space (typed with the spacebar) in the monospaced typeface that your viewer has chosen to use. Hopefully, they'll choose the same one you do.

Here's a typical three-column layout using a standard three-column table. But what if you don't know whether your market uses browsers that support tables? Most likely, they do. But if you're not sure, there are other options.

Classifieds — Old Fairgrounds Tack Shop

1/9/97. In Vermont-**For Sale-Gorgeous AQHA gelding**, foaled June 3, 1983. 15.3 hands. Doc Tom's Peppy has done cross country, and loves to go. Chestnut with star, two flashy white socks. Bloodlines include Doc Bar, Peppy, Jameen Tivio. Tommy has been exposed to many elements, including cattle, pigs, chickens, turkeys, dogs, cats, tractors and other farm equipment, gymkhanas, fairs, shows, and has even brought home the Christmas tree! Asking $3500, negotiable, or let's talk trade for a ranch horse. E-mail tackshop@together.net, or snail mail to Katie Deberville, PO Box 756, Washington, VT 05675, or call 802-883-2290.

1/9/97. In VT-**Dressage Saddle Package**, Silver Fox rarely used, 16", black, doesn't fit my Arab. With cutback head, deeper seat, long slightly padded flaps. Girth, snaffle bridle, irons, leathers. Asking $200. E-mail tackshop@together.net, or snail mail to Liza Deberville, same address and phone as above.

1/9/97-in VT-**AQHA mare**, Ima Son Dee Honey, age 14, 15.2 hands, excellent conformation and muscle. Chrome chestnut, perfect diamond. Bloodlines include Son Dee Bar, Blondys Dude, King Bars. Proven Broodmare. Western, English, shown successfully locally.

Round pen training & professional training. Been exposed to same elements as Tommy, above. Sell, or trade for AQHA stallion, gelding or mare of equal value. E-mail tackshop@together.net, or snail mail to Liza Deberville, address and phone above.

Please send your classifieds to me, and I'll post them in exchange for a link from you to me. I'll also link to your picture(s) on your site. I do not take responsibility for any selling or buying anyone does through these classifieds. Contact each other directly!

In NSCA Mosaic 1.0.3 and other tableless browsers, the Classifieds page comes out looking pretty good. The only change necessary is to add a line break <BR> or paragraph break <P> after the opening image so that the table text doesn't start immediately after the image appears.

Classifieds — Old Fairgrounds Tack Shop

1/9/97. In Vermont-**For Sale-Gorgeous AQHA gelding**, foaled June 3, 1983. 15.3 hands. Doc Tom's Peppy has done cross country, and loves to go. Chestnut with star, two flashy white socks. Bloodlines include Doc Bar, Peppy, Jameen Tivio. Tommy has been exposed to many elements, including cattle, pigs, chickens, turkeys, dogs, cats, tractors and other farm equipment, gymkhanas, fairs, shows, and has even brought home the Christmas tree! Asking $3500, negotiable, or let's talk trade for a ranch horse. E-mail tackshop@together.net, or snail mail to Katie Deberville, PO Box 756, Washington, VT 05675, or call 802-883-2290.

1/9/97. In VT-**Dressage Saddle Package**, Silver Fox rarely used, 16", black, doesn't fit my Arab. With cutback head, deeper seat, long slightly padded flaps. Girth, snaffle bridle, irons, leathers. Asking $200. E-mail tackshop@together.net, or snail mail to Liza Deberville, same address and phone as above.

1/9/97-in VT-**AQHA mare**, Ima Son Dee Honey, age 14, 15.2 hands, excellent conformation and muscle. Chrome chestnut, perfect diamond. Bloodlines include Son Dee Bar, Blondys Dude, King Bars. Proven Broodmare. Western, English, shown successfully locally. Round pen training & professional training. Been exposed to same elements as Tommy, above. Sell, or trade for AQHA stallion, gelding or mare of equal value. E-mail tackshop@together.net, or snail mail to Liza Deberville, address and phone above.

Please send your classifieds to me, and I'll post them in exchange for a link from you to me. I'll also link to your picture(s) on your site. I do not take responsibility for any selling or buying anyone does through these classifieds. Contact each other directly!

In a text-only browser, the Classifieds page is relatively jumbled and definitely difficult to read. Because the code includes a <CENTER>.</CENTER> tag around the image and table, all the text ends up being affected by this code.

```
                    [1]Classified Ads
    1/9/97. In Vermont-For Sale-Gorgeous AQHA gelding, foaled June 3,
    1983. 15.3 hands. [2]Doc Tom's Peppy has done cross country, and loves
    to go. Chestnut with star, two flashy white socks. Bloodlines include
    Doc Bar, Peppy, Jameen Tivio. Tommy has been exposed to many elements,
    including cattle, pigs, chickens, turkeys, dogs, cats, tractors and
    other farm equipment, gymkhanas, [3]fairs, shows, and has even brought
    home the Christmas tree! Asking $3500, negotiable, or let's talk trade
    for a ranch horse. E-mail tackshop@together.net, or snail mail to
          Katie Deberville, PO Box 756, Washington, VT 05675, or call
                              802-883-2290.
    1/9/97. In VT-Dressage Saddle Package, Silver Fox rarely used, 16",
          black, doesn't fit my Arab. With cutback head, deeper seat, long
    slightly padded flaps. Girth, snaffle bridle, irons, leathers. Asking
    $200. E-mail tackshop@together.net, or snail mail to Liza Deberville,
                    same address and phone as above.
    1/9/97-in VT-AQHA mare, [4]Ima Son Dee Honey, age 14, 15.2 hands,
    excellent conformation and muscle. Chrome chestnut, perfect diamond.
    Bloodlines include Son Dee Bar, Blondys Dude, King Bars. Proven
    Broodmare. Western, English, shown successfully locally. Round pen
    training & professional training. Been exposed to same elements as
    Tommy, above. Sell, or trade for AQHA stallion, gelding or mare of
    equal value. E-mail tackshop@together.net, or snail mail to Liza
                    Deberville, address and phone above.
    Please [5]send your classifieds to me, and I'll post them in exhange
    for a link from you to me. I'll also link to your picture(s) on your
    site. I do not take responsibility for any selling or buying anyone
          does through these classifieds. Contact each other directly!
```

```
Classified Ads       VT 05675, or call    Broodmare. Western,
1/9/97. In Vermont-  802-883-2290.        English, shown
FOR SALE-GORGEOUS                         successfully locally.
AQHA GELDING, foaled 1/9/97. In VT-       Round pen training &
June 3, 1983. 15.3   DRESSAGE SADDLE      professional
hands. Doc Tom's     PACKAGE, Silver Fox  training. Been
Peppy has done cross rarely used, 16",    exposed to same
country, and loves to black, doesn't fit  elements as Tommy,
go. Chestnut with    my Arab. With cutback above. Sell, or trade
star, two flashy     head, deeper seat,   for AQHA stallion,
white socks.         long slightly padded gelding or mare of
Bloodlines include   flaps. Girth, snaffle equal value. E-mail
Doc Bar, Peppy,      bridle, irons,       tackshop@together.net
Jameen Tivio. Tommy  leathers. Asking     , or snail mail to
has been exposed to  $200. E-mail         Liza Deberville,
many elements,       tackshop@together.net address and phone
including cattle,    , or snail mail to   above.
pigs, chickens,      Liza Deberville, same
turkeys, dogs, cats, address and phone as Please send your
tractors and other   above.              classifieds to me,
farm equipment,                          and I'll post them in
gymkhanas, fairs,    1/9/97-in VT-AQHA    exchange for a link
shows, and has even  MARE, Ima Son Dee    from you to me. I'll
brought home the     Honey, age 14, 15.2  also link to your
Christmas tree!      hands, excellent     picture(s) on your
Asking $3500,        conformation and     site. I do not take
negotiable, or let's muscle. Chrome       responsibility for
talk trade for a     chestnut, perfect    any selling or buying
ranch horse. E-mail  diamond. Bloodlines  anyone does through
tackshop@together.net include Son Dee Bar, these classifieds.
, or snail mail to                        Contact each other
Katie Deberville, PO Blondys Dude, King   directly!
Box 756, Washington, Bars. Proven
```

In my word processor, I set up my text file in three columns. This process helps to show where manual line breaks should go for setting up a page using the <PRE> or <TT> code. It helps to print this out for visual reference. Note that I used the typeface that I believe will best represent what will show up on-screen in most browsers (in this case, 10-point Courier).

```
Classified Ads       VT 05675, or call    Broodmare. Western,
1/9/97. In Vermont-  802-883-2290.        English, shown
FOR SALE-GORGEOUS                         successfully locally.
AQHA GELDING, foaled 1/9/97. In VT-       Round pen training &
June 3, 1983. 15.3   DRESSAGE SADDLE      professional
hands. Doc Tom's     PACKAGE, Silver Fox  training. Been
Peppy has done cross rarely used, 16",    exposed to same
country, and loves to black, doesn't fit  elements as Tommy,
go. Chestnut with    my Arab. With cutback above. Sell, or trade
star, two flashy     head, deeper seat,   for AQHA stallion,
white socks.         long slightly padded gelding or mare of
Bloodlines include   flaps. Girth, snaffle equal value. E-mail
Doc Bar, Peppy,      bridle, irons,       tackshop@together.net
Jameen Tivio. Tommy  leathers. Asking     , or snail mail to
has been exposed to  $200. E-mail         Liza Deberville,
many elements,       tackshop@together.net address and phone
including cattle,    , or snail mail to   above.
pigs, chickens,      Liza Deberville, same
turkeys, dogs, cats, address and phone as Please send your
tractors and other   above.              classifieds to me,
farm equipment,                          and I'll post them in
gymkhanas, fairs,    1/9/97-in VT-AQHA    exchange for a link
shows, and has even  MARE, Ima Son Dee    from you to me. I'll
brought home the     Honey, age 14, 15.2  also link to your
Christmas tree!      hands, excellent     picture(s) on your
Asking $3500,        conformation and     site. I do not take
negotiable, or let's muscle. Chrome       responsibility for
talk trade for a     chestnut, perfect    any selling or buying
ranch horse. E-mail  diamond. Bloodlines  anyone does through
tackshop@together.net include Son Dee Bar, these classifieds.
, or snail mail to                        Contact each other
Katie Deberville, PO Blondys Dude, King   directly!
Box 756, Washington, Bars. Proven
```

Before I start coding, I check my printout and mark the longest line in each column. This way, I'll be sure to leave enough space between columns at the start, rather than having to realign each line after they are all entered. It helps to count the number of spaces between the first few lines of the first column and the second few lines of the second, and between the second and third, as well.

130

Now comes the tedious part … aligning all the text manually. You can keep open two windows in a text editor and copy (or drag and drop) the lines as you need them, using the printout as a guide to the amount of text to copy. Usually, it's faster just to type the text. Make sure to use the spacebar for spaces between columns; some browsers won't read tabs as the same character width. Note that the links aren't added yet.

After links are added, it's much more difficult to keep track of your alignment.

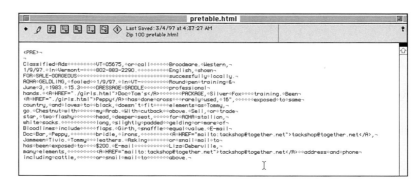

Because the line breaks are manual, links that break in the middle (such as that to Doc Tom's Peppy in the first column) must be linked to twice.

```
<TITLE>Old Fairgrounds Tack Shop - Classifieds</TITLE>

</HEAD>
<BODY bgcolor="#ffffff" text="#000000" link="#999999" vlink="#333333">

<PRE>

Classified Ads          VT 05675, or call      Broodmare. Western,
1/9/97. In Vermont-     802-883-2290.          English, shown
FOR SALE-GORGEOUS                              successfully locally.
AQHA GELDLING, foaled   1/9/97. In VT-         Round pen training &
June 3, 1983. 15.3      DRESSAGE SADDLE        professional
hands. <A HREF="./girls.html">Doc Tom's</A>       PACKAGE, Silver Fox
training. Been
<A HREF="./girls.html">Peppy</A> has done cross    rarely used, 16",
exposed to same
country, and loves to   black, doesn't fit     elements as Tommy,
go. Chestnut with       my Arab. With cutback  above. Sell, or trade
star, two flashy        head, deeper seat,     for AQHA stallion,
white socks.            long, slightly padded  gelding or mare of
```

```
Bloodlines include      flaps. Girth, snaffle   equal value. E-mail
Doc Bar, Peppy,          bridle, irons,          <A
HREF="mailto:tackshop@together.net">tackshop@together.net</A>,
Jammeen Tivio. Tommy    leathers. Asking        or snail mail to
has been exposed to     $200. E-mail            Liza Deberville,
many elements,          <A
HREF="mailto:tackshop@together.net">tackshop@together.net</A>  address
and phone
including cattle,       or snail mail to        above.


</PRE>
</BODY>
</HTML>
```

```
Classified Ads         VT 05675, or call      Broodmare. Western,
1/9/97. In Vermont-    802-883-2290.          English, shown
FOR SALE-GORGEOUS                             successfully locally.
AQHA GELDING, foaled   1/9/97. In VT-         Round pen training &
June 3, 1983. 15.3     DRESSAGE SADDLE        professional
hands. Doc Tom's       PACKAGE, Silver Fox    training. Been
Peppy has done cross   rarely used, 16",      exposed to same
country, and loves to  black, doesn't fit     elements as Tommy,
go. Chestnut with      my Arab. With outback  above. Sell, or trade
star, two flashy       head, deeper seat,     for AQHA stallion,
white socks.           long, slightly padded  gelding or mare of
Bloodlines include     flaps. Girth, snaffle  equal value. E-mail
Doc Bar, Peppy,        bridle, irons,         tackshop@together.net,
Jammeen Tivio. Tommy   leathers. Asking       or snail mail to
has been exposed to    $200. E-mail           Liza Deberville,
many elements,         tackshop@together.net  address and phone
including cattle,      or snail mail to       above.
```

Here are the columns as they'll look in finished form.

But there are drawbacks: Laying out text this way can take a while, and you have to type the first line of the first paragraph of the first column, then the first line of the next paragraph in the next column, and so on. This is especially awkward if you're not sure where your text is going to break. You can try setting up the text you want to put in columns in your word processor using the monospaced typeface size you've chosen—in columns if it supports it—so that you can at least tell where the first column will end and the next will begin. If your word processor doesn't support columns, change your margins to reflect the desired width of your resulting columns, count the lines, and split them accordingly. Make sure you get the layout right the first time: This kind of layout is hell to edit if you need to add or subtract more than a couple of words from within the text.

Keep in mind that it may be tempting to use your Tab key to indent and move text to where you want it. This works in some cases; however, some browsers read a tab as more spaces than does another browser so alignment is sure to be off.

tables and screen readers

People who are used to reading have visually learned that columns are to be read in a certain way—read down one column and then back up to the next. However, screen readers (the software that "reads" a page's text out loud) tend to read directly across the screen, jumbling lines of text together. This is true whether you use <TABLE> tags or the "table-like" method previously mentioned.

The easiest way to solve the screen reader problem is to provide text versions of the information found within your tables, but a more high-tech solution is in the works. According to the Trace Research & Development Center (http://trace.wisc.edu/), proposals have been made to include the <AXES> and <AXIS> tags as supported attributes by screen readers. If so, each entry in a table that appears on-screen would be identified and read in its proper order, as long as the designer places them properly.

<AXIS> and <AXES> tags can be used within <TD> and <TH> references. Generally, AXIS="n" where n defines an abbreviated name for a header cell. If you don't include an abbreviated name, it defaults to the content of the cell.

<AXES> is basically a comma-delineated list of all the AXIS names that identify the rows and column headers that pertain to a cell. This is not only helpful for those who need to use a speech reader to access your tables, but also comes in handy if you need to transfer table contents into a database (because database software needs field names in order to separate cells into the proper fields within a database).

summary

There are some wonderful and unique tables used on the web. One of my favorites is the Discovery Channel Online (http://www.discovery.com). Having consistent tag structures for tables, adding line breaks where applicable, and using alternative text pages or text structures, will add to the overall readability and accessibility of the information you want to share with the users—the main reason many designers choose to use tables in the first place.

Note

Don't forget end tags for those tags that require them. Although some browsers are forgiving, others don't know what to do if a </TR>, </TH>, or so on have not been added. For some helpful information on table tags and their many uses, check out http://www.synapse.net/~woodall/icons/table.htm, part of the Compendium of HTML Elements, complied by (and some written by) Ron Woodall.

frames

"There are no exceptions to the rule that everybody likes to be an exception to the rule."
— *Charles Osgood*

the great cubicle debate

Frames have been applauded and damned for their navigational potential—and the lack thereof. Depending on their designs, they can guarantee consistency in content presentation, or they can wreak havoc on the person new to the web who may not be aware of their proper uses.

Frames are similar to tables in that they allow you to split a page into specific-width blocks, either by specific pixel counts or by percentages of the browser window's width and height. Unlike tables, which simply organize a window's contents, frames break the main window into "subwindows" that contain information from different URLs. Generally, frames are set up to include at least one window that remains constant (this window may contain some sort of navigational graphic or list), in which there are clickable links that change the content in another frame. This frames feature allows you to better control the look and design of your site.

134

Frames allow a web site's information to be presented in a number of subwindows. Usually a site has static subwindows, such as a window that includes a site menu, or a window that displays the site's logo or advertisers. In this case, the main window in which information appears is the subwindow on the lower right.

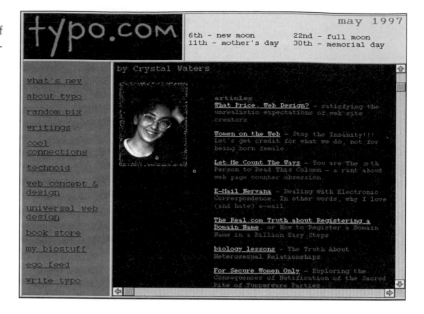

Not all people know that you generally have to hold down the mouse button (for Mac users) or hold down the right mouse button (for Windows users) in order to navigate within a frames window.

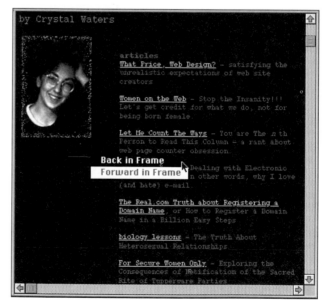

scroll annoyance

To make your frame-based site more accessible, keep it flexible. Don't set up your framed page for a certain size screen; your visitors might view it on a smaller screen. Even a one-inch difference in screen size can turn a seemingly normal-looking screen into a bunch of frames with multiple scroll bars. Not only are scroll bars ugly, but they prevent the viewer from seeing all of the information you intended to show within each frame window.

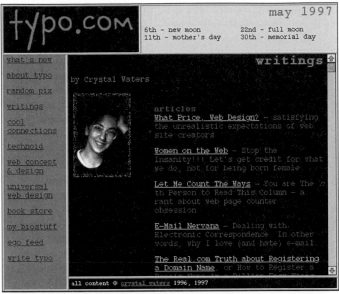

Here's the same URL, but the second image is on a one-inch-smaller-in-diagonal screen. Notice how the scroll bars on the left-hand menu frame have appeared, and almost cut off some of the enclosed text.

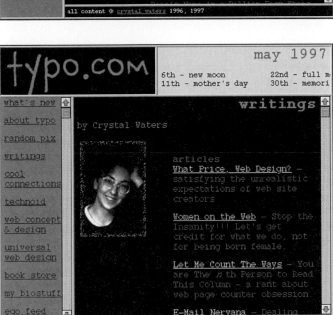

To prevent this, consider using the <FRAMESET> options to specifically control the rows and columns of your frames, either via specifying pixel sizes (best if you think your audience has bigger screens than the one for which you've designed the frames) or percentages of the browser window. Specifying pixel sizes is especially important if your windows *must* be a certain size to show navigational options, a full graphic, or certain text line lengths. Keep in mind, however, that some browsers may override your specified pixel value anyway, in order to fill 100 percent of

the user's window. Using percentages, rather than leaving the frame size determined by the user, (theoretically) guarantees that no matter what the size of the user's browser window, the particular frame will resize itself to match its percentage value.

```
<FRAMESET ROWS="17%,83%">
<FRAMESET COLS="238,*">
```

The "wildcard" option (*) in FRAMESET values sets a "relative size" frame. Used in conjunction with the fixed-pixel values, the wildcard can work fairly well. If you have three horizontal frames, and want the top frame (which encloses your logo) to be 100 pixels high and the bottom frame (which shows your site's advertisers) to be 100 pixels high, you could set your "middle" FRAMESET value as *. The browser then gives the middle frame the remaining space available on-screen.

Frame windows may be tagged so that the user can dynamically resize the window. However, you can also disable frame resizing if you want to make sure that the frame size stays the same.

noframes

Perhaps the most common barrier that a person runs into when they hit a framed site is that their browser simply doesn't support frames.

I highly recommend that you include a descriptive NOFRAMES section within your home page in case someone whose browser doesn't support frames hits your site. Whatever appears between the <NOFRAMES> and </NOFRAMES> tags will show up on the person's screen. Don't take the easy way out used by many of frame-based sites I've seen. These sites simply include a notice such as, "Hey, go download a frame-supporting browser," and maybe a "Netscape Now!" button that links to the Netscape home page. What kind of customer service is that?

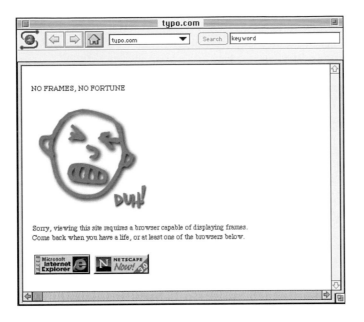

This NOFRAMES page offers nothing more than a kick in the face to the visitor who doesn't have a browser capable of viewing frames. Although it may seem kind to include links to download frames-capable browsers, some people just may not have a system capable of running any of them, or perhaps they just don't feel like being told what to do.

Within your <NOFRAMES> tag, you can provide all of the frame's information and links in a more accessible format. Because the information you're providing in your frames is already in HTML format, all you have to do is provide links to this information via a different navigational structure (a graphical navigation bar or text navigation bar).

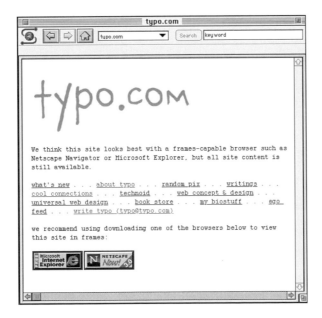

This NOFRAMES alternative may not look all that festive, but it gives the viewer the option to go straight to the site's content or to download the browsers you recommend.

The following NOFRAMES code was used in the example for the preceding figure (inserted below the FRAMESET information in your HTML document):

```
<NOFRAMES>
<BODY>
<TT>
<P>
<IMG SRC="./typoNF.gif" ALT="typo.com" ALIGN=RIGHT
➡WIDTH="288" HEIGHT="99" BORDER="0"><P>
We think this site looks best with a frames-capable
➡browser such as Netscape Navigator or Microsoft Explorer,
➡but all site content is still available.<P>

<A HREF="new.html">what's new</A> . . .
<A HREF="about.html">about typo</A> . . .
<A HREF="pix.html">random pix</A> . . .
<A HREF="writings.html">writings</A> . . .
<A HREF="cool.html">cool connections</A> . . .
<A HREF="technoid.html">technoid</A> . . .
<A HREF="wcd.html">web concept &amp; design</A> . . .
<A HREF="uwd.html">universal web design</A> . . .
<A HREF="store.html">book store</A> . . .
<A HREF="bio.html">my biostuff</A> . . .
<A HREF="ego.html">ego feed</A> . . .
<A HREF="mailto:typo@typo.com">write typo
➡(typo@typo.com)</A>

<P>we recommend using downloading one of the browsers
➡below to view this site in frames:<P>

<A HREF="http://www.microsoft.com/"><IMG SRC="./MIEnow.gif"
➡ALT="download Microsoft Explorer NOW!" ALIGN=LEFT
➡WIDTH="88" HEIGHT="31" BORDER="0"></A> <A
➡HREF="http://www.netscape.com/"><IMG SRC="./netscnow.gif"
➡ALT="download Netscape Navigator NOW!" ALIGN=LEFT
➡WIDTH="88" HEIGHT="31" BORDER="0"></A>
</BODY>
</NOFRAMES>
```

frames and people with impairments

Providing NOFRAMES content is crucial for those who are unable to view a page, either because they have a visual impairment or they choose to enlarge the body text for readability. The

screen readers the visually impaired rely on aren't able to read the information within target frames. Unless you provide an alternative, your site will be inaccessible.

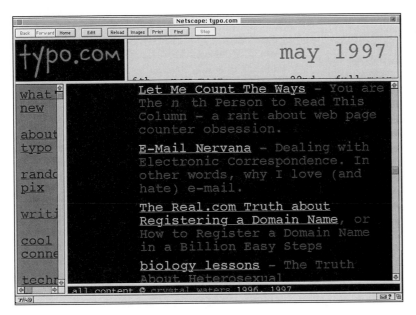

Boosting the base size of the typeface in the browser via the browser's preferences affects the size of type in all frames. However, because some of the frames are fixed in size and don't have scrollbars (such as the yellow frame in the upper right), the content isn't available. Although the left-hand menu frame has scroll bars, the frame is fixed-width, and the user is forced to scroll both horizontally and vertically to read the full text.

Although it won't make your site inaccessible, enlarging the body text will make your frame design very annoying. Chances are (especially because frame windows are relatively small), the enlarged text will be harder to access and read because so little can appear in a window at a time. Viewers will be forced to scroll even more than they would have with the original text in the tiny frame window, especially if you set the frame window to a certain pixel width.

backing out

All kinds of users complain about one navigational aspect of frames: when they click on their browser's Back button (the typical way to navigate one page in a nonframed site), they are backed right out of the site altogether (something you're not particularly fond of people doing). If they've gone a few layers into your site, generally they'll have to start off at the beginning of your site and dig their way back in to get to where they were before they were backed out of the site. This is not intuitive, and can be extremely frustrating.

Although it may not always work, consider including a "Back" button of your own within the target frame window's contents, or be sure that there is a menu available of all the site's contents within one of the frame windows at all times. However, because you never know where your viewers have been, it might be worth your while to include a help file of some sort to teach your visitors how to navigate through a frame site.

other access lessons

Even though users can print each frame separately within Netscape Navigator, this can be a pain if a viewer *wants* to print out the whole page. Netscape prints whichever frame the user clicks on. The same annoyance applies to saving the information to disk—the whole set of frames within the browser page can't be saved in one file; each frame must be saved separately.

In both Netscape Navigator and Internet Explorer, users are limited to printing, mailing, or saving the information in the frame in which they've clicked. Limit the information that you want them to print, mail, or save to one frame—and if there is information that you require from them in a particular frame (such as printing out or mailing an order form that appears in one frame window), remind them to click in the frame first in order to be able to print/save/mail it.

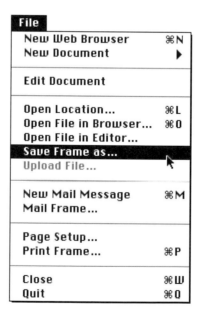

Viewers can also reload or refresh individual frames, or mail the contents of a specific frame if it's been selected by clicking in it.

Here's a site set up using a three-column table. To see what the main difference is between a tabled site and a framed site, let's redo the page using frames for information placement.

With FRAMEBORDERS and BORDERS on (or basically by using the FRAMESET's defaults), you can see how flexible a framed site's layout can become.

In the bottom figure above, the small frames on the left and right have scoll bars turned off, and are a fixed pixel width wide. However, they have a percentage height value of 25 percent of the space the four of them take up vertically. Here's their code:

```
<FRAMESET COLS="94,*,94">
<FRAMESET ROWS="25%,25%,25%,25%">
<FRAME SRC="./tack.html" NAME="tack" SCROLLING=NO NORESIZE>
<FRAME SRC="./saddle.html" NAME="saddle" SCROLLING=
➡NO NORESIZE>
<FRAME SRC="./gifts.html" NAME="gifts" SCROLLING=
➡NO NORESIZE>
<FRAME SRC="store.html" NAME="store" SCROLLING=NO NORESIZE>
</FRAMESET>
```

With all the borders turned off (FRAMEBORDERS=NO, BORDER=0), we end up with a site that looks fairly similar to the table site.

When the framed site appears on the smaller screen, the subwindow in which scrolling is turned on now has its scroll bar showing. Note how the images in the left- and right-hand columns are starting to overlap because they are still struggling to maintain their 25 percent cut of the column's real estate.

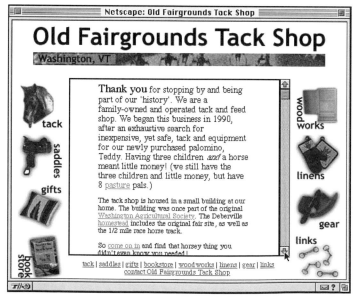

The framed site with borders turned on also has some problems maintaining enough space for everything to show.

Whereas the user has to scroll the entire browser window down to see the rest of the graphics and links, the tabled site better maintains its overall layout and spatial relations.

summary

Many sites jumped at the opportunity to use frames when they were first introduced because they seemed so cool, only to go back to nonframed formats (mostly because viewers had complained about them). Basically, if frames don't add functionality to your site, don't use them. They can cause browser crashes, navigational confusion, or just plain inaccessibility if you don't provide another option to access your site's content.

Tip

If you can't decide whether or not to use frames, why not create one version with tables and another version with frames? Then you can use the table version of your site as the NOFRAMES or low-bandwidth version of your site.

Frames can serve your viewers well, if you maintain consistency of menu placement within a frame to assist in navigation, or a logo within a frame to reiterate the branding of your site. There are obvious plusses and minuses to frames—they are flexible yet one of the least-accessible features to a number of browsers. If your audience is one that has used frames before, they may, by now, be used to the little quirks, such as backing out of a frame or trying to print information in a specific window. However, if you're not sure of your target market's browser usage, you need to add a navigational help section. And don't forget to add a *functional* NOFRAMES or non-frames alternative site.

CHAPTER 9

> *"Look with thine ears."*
> *— William Shakespeare*

sound bytes

do you hear what I hear?

Sound is one of the most misused mediums on the web. No matter how you mix it, it still takes up a ton of bandwidth, and usually serves as little more than window dressing. So why use it? Because sound can add an amazing dimension to your page, making it more interesting and accessible. Coupled with animation, sound can take your page into the realm of flashy multimedia, as well as elevate its status among fellow web designers.

To be successful, however, sound—as must the rest of your web site's elements—must have a point. Most of the surfing world is still strapped to analog modems, which means that if your page has more than a beep or two, it takes too long to download and whoever is visiting your site will most likely move on. Don't lose visitors just because you want to show off.

 RealAudio, from Progressive Networks (http://www.realaudio. com) is perhaps the most widely used sound format on the web.

Thanks to their built-in audio players, the latest incarnations of Netscape Navigator and Internet Explorer make accessing sound and music from your page nearly seamless. This is a good and bad thing. Internet Explorer, for instance, comes with an invisible MIDI file built in, so when someone surfs to a page with a MIDI file embedded in it, a MIDI song starts blaring—every time they go back to that page. In the same way, you can add sound through Java, Shockwave, and WAV files, so your music or sound clips

simply start playing when someone arrives at your site. It's turning into quite a rage because there's no player to configure and no files that the user has to manually download.

the thrill is gone

The first few times someone comes across a page where sound starts playing, it's an eye-opening experience. The addition of sound can even be downright intoxicating to the average passerby. The only problem is that users can't turn it off unless they turn off their speakers. No matter how cool your page is, even the most patient visitor will be able to handle only a few rounds of your MIDI cover of "Just Like Me" from The Captain and Tenille. Even functional sound clips such as "Welcome to my web page, click on the blue button for the index" can be annoying; every time someone jumps back to your main page, the sound plays again. It's almost like a bad joke.

Obviously, in most situations, it's best to let the surfer pick whether to have sound or not. If you like the idea of ambient music wafting in the background, make a second start page for those who would like hear it. You'll probably want to make your default page mute so that you don't drive your viewers nuts with repeated phrases or sound clips.

getting in the mix

From a mechanical standpoint, mixing sound into your site is actually fairly painless—once you decide on a format and buy the necessities, that is. You have a laundry list of sound formats to choose from, and most of them are surprisingly accepted. There are old classics (WAV, AU, and MIDI), as well as new formats created specifically for the web (RealAudio and Shockwave) that provide streaming audio, enabling your audience to begin hearing your audio track as it's downloaded. So which format should you choose? For now the short answer: it depends on what you want to do. I'll discuss the choices in detail later in this chapter. Whichever format you pick, however, remember the cardinal rule: if the format requires a special player, always, always provide a link to where the player can be downloaded.

First, consider the bad news: the price tag for adding sound. If you want to record anything beyond your voice, such as music or any kind of audio, you will probably need an audio capture card. The good news is that your computer may already have one. Look at the back of your computer where you plug in your speakers. If there's an audio-in port (usually a port colored yellow), you're set. After a trip to your local Radio Shack to get the right connector cables, you'll be set for hardware.

You will, however, need software, which can range from free to more than $1,000. For such general sound files as WAV or the Mac's SND format, there are dozens of great shareware programs to download that will let you edit sound. If you're serious about sound and music editing however, you'll probably need a professional program, such as Macromedia's SoundEdit 16, which can quickly run into the hundreds of dollars. And if you want to use either RealAudio or Shockwave, you'll need to buy software that can quickly hit the $1,000 mark, but we'll get to that in a second. First, let's run through the most popular (and cheaper to institute) formats.

the classics: wav, aiff, au

It's safe to say that any computer that has a sound card can play either a WAV (Waveform), AIFF (Audio Interchange File Format), or AU (also known as SunAudio) file. All three formats have been around for years. Most Macs and PCs come with built-in sound players that support them, and the most popular web browsers come with their own players that handle these formats. WAV, AIFF, and AU are all fairly similar in sound quality and file size. WAV was created mainly for the Windows platform; AIFF was created for the Mac; AU for Unix. Because the web originally started on the Unix platform, AU is the most common of the three and often sports the smallest file size. Almost every web browser on all platforms can play AU files, which is good. AU files tend to compress more, but often don't sound quite as nice as WAV or AIFF files, which is not so good. Chances are, you'll want to go with the sound format that *your* platform supports as a default: AIFF for Mac, WAV for PCs, and AU for Unix.

Netscape 3.0 includes the LiveAudio plug-in from EmeraldNet (http://www.emerald.net/), which will play the following embedded files:

MIME type	file extension
audio/basic	.au
audio/x-wav	.wav
audio/x-aiff	.aif, .aiff
audio/x-midi	.mid, .midi

The LiveAudio console allows the user to control sound playing, pausing, stopping, and volume.

The LiveAudio player console.

To embed a sound file in your document that will launch the LiveAudio player console, simply add the following line of code, inserting the name of your sound file within the quotes:

```
<EMBED SRC="nameofsound.wav"  HEIGHT=60  WIDTH=144>
```

If you want the LiveAudio player to open in its own window, simply include a link to the sound file:

```
<A HREF="nameofsound.wav">nameofsound.wav</A>
```

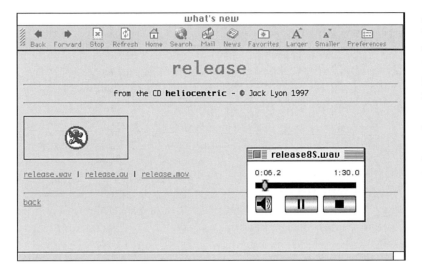

Here are the results of both an embedded LiveAudio player, and one appearing in its own Netscape window.

Although Internet Explorer 3.0 won't honor the <EMBED SRC> tag (as you can see by the broken plug-in icon), it does have a pop-up audio player that allows users to control sound playing, stopping, and volume. The audio player automatically appears after clicking on an A HREF link to a .wav, .au, .aiff, or .mov audio file, and the file has been downloaded to your computer.

The good news is that making a sound file in these formats on either a Mac or a PC is painless. On a PC running Windows 95 for instance, all you have to do is open up the Sound Recorder and start recording with your microphone or plug in an audio player, such as your stereo, to your sound card. Save the sound clip you recorded as a WAV file, and you're finished. If you want to get fancy, there are also several sound editing applications on the web

that are freely downloadable. Check out The Cross Platform Page: Audio Formats site (http://www.mcad.edu/Guests/EricB/ xplat.aud.html) for links to popular sound editing utilities for both Macs and PCs.

So why not use one of these three formats without question? Because WAV, AIFF, and AU files that are longer than a couple of seconds in length can quickly get huge—no way anyone would want to download them unless they're absolute must-hears. Even when you dabble in compression and kHz rates to lower the file size, anything more than a few seconds of audio can easily be bigger than a megabyte. But, if you have a small digital recording to post and want zero guesswork from your audience, any of these three formats is your pick. They're easy to create, easy to play, and easy to integrate into your page because none of them require special plug-ins, players, or usually even configuration.

digital tunes: midi and mod

So what if you like the idea of ambient music pinging in the background? If you don't mind making it from scratch, either MIDI or MOD format is a good pick.

midi

Both major platforms and both major browsers offer common MIDI players. MIDI's biggest advantage is that its files are amazingly small. A three-minute song, for instance, can take only a few seconds to download. That's because a MIDI file isn't a sound file at all, but rather directions for your sound card to play a song from among all the sounds built into your sound card. Think of it as a conductor, and your sound card the orchestra. The bad news: MIDI still sounds a lot like the kind of music you could crank out of a $50 synthesizer. Its range is limited, and any song you can create most visitors will find tacky at best.

MIDI definitely can have a place on your site. But, as mentioned before, you'll want to make it a selective choice. There are already several pages on the web that start playing MIDI songs the second you surf to them, and after a few minutes, the annoyance factor is right up there with elevator music. Developing MIDI music is easy enough. It's a much easier process if you have a MIDI keyboard (you can get a satisfactory one for around $100). There is also a slew of MIDI composing programs.

Midplug (http://www.ysba.com/mid-plug_index.html) is a MIDI-playing plug-in available for both Netscape and Internet Explorer.

Crescendo, from LiveUpdate (http://www.liveupdate.com/), is another MIDI-file plug-in choice for both Netscape and Internet Explorer.

mod

The MOD format offers a little higher quality and range in terms of digital music. Rather than leaving all the work to the sound card, and its limited sound collection, a MOD file has two parts: its sound library and the actual song. The song part works a lot like a MIDI file. It provides simple directions for what the sound library needs to play. Because a MOD file comes with its own custom library, you have a lot more flexibility, but you'll also have a bigger file. MOD also isn't very standardized on the web. There are an apt amount of MOD creators and players for either platform, but most of them are quirky shareware, created by hobbyists, and it's far more likely someone coming to your site will have a MIDI player than have a MOD player.

If one of your big goals for your site is low bandwidth, MIDI may add a nice multimedia touch, but again, its sound quality isn't so hot. If you love the idea of adding music to your web site, there are other ways to do it that will add file size but give you infinitely better sound quality.

super audio: mpeg 1 & 2

Yes, MPEG is primarily for a video format, but it has an entire channel dedicated for stereo sound. Although MPEG has been around for some time, it's about to make a huge comeback in the guise of DVD (digital video disc). The upcoming DVD video standard is really nothing more than MPEG-2 video. In the next couple of years, it's probable that plenty of people will have software MPEG-2 players that came with their systems. And there are plenty of MPEG players available for download now for the most popular platforms. As far as sound quality goes, you can't get much

> **Note**
>
> To embed a background sound that will play in Internet Explorer 3.0 and up, you can use the <BGSOUND> tag, and specify what sound file to play (.wav, .au, or MIDI file). Add the LOOP attribute to determine how many times the sound will play when someone goes to that page:
>
> ```
> <BGSOUND SRC="nameofsound
> .wav LOOP=5>
> ```
>
> In this case, the sound would be played five times. Each time a visitor goes back to the page, the sound starts playing over again. If you want the sound to keep playing rather than ending after a specific number of times, use the tag LOOP=INFINITE.

152

better than MPEG-2 because it uses the Dolby Surround Sound (or the AC3) standard—the stuff you hear in movie theaters. Unfortunately, it's no secret that the MPEG files can be gigantic.

MPEG-1 can play at up to 48 MHz, or CD-audio quality, and also has room for compression, but its file sizes are overwhelming for anyone on an analog modem. From the development end, MPEG encoders aren't cheap, and most of the popular sound-editing packages don't support either MPEG-1 or -2. If you have sound clips that you want people to hear at the best quality possible, however, MPEG is a fair pick that's going to get better over time.

Some MPEG plug-ins include the InterVU Player (http://www.intervu.com/), the StreamWorks player (http://www.xingtech.com/sw_now.html), and Net Toob (http://www.duplexx.com/).

InterVU

webcentric sounds: RealAudio, Shockwave, Voxware, and Talker

The plug-in and web browser war rages on, and in its wake there are dozens of ways to create and play sound developed specifically for the web. And of course, none is compatible with the next. Although plug-in and ActiveX controllers bring a limitless amount of functionality to the web, there's already been a backlash. Many of us have long felt like we have reached the point where we've downloaded one plug-in too many. The result is that if your site requires yet another obscure plug-in, chances are no one is going stay around long enough to download it.

That's not to say you shouldn't use a sound format that requires a proven plug-in. In fact, in many situations, the best way to deliver your audio message is through one of the popular new web audio formats: RealAudio, Shockwave, Voxware, or Talker. They offer streaming (playing while downloading), so there's nearly instant gratification for your audience, and file sizes are small. Each one offers a unique service, but as a good rule of thumb, you will at the very most want to use only one for your site.

RealAudio

Without contest, RealAudio is the most popular sound plug-in available on the web today, and—believe it or not—it's quickly becoming a standard. And for good reason. Although its sound quality is definitely up for critique, it streams audio well. With a 28.8 Kbps modem and the plug-in, you can instantly begin listening to a sound file that can go on for hours. In a perfect virtual world, you'll be able to hear the sound file uninterrupted. But, the web is far from perfect, and bandwidth hiccups often occur. Often the audio stream will be interrupted or become glitchy as the player waits for more of the sound file to be downloaded.

Progressive Networks RealAudio: http://www.realaudio.com.

The RealAudio Encoder, free for the download, allows you to translate a number of sound file formats into RealAudio formats.

As you can imagine, sound quality can range from a bit better than an AM radio to a garbled mess. Because of this, RealAudio probably isn't the best choice for ambient background music or for high-quality sound clips. Instead, it's great for quick samples of sounds, spoken messages, and live simulcasts. RealAudio can broadcast in real time—several radio stations are broadcasting their programming over the web at the same time it goes over the airwaves. That's an amazingly powerful use of the technology. For links to hundreds of RealAudio sound sources, a great starting point is the RealAudio site itself (http://www.realaudio.com/).

RealAudio is available in many flavors—from RealAudio 2.0–14.4 for basic rough-edges text files up to high-end stereo (best if accessed via ISDN or faster).

```
RealAudio 2.0 - 14.4
RealAudio 3.0 - 28.8 Mono, narrow response
RealAudio 3.0 - 28.8 Mono, medium response
RealAudio 3.0 - 28.8 Mono, full response
• RealAudio 3.0 - 28.8 Stereo
RealAudio 3.0 - ISDN Mono
RealAudio 3.0 - ISDN Stereo
RealAudio 3.0 - Dual ISDN Mono
RealAudio 3.0 - Dual ISDN Stereo
RealAudio 2.0 - 28.8
```

Anyone surfing the web with Navigator or Internet Explorer can use RealAudio as well. There's a free RealAudio player available for Mac, PC, and most flavors of Unix. Unfortunately, there's a big downside for you, the web developer, and that's cost. The player is free (a boon to your visitors), as is the RealAudio Encoder that let's you convert standard sound files into RealAudio. But from the developer end, you're going to need a server. The basic RealAudio server comes with the Encoder and the ability for five people to be connected to it at once, and costs $495. The good news is that if you're using an Internet Service Provider, they may already have the RealAudio Server installed, and you'll have to pay only a little bit extra every month to use it. If they don't, check out RealAudio's web site for a list of Internet Server Providers that do. Like the player, both the RealAudio Encoder and Server have Windows, Mac, and Unix versions.

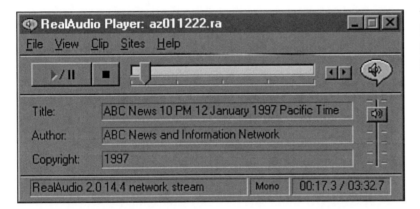

The Windows and Macintosh RealAudio players in action. Each player gives the user control over playing, stopping, and volume.

RealAudio really has something going. Hundreds of sites are already using it including ABC, NPR, and even House of Blues. Everything, including the server, is free to try out. Check it out at http://www.realaudio.com.

Shockwave

Macromedia's Shockwave works much like RealAudio does, except it doesn't require its own special server software. But that doesn't mean it comes cheap. You need Macromedia Director, which costs around $900 on the street. And to really take advantage of Shockwave's quality audio streaming, you'll also need one of Macromedia's audio tools (such as SoundEdit 16 plus Deck II for around $419). Your overall price tag could hit more than $1,300. But, as you already know, there's a lot more that you can do with Shockwave than sound.

Macromedia Shockwave—
http://www.macromedia.com/.

The big advantage to using Shockwave is that it's probably the most popular browser plug-in to date. Netscape and Microsoft both have enhanced versions of their browsers that come with the Shockwave player preinstalled. Even people who hate plug-ins end up getting Shockwave because so much of the web is already using it.

Another big plus to Shockwave is that you have complete control over how people access and play your sound files, which can improve the usability and accessibility of your site dramatically. Capitol Records (http://www.hollywoodandvine.com/), for example, has created an entire virtual jukebox on its site through Shockwave. All you do is pick a song, and it starts streaming in, with audio quality that's surprisingly good. Of course, it helps to be a whiz at Director to create these files, which doesn't come easy. If you have an entire music concept in your head, it's best to go with Director. And Director's also a good pick if you want to play a lot of music on your site. Because there are no external players needed for Shockwave, music can be seamless.

Macromedia Shockwave: http://www.macromedia.com/

Voxware and Talker

Both Voxware ToolVox and Talker are Netscape-only plug-ins. Although Voxware is available for both Windows and Mac, Talker is available only for the Mac. Despite the strict requirements, both plug-ins bring voice to the web in a clever way. Rather than downloading sound clips, these plug-ins use a speech-to-text engine that simply reads text to you. It's a great solution if you'd like to add a daily announcement or audio-based navigation aids, which can greatly enhance your site's ease of use.

Voxware ToolVox: http://www.voxware.com/.

Voxware comes with its own set of voices (the company calls them voice fonts), and there is a healthy list to choose from. Talker uses the text-to-speech engine and voices already available

MVP Solutions Talker: http://www.mvpsolutions.com/PlugInSite/Talker.html.

in Mac System 7.5—it merely connects it to the web. Hopefully, both these plug-ins will broaden their support for browsers and platforms soon because they're a great way to add voice to your site without requiring much bandwidth.

resist temptation

By the time you read this, there will probably be yet another crop of the latest and greatest streaming audio formats, but don't get pulled in by technolust. If it's new or serves only an obscure niche, most people coming to your site aren't going to be equipped to hear it, and your message won't be received.

not-so-stupid sound tricks

So you want to add sound to your site? It can either be a great enhancement or a sure-fire way to irritate people enough that they'll never want to come back. Whether you want to use universal WAV files or cutting-edge streaming technology, there are a few tricks you'll want to use.

smaller is better

First and foremost, keep your sound files as small as possible. With each format there are ways to compress audio without completely destroying your audio quality. Standard sound files such as WAV, AIFF, and AU can all run at various kHz rates. The smaller the rate, the smaller the file.

```
╔══════════ SoundApp Status ══════════╗
   Name: releaseS.mov

   Type: AIFF (stereo) @ 22050 Hz
Encoding: 16-bit linear (PCM)
   Time: 1:30.0        Size: 7752.0 K
  Status: Converting to Windows Wave...
  Volume: 100 %     Memory: 603.7 K / 15823.0 K

 ███████████░░░░░░░░░░░░░░░░░░░░░░░░░░░░
```

Many shareware applications, such as SoundApp for the Macintosh, give you a number of sound conversion choices. Besides switching to another format, SoundApp also lets you choose the quality of the file to which you're converting. Try a search on the net for "sound converters" for shareware before you pay a high price for a commercial product.

Many sites offer sound files on the web at either 8 or 11 kHz, which is passable for voice or small music clips. Ultimately, if it's a choice between file size and quality, you'll probably want to opt for a smaller file. Most sound editing utilities will let you tweak

the kHz rate to your heart's content. Streaming technologies, such as RealAudio and Shockwave, also let you crunch down your audio so that it can fit through the tiny 28.8 Kbps pipe. Take some time with the package you chose and see how small you can get your files. Often, the default settings won't be enough.

options are standard

Although it may seem like a huge time sink, it's also a great idea to offer the same sound clips in more than one format. For instance, several sites let you listen to sound clips either through RealAudio or AU files. The links to each reside side by side. This is especially important to do if one of your supported sound formats requires a plug-in. Those with short attention spans will want to go with what they can download right away, even if it is a bigger file.

This page presents a number of different sound file formats in various levels of quality (and file size), as well as an option to download an optional plug-in for some of the files.

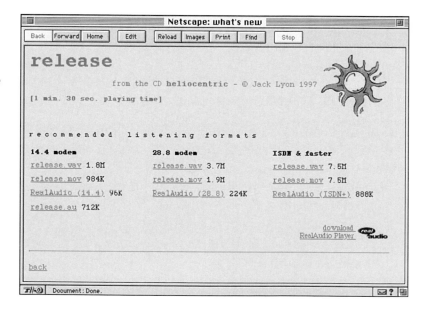

links, links, links

Finally, always remember to add links to every plug-in, player, or ActiveX control that someone could ever possibly need. Even for popular formats, it's not a bad idea to have a link to a sound player—just in case.

sound off

A major oversight by many sites that use sound for navigational or entertainment purposes is not providing an alternative for people who can't hear the sounds. Alternatives to sound files, text transcripts of sound files such as radio broadcasts, or captioning QuickTime movies are crucial for access and for the understanding of what's going on. Not only the hearing impaired will benefit.

Consider the many other situations of "forced quiet" environments, for example, where sound may not be appreciated. There are many working environments in which sounds are intrusive, such as open offices, classrooms, and libraries, or even in the home. Offering text alternatives to sound clips, or captioned movies, not only assists people who are hearing impaired, but avoids the annoyance (or trouble!) factor in places where people must work closely together or where quietness is requested or enforced. There are some cases where people can wear headphones to hear sound tracks, but this could potentially be detrimental. For example, co-workers have to bug each other to listen to them; bosses could get annoyed that employees aren't able to hear their phone ringing (not to mention that the employee could miss an important call from a client); there may be a sort of "dress code" policy against headphones (they don't look "professional"); a parent gets angry that his or her child doesn't hear the call to dinner.

transcripts

Transcribing text can take a heck of a long time, and unless you have experience as a transcriptionist, may seem a lot less than worth the trouble.

Some transcriptionists charge by the word; some by the resulting number of pages from a transcript. Prices per word seem to run about $12 per 1,000 words. That means a transcript of this chapter, if spoken, would cost about $48. Those who charge by the page cost around $2 per finished page, which could be from 20 to 50 pages of a 60-minute recording, depending on interruptions and speech rate. If this chapter were read straight through without interruption at a normal rate of speech, it would cost about $40.

One way around this is to use speech-to-text software, otherwise known as voice-recognition software. Although it's still not 100 percent accurate, there are still tons of packages out there that do a great job of recognizing a person's speech patterns (they generally have to be "trained" to your voice) and translating your words into a text file. However, unless your recordings are of one voice only, training and retraining the voice-recognition software will probably be more of a pain in the butt than hiring a transcriptionist. If you are interested in this kind of software, however, take a look through the listings on Yahoo!: http://www.yahoo.com/Business_and_Economy/Companies/Computers/Software/Voice_Recognition/.

Voice-recognition software also assumes that you will (or the speaker will) be speaking directly into the computer's microphone for immediate translation. Unless you are rereading a speech from a written-out speech, this may be difficult to arrange, but then if it's already written out, there's your transcript!

However you manage to get your transcript typed, it's a great service to include a text or HTML file for those who can't or won't wait around for a sound file to download, or for those who are unable or unwilling to hear a sound file.

summary

Sound really has yet to truly find its place on the web. Technologies such as RealAudio and Shockwave that deliver endless, real-time audio bring a new medium to the web effectively. But before you're romanced into the world of sound, realize that the trick is to include sound only if you really need to. There's nothing wrong with adding audio-based navigational directions to your site, or even a sound effect or two. Just please keep the "Tie a Yellow Ribbon Around the Old Oak Tree" renditions to a minimum. We're trying to enjoy your site over here.

movin' & shakin'

adding descriptions & captions to movies

The ability to have moving pictures on the web sparked a number of sites to begin adding server-push animations and moving images, which were then superseded by GIF animations, Shockwave files, QuickTime movies, and other eye-catching gizmos. There's no doubt that movement catches the eye. Unfortunately, a great many sites use a great many gizmos that end up overwhelming viewers instead of informing them. Gratuitous gadgets soon lose their luster to site visitors, especially when users are forced to download a huge file that they either can't access or receive no value from.

Web sites become web designer's and programmer's portfolio pieces instead of sites developed with their users in mind. Most people don't have the speed, the time, the browser, the plug-ins, or the patience to wait around for an applet to execute or a GIF animation to fulfill its loop when they'd rather be accessing the information that a site holds.

If you are going to go to the trouble to include picture shows in the form of GIF animations or QuickTime movies, what can you do to make the experience less painful for your viewers? How can you make them not just more tolerable, but more accessible to more people?

Although not every format can become easily transformed into an accessible file, there are a few options we'll explore in this chapter.

offering alternatives

Offering smaller or lower-resolution clips as a preview or an alternative to larger files, such as a QuickTime movie or Shockwave file, gives your viewers a choice based on their connection speed, amount of patience, and desire for the kind of file they wish to view. An alternative or preview can be in the form of still-image shots, exported sound files, shorter movies, or movies of different screen size (that is, 160×120 versus 320×240 pixels).

Turntable Media (http://www.
turntable.com/) offers its visitors a
choice among a small audio version
of a file (900k), a medium-sized
QuickTime movie version (1.8 m),
and a large-sized version (6.8 m) for
those who have the desire, time,
and bandwidth to wait for the
goodies to arrive. Note that the site
designer was courteous enough to
warn visitors of the actual size of
the files, rather than simply listing
the file names.

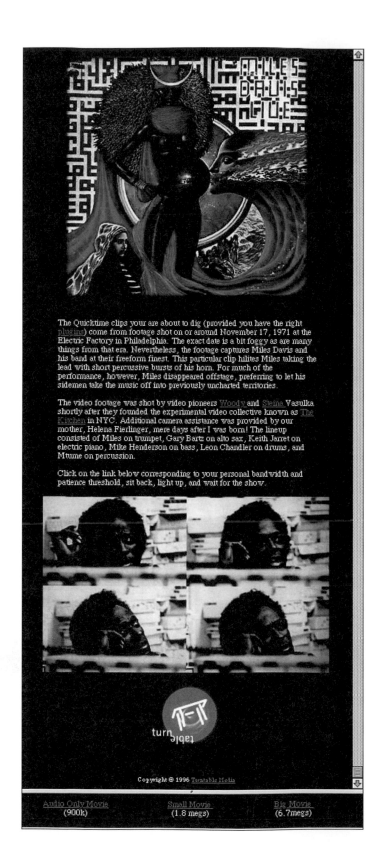

movie thumbnails

It's considerate to give your visitors a taste of upcoming movies or files about to be presented—the more they know about a file before they download it, the more they are likely to make an educated decision about whether the download is worth it to them. Like thumbnails of large still-image graphics, thumbnails for the movie can simply be smaller versions of a frame or frames of the movie that you are offering for download.

To preview the movie *Image Outlaws*, there were four stills captured from the movie to act as teasers. The menu gives the viewer a number of download and viewing options.

The movie Outlaws.mov, by Dana Atchley (http://www.nextexit.com), shown at 160×120 pixels and at its full size of 320×240 pixels. Cutting screen size in half also cuts file size in half.

creating descriptive transcripts

A potentially easy way to add an option for your visitors is to include the transcripts of those movies or files that include narrative and/or song lyrics. It's easy because, if you've created a movie that has a script or lyrics, you probably already have the text and lyrics available, probably in electronic format.

You can either create a downloadable text file or create an additional web page with the text included. In this case, a few added tags to the already existing text file was relatively simple to put together:

```
<code><font COLOR="#ffcc00" size=8>Image Outlaws</font>
</code>

<p>
<font size=4>
<BLOCKQUOTE>
<IMG SRC="./outlaw1.jpg" ALIGN=RIGHT WIDTH="108"
➡HEIGHT="81" BORDER="0" ALT="Greetings from the Image
➡Outlaws">
<I>narrator:</I><P>
There is an exit along the way<BR>
where the locals drive pickup trucks<BR>
with bumper stickers that read...<BR>
"When Images are Outlawed...<BR>
only Outlaws will have Images."<P>


<IMG SRC="./outlaw2.jpg" ALIGN=RIGHT WIDTH="108"
➡HEIGHT="81" BORDER="0" ALT="Image outlaw driving a truck
➡and drinking a beer">
We know, of course, that humans<BR>
first began to hunt for food<BR>
for sustenance.<BR>
The evolution from hunting for food<BR>
to hunting images came in stages,<BR>
and early marksmen often confused<BR>
images with reality.<BR>

Shooting signs was just one stop<BR>
<IMG SRC="./outlaw3.jpg" ALIGN=RIGHT WIDTH="108"
➡HEIGHT="81" BORDER="0" ALT="Image outlaw shooting a deer-
➡crossing caution sign">
along the way.<P>


<I>singing:</I><P>

Load up your shotgun...<BR>
keep your eyes peeled for game...<BR>
why don't you roll down your window...<BR>
then take careful aim...<BR>

<IMG SRC="./outlaw4.jpg" ALIGN=RIGHT WIDTH="108"
➡HEIGHT="81" BORDER="0" ALT="Deer-crossing caution sign
➡hanging on a wall">

<I>sound of two gunshots</I><BR>
bag yourself a caution sign...<BR>
the hunting's good this fall...<BR>
just tie it to your fender...<BR>
then go hang it on the wall...<BR>
```

```
<p>

</BLOCKQUOTE>


© Dana Atchley - <A
HREF="http://www.nextexit.com">http://www.nextexit.com</A>
<p>
<a href="./welcome.html">back</a><P>
```

The *Image Outlaws* transcript translated easily to a web page. Because the thumbnail images were already in the viewer's cache (because the web site visitor went to the introductory page first, where the images were initially loaded), adding them here doesn't add any additional downloading time for the viewer.

captioning movies

A rarely utilized feature of QuickTime is its capability to include multiple tracks. Besides video and sound, QuickTime also has tracks available for text, which is ideal for captioning a movie clip.

To caption an existing QuickTime movie, you'll need to have access to a Macintosh, a copy of SimpleText (the text editor), and a copy of MoviePlayer 2.1 or higher and its plug-ins: Authoring Extras and Goodies. SimpleText, MoviePlayer, and the plug-ins are downloadable from ftp://ftp.info.apple.com/Apple.Support.Area/Apple.Software.Updates/US/Macintosh/Utilities/.

The National Center for Accessible Media in Boston houses a number of examples of QuickTime movies that have had captions added to their text track. Check them out at http://www.boston.com/wgbh/pages/ncam/captionedmovies.html.

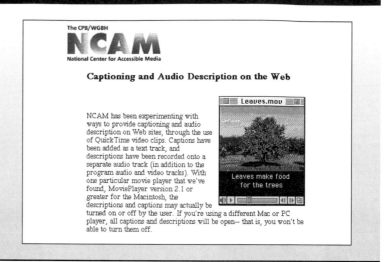

1. The MoviePlayer plug–ins have to be in the same folder as MoviePlayer.

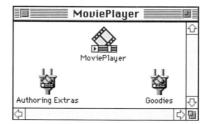

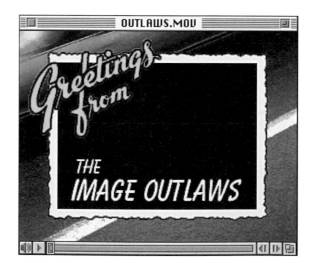

2. The first step is to open the movie you'd like to caption in MoviePlayer. In this format, there's no text track showing yet; just the opening screen of the film itself. Make sure that the player's slider is all the way to the left, at the very first frame of the movie.

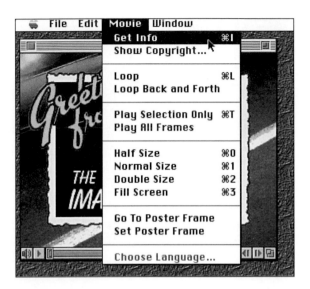

3. Choose Get Info from the Movie menu, or press Command+I.

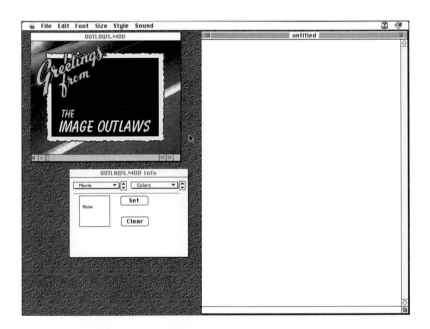

4. Launch SimpleText, and arrange the movie window, the Get Info window, and the SimpleText window in a way that allows you to see all three clearly.

5. To enable the text track, you've got to launch SimpleText and press Return one to three times, depending on how many lines you think you'll want to have each caption be. In *Image Outlaws*, I wanted only one line to show, so I pressed return only once.

6. Select All in SimpleText to grab your blank line(s). Copy them (Command+C), and then click on your movie to make MoviePlayer the active application. While holding down the Option key, choose Add from the Edit menu. Now you'll see a blank white line (or more, depending on what you chose in SimpleText) below your movie.

If you slide the MoviePlayer slider toward the left, you'll see that a black bar was added below the image. A text track has now been added, even though you didn't actually enter any text yet. Adding the text is the tedious part.

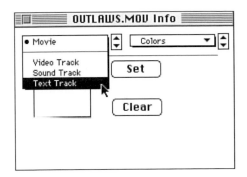

7. In the Get Info box, you'll see that there's now a text track available as a choice in the left-hand pop-up menu. Select Text Track.

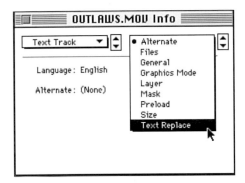

8. In the Get Info right-hand pop-up menu, choose Text Replace.

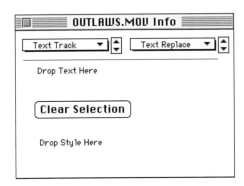

9. Here's your Get Info window ready for work.

outlaw.txt

```
<music fades in>
<sound of car horn blaring as it goes by>

There is an exit along the way
where the locals drive pickup trucks
with bumper stickers that read...
"When Images are Outlawed...
only Outlaws will have Images."
We know, of course, that humans
first began to hunt for food
for sustenance.
The evolution from hunting for food
to hunting images came in stages,
and early marksmen often confused
images with reality.
Shooting signs was just one stop
along the way.

<music fades up>

<singing> Load up your shotgun...
keep your eyes peeled for game...
why don't you roll down your window...
then take careful aim...
<sound of two gunshots>
bag yourself a caution sign...
the hunting's good this fall...
just tie it to your fender...
then go hang it on the wall...

<music continues>

<car horn blaring>

<gunshot>

<gunshot>

<music fades out>

© Dana Atchley – http://www.nextexit.com
```

10. Now open your text file in SimpleText. It helps if you break lines (with hard returns) at the points where they are as long as you'd like them to appear on the caption area. In the case of the Image Outlaws movie, which has music and sound effects, action and background explanations are included in brackets, such as <music fades in>, <singing>, and <sound of two gunshots>.

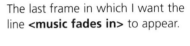

The first frame in which I want the line **<music fades in>** to appear.

The last frame in which I want the line **<music fades in>** to appear.

11. To insert text that captions a certain part of the movie, drag the slider to the beginning of the arca, or move frame by frame (using the left and right arrow keys on your keyboard) to the starting point. This can take some trial and error; I had to listen to the movie a number of times and "eye" where I want a certain line of text to end. Note: Since you placed the blank line of text in the text track, there is a portion of the movie already selected. Look closely at your slider bar, and you'll see that a small section of it is darkened. Before you select a new section of the movie, click anywhere else on the bar to deselect the section already selected.

12. When you've sort of eyed the frames where you want to insert a line of text, drag your slider to the first frame in which you want to insert text. Then hold down your Shift key, and press the play button on the movie. Stop the movie at the frame on which you want your line to end. If you accidentally go past, simply press your left arrow key back to the frame where you want the text to end.

There's now a black area on the play bar. This is the area of the movie that you just selected.

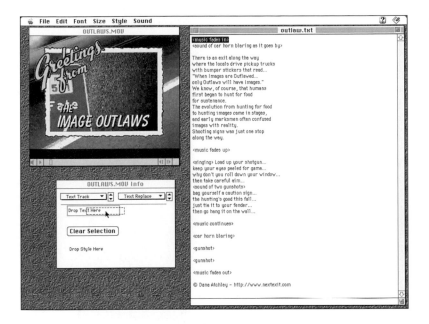

13. Making SimpleText your active application, select the text you wish to insert, and drag-and-drop it on the words Drop Text Here in the Get Info box.

If you slide your play bar back into the area you selected, voilà, the text appears.

choosing caption type

Before we put all the text in, it's best to decide what typeface you want, since you can have only one typeface and typestyle throughout the whole movie. Some typefaces and styles are too small, some too hard to read, and some are too large to fit on the limited size of the bar.

You could make text small and try to fit a lot of it within the caption, but this can distract people from the movie because they'll be so busy reading, they won't get a chance to see what's happening. It's also important to leave text on long enough for people to read *and* see what's going on.

Keep in mind, too, that MoviePlayer text tracks only allow for text to be center aligned, so the more lines of text there are, the more difficult it is to read.

Here are a few examples of different basic typefaces and styles. Some are easy to read, but the lines would have to be shortened. Others are too compact or simply not easy to read on-screen.

To determine the style you want for your text, change the text in SimpleText, and then drag some of the text on to the words Drop Style Here. The style will change throughout the movie.

The final choice in this case is a sans serif typeface that is large enough to read, and fits a comfortable amount of reading material on each line. ("where the locals drive pickup trucks" is 36 characters long; near the recommended maximum length for a line of text to be most readable.)

<music fades in>
<sound of car horn blaring as it goes by>
There is an exit along the way
where the locals drive pickup trucks
with bumper stickers that read…
"When Images are Outlawed…
only Outlaws will have Images."

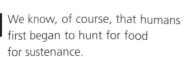

We know, of course, that humans
first began to hunt for food
for sustenance.
The evolution from hunting for food
to hunting images came in stages,
and early marksmen often confused
images with reality.
Shooting signs was just one stop
along the way.
<music fades up>

We know, of course, that humans

first began to hunt for food

for sustenance.

The evolution from hunting for food

to hunting images came in stages,

and early marksmen often confused

images with reality.

Shooting signs was just one stop

along the way.

<singing> Load up your shotgun…
keep your eyes peeled for game…
why don't you roll down your window…
then take careful aim…
<sound of two gunshots>
bag yourself a caution sign…
the hunting's good this fall…
just tie it to your fender…
then go hang it on the wall…
<music continues>

178

<car horn blaring>

<gunshot>

<music fades out>

© Dana Atchley - http://www.
nextexit.com

The finished product. Note that there are some blank black lines under some of the images. In these cases, I had to drag-and-drop blank lines from SimpleText to the Get Info box—if I hadn't, this space with no text would be white, and show up as flashes of white as the movie plays.

An important thing to remember is to balance the appearance of the text at the same time as the narrative, and also keep the text on-screen long enough for easy reading. The best way to test this is to play the movie as you go along (with the sound off!) to see whether you can keep up with the text and pay attention to the movie at the same time.

summary

Whether you use QuickTime or ShockWave files to bring motion to your visitors' desktops, adding captioning or descriptive text can assist some visitors in better interpreting your content. It takes a bit of extra work on your part, but it potentially brings the key part of the movie—the message—to more of your market.

Note

179

more information on captioning

The Caption Center at WGBH:
http://www.boston.com/wgbh/caption

Closed Captioning Web:
http://www.erols.com/berke/

The Caption FAQ:
http://www.caption.com/capfaq/

color & contrast

the eyes have it

A crucial element for web site accessibility is the contrast between the text or other elements, and the background of the pages. The easiest way to check this is, if you can't read it, your audience won't be able to read it either. The default color scheme for most browsers is a gray background with black text, blue links, and purple visited links. Although this color scheme is adequate for basic reading comfort and understanding navigation, it's also pretty boring.

This is default text on a default background.

This is a default link on a default background.

This is a default visited link on a default background.

The default color scheme for most browsers is highly readable, but not that exciting.

importance of contrast

Although different platforms and different monitor settings will make colors appear different, viewing a site on nearly any monitor with any graphic browser will give you enough of an approximation of the readability of that page's information. True, PC monitors tend to show colors darker than Mac monitors, but if two colors contrast strongly on the Mac, they should still contrast strongly on a PC.

Note

color cues: definitions of color attributes

hue   The color attribute identified by color names, such as "red" or "yellow."

value   The degree or lightness or darkness of a color.

saturation   The relative purity of a color; also referred to as intensity. The "brighter" the intensity of a color, the more saturated it is. New jeans are saturated with blue; faded ones are less saturated blue.

chromatic hues   All colors other than black, white, and gray.

neutral colors   A black, white, or gray; otherwise known as "non-chromatic hues."

monochromatic   Refers to a color combination based on variations of value and saturation of a single hue.

This image combines various values of the color purple. The closer two hues are in value to one another, the less contrast there is.

Even when combining colors of different hues, their respective values (darkness or lightness) affect the contrast between the two colors.

This image shows variations of both same and different hues, and similar and contrasting values.

If you're not up for learning color theory or studying color wheels for ideal color combinations, a quick way to test the contrast of your colors is to change your monitor settings (or the image itself) to a grayscale setting. Note how even though there are a number of colors on the original, those with similar value settings (percentage of brightness) seem to fade into the background.

Change your monitor or image settings to black-and-white (bitmapped) to further prove the contrast variables of your color choices.

multicolored backgrounds

There's not a whole lot you can do to make a multicolored, patterned background into an ideal setting for text, unless you drastically change the overall contrast and brightness of the background image. Choosing a color of text that contrasts with all of the background colors is a pretty impossible task.

Tip

Want to make sure your entire site is easily readable? Set your monitor to black-and-white, and browse through your site, taking note of those pages that aren't easily readable. Then change the text or the background color so that the differences in their values are greater.

This example is (hopefully!) a bit extreme in the overwhelming-colors department, but it does drive home the importance of background patterns, its color value, and the contrast between background colors and the chosen type color.

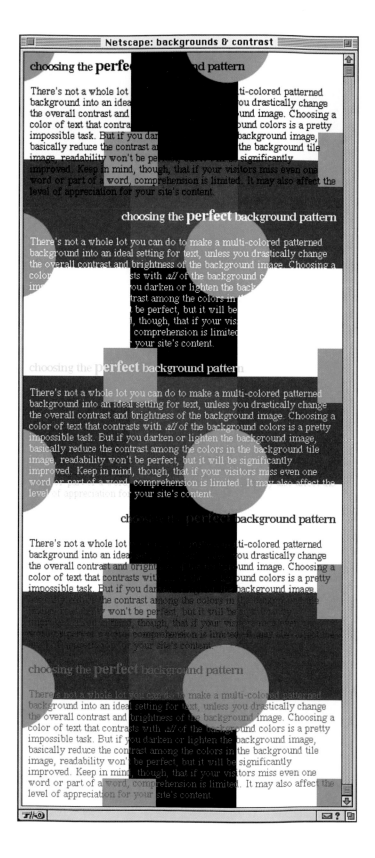

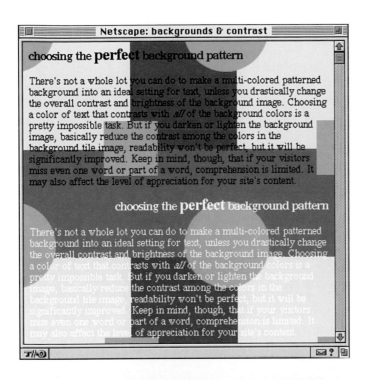

But if you darken or lighten the background image—basically reduce the contrast among the colors in the background tile image—readability won't be perfect, but it will be significantly improved. Keep in mind, however, that if your visitors miss even one word or part of a word, comprehension is limited. It may also affect the level of appreciation for your site's content.

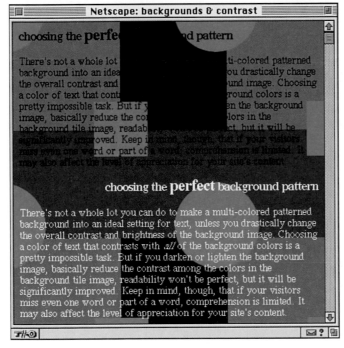

If the background is lightened or darkened, there's more of a chance that your choice of text color will contrast against it. In this case, it's obvious that the darker text contrasts best with the lighter background, and vice versa.

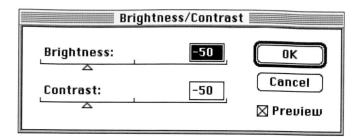

picking out colors

When you're out shopping for colors to use on your site, your best bet is to stick to the browser-safe color palette. Although designers can choose to use any colors a monitor can handle, the 216 browser-safe colors are guaranteed not to dither on-screen. Dithering is what happens when a color is not available in the application's palette, and the browser tries to compensate by combining pixels of other colors to accommodate.

The original image.

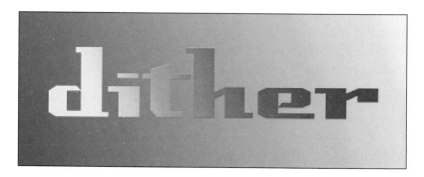

The image as viewed in a browser that supports only 216 colors. Notice the banding and the dithering because the browser can't handle the multitude of colors.

A close-up of the dithering effect.

Dithered colors look spotty or rough, whereas browser-safe colors retain smoothness on-screen. To get the best effects, choose colors from the browser-safe palette for your images and backgrounds. This will be helpful when trying to match up image or background tile colors with text colors, or image colors with background colors. If you create an image in Photoshop, for example, and it consists of the RGB values of R:255, G:051, and B:051, you can match it up with the hex value that you may use in your HTML code for the background color or one of the text colors (in this case, #FF3333).

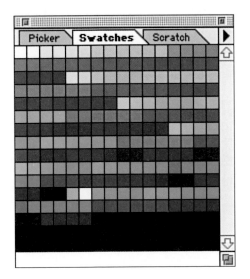

The 216-color, browser-safe CLUT (color lookup table), loaded into the Photoshop Swatches palette. The CLUT, free for the download, can be found for the Mac at ftp://ftp. adobe.com/pub/adobe/photoshop/ mac/3.x/web216m.sit, and for Windows at ftp://ftp.adobe.com/ pub/adobe/photoshop/win/3.x/ web216w.zip.

For easy access to browser-safe colors, go to http://www.lynda.com/hex.html and download one or both of the palettes (one is arranged by hue; one by value). Open up the palette in the art program of your choice and use the Eyedropper tool to select the browser-safe colors as you need them.

readable blends

What color combinations are the most readable? It's generally accepted that the best color scheme for reading is black text on a white background (you might have noticed that most books and magazines are printed with black text on white paper). Black text on white paper is high contrast, and high contrast is easier to read than low contrast.

However, because a person viewing a monitor is staring straight at a light source, black text on a white background isn't the most comfortable to look at for long periods of time. It can help readers if you take the contrast down just a touch, especially if you're asking them to read a lot of text. This could also mean using a light color rather than white in combination with black (either as a background or text color). On-screen, it generally seems that black and yellow make the highest readability combination.

Reading large amounts of black text on a white background can get tiring when viewed on-screen: BGCOLOR="#FFFFFF" TEXT="#000000".

```
Then, at 3:00 in the morning, I found myself reading the dictionary.
Adrenal. Boot. Cow. Dynapolis. Emu. All either taken or dumb. I got to the
h's and decided to start from the back. Zip. Taken. Zig. Taken. Zag.
Taken. I thought about reading a book on mythology or pick out a character
from a Neil Gaiman book. But did I really want people to have to think
about the depth of meaning of my domain name?

In frantic sleep-deprived mode, I tried making up words. Believe it or
not, zeg.com is still available (at press time, that is)! Zeg. Original,
yes. Could I make it into an anagram? Zephyr Entertainment Group. Zippo
Enlightment Guru. I then took my temperature, and it appeared normal.

I flipped some pages, and there was a word. One that's not only easy to
spell, but one that described a serious and passionate pastime of mine:
typo. I typed it in, slowly and carefully, all the time mumbling a prayer
to the InterNIC gods that I would maintain this site with every ounce of
my being (at least outside of business hours) if they only let it be
available. "No match for 'TYPO.COM'. " I tried it again. And again. And
again, just to make sure. Bingo. I immediately sent off a letter to Jim:
"Guess what? I FINALLY found a domain name that's actually not taken (I
know you don't believe me after all this, but give it a try...)..."
```

```
Then, at 3:00 in the morning, I found myself reading the dictionary.
Adrenal. Boot. Cow. Dynapolis. Emu. All either taken or dumb. I got to the
h's and decided to start from the back. Zip. Taken. Zig. Taken. Zag.
Taken. I thought about reading a book on mythology or pick out a character
from a Neil Gaiman book. But did I really want people to have to think
about the depth of meaning of my domain name?

In frantic sleep-deprived mode, I tried making up words. Believe it or
not, zeg.com is still available (at press time, that is)! Zeg. Original,
yes. Could I make it into an anagram? Zephyr Entertainment Group. Zippo
Enlightment Guru. I then took my temperature, and it appeared normal.

I flipped some pages, and there was a word. One that's not only easy to
spell, but one that described a serious and passionate pastime of mine:
typo. I typed it in, slowly and carefully, all the time mumbling a prayer
to the InterNIC gods that I would maintain this site with every ounce of
my being (at least outside of business hours) if they only let it be
available. "No match for 'TYPO.COM'. " I tried it again. And again. And
again, just to make sure. Bingo. I immediately sent off a letter to Jim:
"Guess what? I FINALLY found a domain name that's actually not taken (I
know you don't believe me after all this, but give it a try...)..."
```

Lots of white text on a black background doesn't sit all that well for long reading sessions, either.

To cut down on the harshness of black on white or white on black, try changing to a slightly off-black or off-white, or light values of other colors.

```
Then, at 3:00 in the morning, I found myself reading the dictionary.
Adrenal. Boot. Cow. Dynapolis. Emu. All either taken or dumb. I got to the
h's and decided to start from the back. Zip. Taken. Zig. Taken. Zag.
Taken. I thought about reading a book on mythology or pick out a character
from a Neil Gaiman book. But did I really want people to have to think
about the depth of meaning of my domain name?

In frantic sleep-deprived mode, I tried making up words. Believe it or
not, zeg.com is still available (at press time, that is)! Zeg. Original,
yes. Could I make it into an anagram? Zephyr Entertainment Group. Zippo
Enlightment Guru. I then took my temperature, and it appeared normal.

I flipped some pages, and there was a word. One that's not only easy to
spell, but one that described a serious and passionate pastime of mine:
typo. I typed it in, slowly and carefully, all the time mumbling a prayer
to the InterNIC gods that I would maintain this site with every ounce of
my being (at least outside of business hours) if they only let it be
available. "No match for 'TYPO.COM'. " I tried it again. And again. And
again, just to make sure. Bingo. I immediately sent off a letter to Jim:
"Guess what? I FINALLY found a domain name that's actually not taken (I
know you don't believe me after all this, but give it a try...)..."
```

Black text on light gray background: BGCOLOR="#CCCCCC" TEXT="#000000".

```
Then, at 3:00 in the morning, I found myself reading the dictionary.
Adrenal. Boot. Cow. Dynapolis. Emu. All either taken or dumb. I got to the
h's and decided to start from the back. Zip. Taken. Zig. Taken. Zag.
Taken. I thought about reading a book on mythology or pick out a character
from a Neil Gaiman book. But did I really want people to have to think
about the depth of meaning of my domain name?

In frantic sleep-deprived mode, I tried making up words. Believe it or
not, zeg.com is still available (at press time, that is)! Zeg. Original,
yes. Could I make it into an anagram? Zephyr Entertainment Group. Zippo
Enlightment Guru. I then took my temperature, and it appeared normal.

I flipped some pages, and there was a word. One that's not only easy to
spell, but one that described a serious and passionate pastime of mine:
typo. I typed it in, slowly and carefully, all the time mumbling a prayer
to the InterNIC gods that I would maintain this site with every ounce of
my being (at least outside of business hours) if they only let it be
available. "No match for 'TYPO.COM'. " I tried it again. And again. And
again, just to make sure. Bingo. I immediately sent off a letter to Jim:
"Guess what? I FINALLY found a domain name that's actually not taken (I
know you don't believe me after all this, but give it a try...)..."
```

Black text on light yellow background: BGCOLOR="#FFFFCC" TEXT="#000000".

Black text on light purple background: BGCOLOR="#CCCCFF" TEXT="#000000".

Then, at 3:00 in the morning, I found myself reading the dictionary. Adrenal. Boot. Cow. Dynapolis. Emu. All either taken or dumb. I got to the h's and decided to start from the back. Zip. Taken. Zig. Taken. Zag. Taken. I thought about reading a book on mythology or pick out a character from a Neil Gaiman book. But did I really want people to have to think about the depth of meaning of my domain name?

In frantic sleep-deprived mode, I tried making up words. Believe it or not, zeg.com is still available (at press time, that is)! Zeg. Original, yes. Could I make it into an anagram? Zephyr Entertainment Group. Zippo Enlightment Guru. I then took my temperature, and it appeared normal.

I flipped some pages, and there was a word. One that's not only easy to spell, but one that described a serious and passionate pastime of mine: typo. I typed it in, slowly and carefully, all the time mumbling a prayer to the InterNIC gods that I would maintain this site with every ounce of my being (at least outside of business hours) if they only let it be available. "No match for 'TYPO.COM'. " I tried it again. And again. And again, just to make sure. Bingo. I immediately sent off a letter to Jim: "Guess what? I FINALLY found a domain name that's actually not taken (I know you don't believe me after all this, but give it a try...)..."

Black text on light green background: BGCOLOR="#CCFFCC" TEXT="#000000".

Then, at 3:00 in the morning, I found myself reading the dictionary. Adrenal. Boot. Cow. Dynapolis. Emu. All either taken or dumb. I got to the h's and decided to start from the back. Zip. Taken. Zig. Taken. Zag. Taken. I thought about reading a book on mythology or pick out a character from a Neil Gaiman book. But did I really want people to have to think about the depth of meaning of my domain name?

In frantic sleep-deprived mode, I tried making up words. Believe it or not, zeg.com is still available (at press time, that is)! Zeg. Original, yes. Could I make it into an anagram? Zephyr Entertainment Group. Zippo Enlightment Guru. I then took my temperature, and it appeared normal.

I flipped some pages, and there was a word. One that's not only easy to spell, but one that described a serious and passionate pastime of mine: typo. I typed it in, slowly and carefully, all the time mumbling a prayer to the InterNIC gods that I would maintain this site with every ounce of my being (at least outside of business hours) if they only let it be available. "No match for 'TYPO.COM'. " I tried it again. And again. And again, just to make sure. Bingo. I immediately sent off a letter to Jim: "Guess what? I FINALLY found a domain name that's actually not taken (I know you don't believe me after all this, but give it a try...)..."

Gray text on black background: BGCOLOR="#000000" TEXT="#CCCCCC".

Then, at 3:00 in the morning, I found myself reading the dictionary. Adrenal. Boot. Cow. Dynapolis. Emu. All either taken or dumb. I got to the h's and decided to start from the back. Zip. Taken. Zig. Taken. Zag. Taken. I thought about reading a book on mythology or pick out a character from a Neil Gaiman book. But did I really want people to have to think about the depth of meaning of my domain name?

In frantic sleep-deprived mode, I tried making up words. Believe it or not, zeg.com is still available (at press time, that is)! Zeg. Original, yes. Could I make it into an anagram? Zephyr Entertainment Group. Zippo Enlightment Guru. I then took my temperature, and it appeared normal.

I flipped some pages, and there was a word. One that's not only easy to spell, but one that described a serious and passionate pastime of mine: typo. I typed it in, slowly and carefully, all the time mumbling a prayer to the InterNIC gods that I would maintain this site with every ounce of my being (at least outside of business hours) if they only let it be available. "No match for 'TYPO.COM'. " I tried it again. And again. And again, just to make sure. Bingo. I immediately sent off a letter to Jim: "Guess what? I FINALLY found a domain name that's actually not taken (I know you don't believe me after all this, but give it a try...)..."

Then, at 3:00 in the morning, I found myself reading the dictionary. Adrenal. Boot. Cow. Dynapolis. Emu. All either taken or dumb. I got to the h's and decided to start from the back. Zip. Taken. Zig. Taken. Zag. Taken. I thought about reading a book on mythology or pick out a character from a Neil Gaiman book. But did I really want people to have to think about the depth of meaning of my domain name?

In frantic sleep-deprived mode, I tried making up words. Believe it or not, zeg.com is still available (at press time, that is)! Zeg. Original, yes. Could I make it into an anagram? Zephyr Entertainment Group. Zippo Enlightment Guru. I then took my temperature, and it appeared normal.

I flipped some pages, and there was a word. One that's not only easy to spell, but one that described a serious and passionate pastime of mine: typo. I typed it in, slowly and carefully, all the time mumbling a prayer to the InterNIC gods that I would maintain this site with every ounce of my being (at least outside of business hours) if they only let it be available. "No match for 'TYPO.COM'. " I tried it again. And again. And again, just to make sure. Bingo. I immediately sent off a letter to Jim: "Guess what? I FINALLY found a domain name that's actually not taken (I know you don't believe me after all this, but give it a try...)..."

Light yellow text on black background: BGCOLOR="#000000" TEXT="#FFFFCC".

Then, at 3:00 in the morning, I found myself reading the dictionary. Adrenal. Boot. Cow. Dynapolis. Emu. All either taken or dumb. I got to the h's and decided to start from the back. Zip. Taken. Zig. Taken. Zag. Taken. I thought about reading a book on mythology or pick out a character from a Neil Gaiman book. But did I really want people to have to think about the depth of meaning of my domain name?

In frantic sleep-deprived mode, I tried making up words. Believe it or not, zeg.com is still available (at press time, that is)! Zeg. Original, yes. Could I make it into an anagram? Zephyr Entertainment Group. Zippo Enlightment Guru. I then took my temperature, and it appeared normal.

I flipped some pages, and there was a word. One that's not only easy to spell, but one that described a serious and passionate pastime of mine: typo. I typed it in, slowly and carefully, all the time mumbling a prayer to the InterNIC gods that I would maintain this site with every ounce of my being (at least outside of business hours) if they only let it be available. "No match for 'TYPO.COM'. " I tried it again. And again. And again, just to make sure. Bingo. I immediately sent off a letter to Jim: "Guess what? I FINALLY found a domain name that's actually not taken (I know you don't believe me after all this, but give it a try...)..."

Pink text on black background: BGCOLOR="#000000" TEXT="#FFCCCC".

Then, at 3:00 in the morning, I found myself reading the dictionary. Adrenal. Boot. Cow. Dynapolis. Emu. All either taken or dumb. I got to the h's and decided to start from the back. Zip. Taken. Zig. Taken. Zag. Taken. I thought about reading a book on mythology or pick out a character from a Neil Gaiman book. But did I really want people to have to think about the depth of meaning of my domain name?

In frantic sleep-deprived mode, I tried making up words. Believe it or not, zeg.com is still available (at press time, that is)! Zeg. Original, yes. Could I make it into an anagram? Zephyr Entertainment Group. Zippo Enlightment Guru. I then took my temperature, and it appeared normal.

I flipped some pages, and there was a word. One that's not only easy to spell, but one that described a serious and passionate pastime of mine: typo. I typed it in, slowly and carefully, all the time mumbling a prayer to the InterNIC gods that I would maintain this site with every ounce of my being (at least outside of business hours) if they only let it be available. "No match for 'TYPO.COM'. " I tried it again. And again. And again, just to make sure. Bingo. I immediately sent off a letter to Jim: "Guess what? I FINALLY found a domain name that's actually not taken (I know you don't believe me after all this, but give it a try...)..."

Beigish-orange on black background: BGCOLOR="#000000" TEXT="#FFCC99".

type size and style

Type size also increases readability, but if the color contrast isn't there to begin with, then you're tackling the wrong problem. However, when using proper color combinations of high contrast, adding to the text size also increases overall readability.

If the color contrast is there, changing the type size or style also adds to reading ease.

> Then, at 3:00 in the morning, I found myself reading the dictionary. Adrenal. Boot. Cow. Dynapolis. Emu. All either taken or dumb. I got to the h's and decided to start from the back. Zip. Taken. Zig. Taken. Zag. Taken.
>
> I thought about reading a book on mythology or pick out a character from a Neil Gaiman book. But did I really want people to have to think about the depth of meaning of my domain name?
>
> In frantic sleep-deprived mode, I tried making up words...

color blindness

Color blindness, a genetic disorder of color deficiency, affects one out of every 12 men and approximately one in every 200 women. These people are unable to see the full spectrum of colors, and may have difficulty reading or viewing certain combinations of colors. A colorblind person has a lack of a color receptor (either red, green, and/or blue); the most common form is red-green color blindness. If a red-green colorblind person sees a red object and a green object that are of about equal value (brightness), the red object will appear darker than the green one.

So, the key here (no matter what color or colors the person has problems with) is the fact that if the respective colors are of equal brightness, the colorblind viewer won't be able to view, for example, red text on a green background. However, if the contrast between the two colors (that is, their relative brightness, or color value) is great enough, then the prospects of viewing become easier.

If any of your web site's navigational cues are color based, such as "click on the red dot to vote *no*, or click on the green dot to vote *yes*," then a person with color blindness may not be able to get to where you're trying to help them to go. Try adding text cues to any color-based scheme, such as labeling buttons on a navigational bar. Another option is to use shapes as the differing aspect of each choice—for example, a check mark for yes, and an X for no.

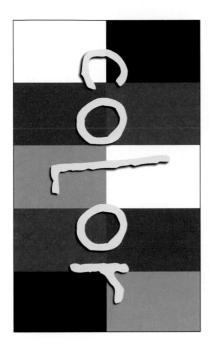 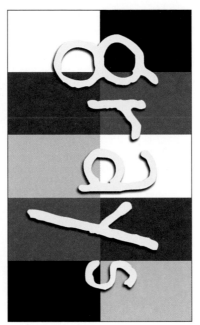

Colors of equivalent value can be difficult to view for a person with colorblindness. One way to check for various combinations of colors that will work for most audiences, including those with colorblindness, is to test images and sites in grayscale mode.

summary

Again, the rule of thumb is that if you can't read your web pages, others probably can't either. Variations of color hues is not so important as a contrast in color value when it comes to enhancing contrast and readability on your site. There are no rules about those colors you choose for your site, but before you start using every "palettable" color in the rainbow, test your images and color schemes in both grayscale and black-and-white to make sure the view is clear.

Tip

Those methods utilized to help those who are colorblind also benefit those who visit your site using a monochrome or grayscale monitor.

Using shapes as a navigational visual cue, rather than using colors, also can assist those with cognitive impairments.

CHAPTER 12

> *"There are two kinds of people, those who do the work and those who take the credit. Try to be in the first group; there is less competition there."*
> *— Indira Gandhi*

the importance of html

the multi-accessible standard

Learning HTML these days can be easy, especially with all the new-fangled HTML editors out there that can do a lot of the work for web designers. The thing is, as easy as HTML can be to learn, it's just as easy to screw it up.

What saves many a page from disaster is that many browsers are "forgiving." A number of tags may seem to give the same or similar result, such as using a <FONT SIZE="*n*"> tag versus an <H1> tag, or placing a font attribution tag within or without a paragraph tag. However, for best results, HTML tags should be placed in a certain order to be as accessible as possible to as many browsers as possible.

For example, let's say you use a <CENTER> tag to center your page's introductory text, and then place the rest of the page in a table. In browsers that support tables, the text within the <TABLE> specifications won't be affected by the <CENTER> tag because font styles and layout attributes for the content within a table must be specified within the table for it to have an effect. But on a browser that doesn't support tables—if you've forgotten to put an ending </CENTER> tag after your introductory text—all the following text will be centered. Basically, if there is an ending tag for whatever style or attribute you've specified for a section of your page, use it.

sgml: the basis of html

Standard Generalized Markup Language (SGML) is the structure documentation format on which HTML is based. Basically, for all of us to be able to view web sites, we must be presented with a common format so that all platforms, operating systems, and browsers can view the same information in the same way. The goal is to make all information "portable," viewable, and navigable among different systems.

The most basic level of commonality is ASCII text. But text by itself, although it can contain important content, isn't easily navigable. Two of the things that make the web so cool are that text can be presented in a variety of ways and that it can include hyperlinks to other pages or areas of pages. This is how HTML coding enhances text and the presentation of images.

HTML, and the standards of its structure that are always being challenged, changed, and debated, is the core of the web and how it appears. Why is it challenged? Because, as browser competitors battle it out, they need to have something unique so that people can tell the difference—not to mention the fact that designers push coding to its limits and ask for more and more features. A new feature is developed or discovered, and it takes time for the various committees and browser companies to all agree on what becomes a "standard"—something that all browsers, ideally, will then support.

logic and structure

The purpose behind HTML and its standards is to logically describe the structure of the information on a page—not to describe what it represents in function and meaning, not a particular "look." For example, a line tagged as a header is meant to *be* a header, not necessarily have a particular font size. Within the HTML confines, the tags <H1>…</H1>, <H2>…</H2>, and <H3>…</H3> each describe levels of headers, with <H1> being the most important, or highest level, and <H3> being the least important, or a lower-level division of information within the tagged text.

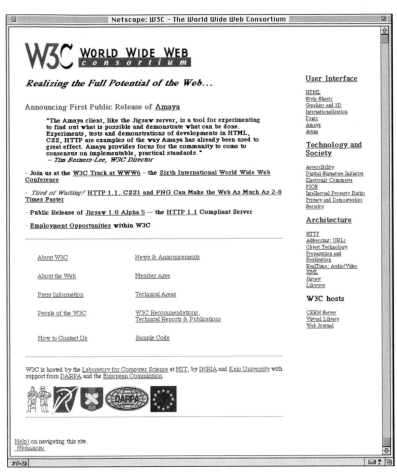

To keep up on current and proposed HTML standards and web technology, drop by W3C (World Wide Web Consortium) at http://www.w3.org.

the significance of function

The easiest way to describe the significance of HTML "meaning" versus "look" is to consider how screen readers, those programs that people with visual impairments use to access web pages, use the tags for easier navigation.

Sighted users are able to scan a page visually, and see headlines and subheads that cue them to points on a page at which new sections begin and end. However, because a person with a visual impairment may not be able to differentiate these subheads from the main body text visually, on improperly structured HTML pages they are forced to have the screen reader read the entire text out loud before they can find what they may (or may not) have been looking for within the parameter of the page. This might be tolerable if web pages were all short, but unfortunately, that's not the case. Long pages of text can easily become a frustrating frontier to

visitors relying on screen readers. Imagine reading this book if there were no headlines or subheads, and all of the text ran from one paragraph to another without a break—and I told you that you had to read it this way if you wanted to find out if any information within a chapter might be of interest?

If you use proper HTML coding, you can save your audience such frustration. Screen readers generally take advantage of <H1>...</H1>, <H2>...</H2>, and <H3>...</H3> header tags by giving visually impaired users the option to get an overview of the page structure. By directing the screen reader to read only the <H1>...</H1> headings, for example, users are able to scan the page for sections they may be interested in reading. If the other logical-structure tags are used, then within a section, subsections can be scanned for an even more precise reading choice. If the users don't find a headline compelling after it is read aloud, they can instruct the screen reader to skip ahead to the next heading.

where tags belong

Sometimes designers think it's enough to include beginning and end codes—as long as the tags are there, what does it matter where they go? True, chances are that one of the Big Browsers will probably interpret your tags the way you thought you intended, but others will simply ignore the tags.

An inexhaustible resource for HTML elements, and their acceptable constructs and required structure is available within the HTML Elements List section of the HTML Reference Manual hosted by Sandia National Laboratories (http://www.sandia.gov/sci_compute/elements.html or http://orion.postech.ac.kr/~handol/www/html/html_elem.html). The complete manual is available at http://www.sandia.gov/ sci_compute/html_ref.html.

Sandia National Labs maintains a comprehensive guide to HTML and its elements and standards at http://www.sandia.gov/sci-compute/html_ref.html. Although it was written as an in-house design conformance document, it's loaded with information for the rest of us.

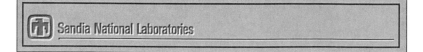

Resources for HTML Standards and Constructs

The original HTML 2.0 standards documentation—ftp://ds.internic.net/rfc/rfc1866.txt—both historical and informative resource on the guts of HTML.

SGML Basics—http://www.sil.org/sgml/sgml.html—a primer about Standard Generalized Markup Language.

Composing Good HTML—http://www.sil.org/sgml/sgml.html—what do to, what not to do, and how to check out your source code for best results.

The HTML 3.0 Hypertext Document Format—http://www.w3.org/ pub/WWW/Arena/tour/ start.html—a brief slide show of the proposed standards for HTML 3.x, which includes text wrapping around images, embedded virtual reality models, and fill-out forms.

Netscape Extensions to HTML 2.0—http://www.netscape.com/assist/net_sites/html_extensions. html—includes tagging structures for tables, backgrounds, and META tag dynamic documents.

Netscape Extensions to HTML 3.0 Proposals—http://www.netscape.com/assist/net_sites/ html_extensions_3.html—includes references to tags for font attributes and embedded objects.

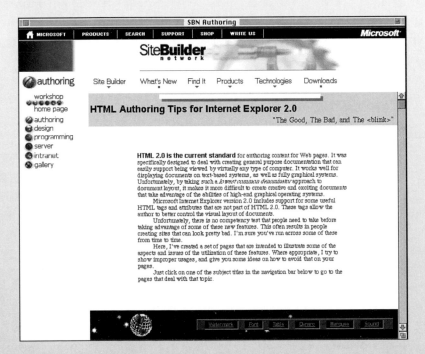

Microsoft's HTML Authoring Tips for Internet Explorer 2.0—http://www.microsoft.com/workshop/author/ other/ie20tips-f.htm—part of Microsoft's Site Builder's Workshop, this guide touches on font attributes, sounds, tables, and other Explorer features.

Browser By Design's HTML Resource pages—http://www.browserbydesign.com/resources/appa/apa1.htm— includes an extensive chart that list HTML tag and attribute support by browser.

html checkers

To help ensure proper tag placement and command syntax, try an HTML validation program. Validation tools serve as HTML grammar checkers: you run your document through the validator, and it supplies a list of (or points you to) incomplete tags, tags that aren't supported on a particular browser, or suggestions that will make your page more accessible overall. Some validators even go as far as to explain in exact detail what the consequences will be if you don't fix the inconsistencies within your coding.

Of course, using a validation tool does not guarantee that your page will look great. That's the challenge—to use HTML within its limits to create a site that looks great, but doesn't leave anyone out in the cold.

A popular online HTML validation checker is hosted by **WebTechs** at http://www.webtechs.com/html-val-svc/. Simply type the URL you'd like it to check, and off it goes. The service also allows you to test a section of code: type your test code and click to get the service's comments. At the time of this writing, WebTechs Validation service checks compliance for HTML Level 2, Level 3, Level 3.2 (Wilbur), Level 3.2 (Cougar), Mozilla, SoftQuad, AdvaSoft, Microsoft IE, and the Microsoft IE 3.0 Beta.

Doctor HTML (http://imagiware.com/RxHTML.cgi) takes your inventory a bit differently. This site checks spelling, document structure, image syntax, image analysis, table structure, form structure, and verifies hyperlinks. It breaks the document into sections and gives detailed reports (if requested) that direct you to the specific line of code in which a problem is suspected.

Weblint (http://www.khoros.unm.edu/staff/neilb/weblint.html) is a Perl script that checks syntax and HTML style. Available for Unix, Mac, Windows NT, and OS/2 platforms, Weblint is downloadable freeware that performs a variety of tests, including checking for basic structure and syntax, context (where a tag must appear within a certain element), and overlapped or illegally nested elements; flags obsolete elements; HTML that is not portable across all browsers; and will even check to see whether your images contain <ALT> tags (among other features). In addition, it flags mark-up embedded in comments, which can confuse some browsers.

Several sites now offer web-based interfaces to the Weblint syntax and style checker for quick access to its features. All you have to do is type the URL you'd like to check, and in some cases, choose those specific attributes of code and structure you'd like examined. Some of these include:

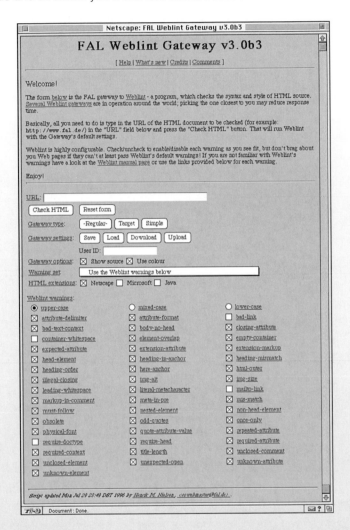

EWS Weblint Gateway—http://www.fal.de/cgi-bin/WeblintGateway

FAL Weblint Gateway v3.0b3—http://www.fal.de/cgi-bin/WeblintGateway

University of South Australia, Weblint Checking by URL—http://www.netspot.unisa.edu.au/weblint/

Chemnitz University of Technology, HTML-Prüfung mit weblint (German interface)—http://www.tu-chemnitz.de/~fri/www/html-test.html

Masayasu Ishikawa's Japanese Weblint interface—http://saturn.aichi-u.ac.jp/~mimasa/jweblint/

An updated list of gateways can be found on the Weblint site (http://www.cre.canon.co.uk/~neilb/weblint/gateways.html)

The nifty **Bobby** (http://www.cast.org/bobby/) was created by Josh Krieger for CAST (Center for Applied Special Technology) with the express objective of helping to check web pages for missing accessibility features. Among the many coding aspects and common mistakes that Bobby checks for are:

Missing ALT text for images

Missing ALT text for imagemap hot spots

Missing ALT text for Java Applets

Web pages taking longer than one minute to download using a 14.4 Kbps modem

Separation of adjacent hypertext anchors by more than a new line

Invalid attribute errors

Invalid attribute assignment errors

Invalid element errors

Client-side imagemap: XXX contains a hypertext link: YYY which is accessible only through the imagemap

Link names containing ambiguous phrases (that is, click this)

BLINK and MARQUEE tags that cannot be read by screen readers

Download sizes following audio and video files

The use of both server- and client-side imagemaps

AREA tags occurring outside a MAP definition

Too many words in link text

Client-side imagemap: XXX is not defined

Missing NAME attributes for client-side imagemaps

Missing SRC attributes for IMG tags

The lack of a server-side imagemap specification when ISMAP is used

Client-side-pull that makes pages inaccessible to screen readers

HTML forms that are not accessible without a mouse

Background images that make pages unreadable

Within word font changes that confuse screen readers

Smileys :) or ;) that are troublesome for screen readers :(

HTML tables that are often incorrectly read by screen readers

Too many words in ALT text

The lack of a text-only link

Movie files requiring descriptive text

Audio files requiring descriptive text

Bobby can check for compatibility with one browser, or, using its advanced options, can check multiple browsers and versions of browsers at once (America Online, Microsoft Internet Explorer, Mosaic, Netscape Navigator, Lynx, and HTML various standards).

Bobby gives you the option to validate your URL's code among 13 browsers and HTML standards.

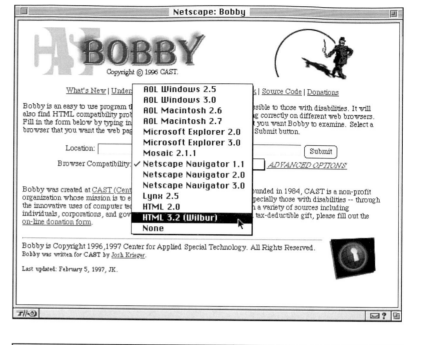

Bobby's advanced options give you the ability to check multiple browsers and standards concurrently, with a choice of graphical output or text output. It even lets you check local files that aren't posted to your server yet.

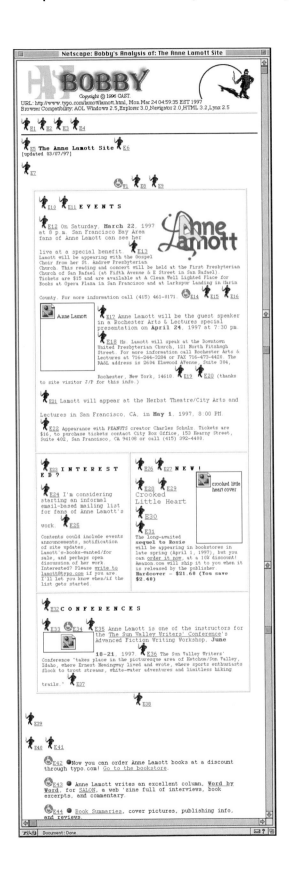

After you choose the browsers you want to check, Bobby gives both a graphical representation of the site (if that's the option you chose), with error points marked with con-structual and access warnings, and a text report of those errors it found.

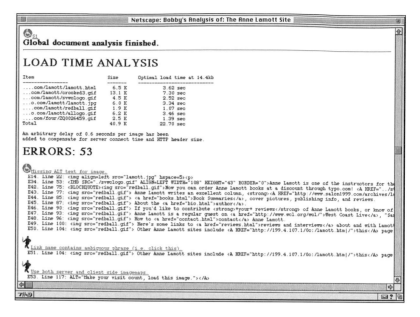

Krieger also created **Liz**, a program that allows Netscape Navigator to preview web pages as they would appear on all of the major web browsers. Although Liz isn't exactly an HTML val-idator, it acts as a sort of visual effect validator—to help you assess whether the code you specified for one browser will appear as you expected in other browsers.

summary

Our humble friend HTML is a significant cross-platform, multi-accessible standard, and it helps even more when you pay atten-tion to the rules. Even if browsers are "forgiving," stick to the standards, or at least as close as you can. A simple oversight can render your page tediously ugly or boring, or even completely unreadable.

CHAPTER 13

"Life is trying things to see if they work."
— *Ray Bradbury*

the text-only option

ASCII doesn't have to be boring

The term "text-only design" first brings to mind visions of bland, black, 12-point Times-Roman text flowing in an uninterrupted river down the length of a long long *long* gray web page. Maybe, if slightly inspired, the text-only design will also include some bold or italic typefaces, or maybe a headline here or there. Not to mention the spurts of blue and purple that generally signify links and visited links, respectively (depending on what browser you're using). Oh yeah, and some underlines for the same.

the benefits of text-only sites

The most obvious benefit of text-only sites is that they *are* accessible in many ways:

> all browsers can access text
>
> they can be read out loud by screen readers
>
> text is cut-and–pastable

text appearance

In most browsers, the user can change his default typefaces to suit his fancy. This can wreak havoc on your intended design, of course. You can request users to use certain typefaces, as well, but if someone has to change the typefaces every time he comes to your site, or if he doesn't have the typefaces you require, he may be inspired to move on.

Most browsers let users change the default typefaces for both proportional and fixed-width (monospace) fonts. They can choose any typestyle that happens to be installed on their system.

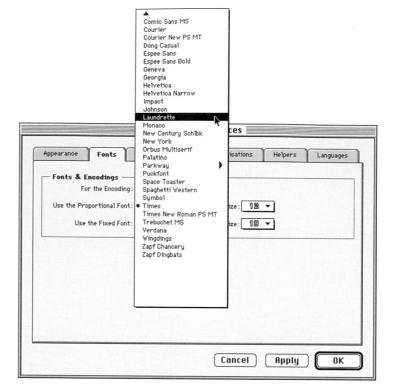

There's not a lot you can do to help those who need to increase your type size to be able to read it more easily. Test your site's text at various sizes; see how well it reads, and how graphics interact with the text. If you've used forced line breaks to make text wrap at certain points (with <BR> or <P> tags), then reading might become extremely awkward due to the text being larger because the tags have been moved.

Users can generally change default font sizes through their browser's settings. You can also change your default font sizes to test how these varying font sizes look on your pages—how text breaks, wraps, and reads.

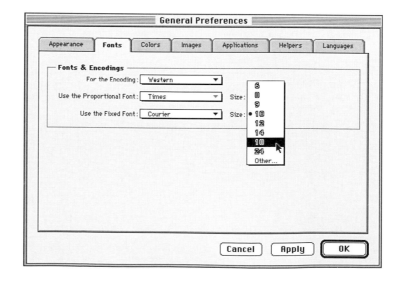

You can make all text part of graphics files for ultimate control over text appearance, but that starts up a whole new ball of wax. The problems include risking large file sizes and longer download times for users, as well as yet another barrier to those who are visually impaired.

controlling text function and size

There are a number of tags that are available, which give you options to control the look of the text on your site. The first of these are known as block elements, which break text into specific hierarchical structures, such as headings, subheads, and paragraphs. Block elements require both beginning and end tags (such as <H1>heading</H1> or <P ALIGN=RIGHT> right-aligned paragraph here</P>). These are considered "descriptive markup" tags because they not only change the *look* of the text within the tag, but they also specify to the browser the *function* of the tag's content and help to define the overall structure of the page.

headings

Headings within a document are specified by H1, H2, H3, H4, H5, and H6, with the lower number (H1) ranking in highest importance, and the highest number (H6) ranking in lowest importance. It just so happens that in HTML syntax, H1 tags around text make it appear in a larger type size than those following, and the sizes of each heading definition get smaller as their number-reference gets larger.

A heading tag doesn't need line breaks <BR> or paragraph breaks <P> between it and the body text; the code itself inserts a space between the two.

Heading level one, <H1>Heading 1</H1>, with default body text.

Heading 1

Why create a web page? The answer is threefold: First of all, because I can, and I must. It's not like coding a page is a glamorous process, nor is it anything new to me. It's just that I finally have an excuse to let my inner-coding-child fly free - plus, I have an executive order to do so.

Heading level two, <H2>Heading 2</H2>, with default body text.

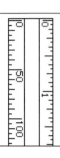

Heading 2

Second, having a Web page is extremely ego-satisfying; we creative types are all confessional exhibitionists at heart. Third, and most importantly, and always remember, we coders are not doing it for you - a personal Web page is a confirmation of one's being. One's existence in the ether if you will. "I have a reason to live!" we cry. "My public needs me to update my virtual plant-watering schedule!"

Heading level three, <H3>Heading 3</H3>, with default body text.

Heading 3

So, now I've turned into a selfish monster when I'm looking at sites. On the outside, I'm a mild-mannered editor looking for stuff that our readers will learn from or be entertained by; and when no one's looking, I'm viewing source and laying out fantasy pages in my head Who - or what - else can I dedicate pages to? My dislike of sweet potatoes? The revival of go-go boots?

Heading level four, <H4>Heading 4</H4>, with default body text.

Heading 4

I got me some links to sites, mail-to forms, and MY favorite, you-are-visitor-number-n-to-my-page codes (the latter gives me reason to squeal gleefully that "I've had another visitor to my page, and it wasn't ME!!"). By the way, have you gone to look at it yet? I'll wait here while you do.

Heading level five, <H5>Heading 5</H5>, with default body text.

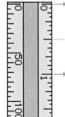

Heading 5

For the record, I can't take all the credit (or blame) for my sudden expertise; Kathy helped me out a lot along the way mostly by gently reminding me that "that is an unsupported feature of [my] web page," to look at Netscape's Creating Net Sites section, or to leave her alone. In return, my goal is to make sure that my home page is always better than hers.

211

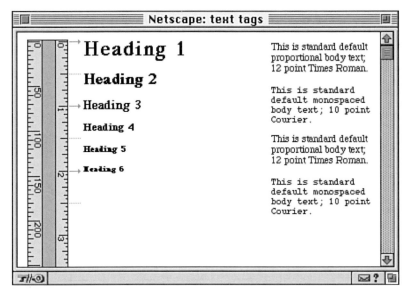

Heading level six, <H6>Heading 6</H6>, with default body text.

Netscape Navigator: all of the heading settings, from highest importance to lowest.

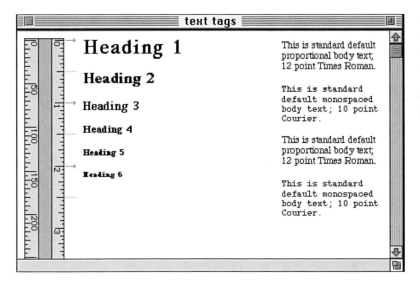

Microsoft Internet Explorer: all of the heading settings, from highest importance to lowest. Note that the headings tags take up more vertical room than in Netscape Navigator, even though the type sizes are the same.

NCSA Mosaic: all of the heading settings, from highest importance to lowest. Some of the type styles appear slightly different from the other two browsers, and the spacing before and after each heading is slightly more than Netscape and Explorer.

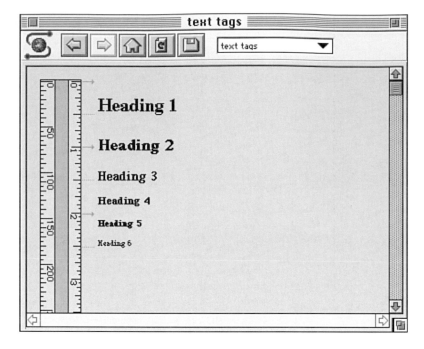

It should be noted that all of the heading tags may include one of the alignment specifications: ALIGN=RIGHT, ALIGN=CENTER, or ALIGN=LEFT. The structure for this coding is <H1 ALIGN=CENTER>*centered header here*</H1>. The end tag also affects the centering (or other alignment) code.

font attribution tags

Using a <FONT SIZE=*number*> tag around text also changes its size, at least in the most popular browsers. The key point here is that the <FONT SIZE> tag changes *only* font size, and doesn't mark a particular section of text with any structural significance. For example, if a person who is blind uses a screen reader to scan your page, and all of your titles and subtitles are formatted with <FONT SIZE> tags, the person won't be able to differentiate between body text and headings because this tag doesn't alert the screen reader to any hierarchical differences among the text within FONT tags and the text that's not.

Coding with the <FONT SIZE> tag can be structured two different ways. One is to specify the actual "number" size of the font (1 through 7), or to give a value range of "+" or "−" a certain number that is relative to the BASEFONT size. The default BASEFONT of a document is 3.

Font Size="7"

Why create a web page? The answer is threefold: First of all, because I can, and I must. It's not like coding a page is a glamorous process, nor is it anything new to me. It's just that I finally have an excuse to let my inner-coding-child fly free - plus, I have an executive order to do so.

<FONT SIZE="7">Font Size="7"</FONT>, with default body text.

Font Size="6"

Second, having a Web page is extremely ego-satisfying; we creative types are all confessional exhibitionists at heart. Third, and most importantly, and always remember, we coders are not doing it for you - a personal Web page is a confirmation of one's being. One's existence in the ether if you will. "I have a reason to live!" we cry. "My public needs me to update my virtual plant-watering schedule!"

<FONT SIZE="6">Font Size="6"</FONT>, with default body text.

Font Size="5"

So, now I've turned into a selfish monster when I'm looking at sites. On the outside, I'm a mild-mannered editor looking for stuff that our readers will learn from or be entertained by; and when no one's looking, I'm viewing source and laying out fantasy pages in my head Who - or what - else can I dedicate pages to? My dislike of sweet potatoes? The revival of go-go boots?

Font Size="4"

<FONT SIZE="5">Font Size="5"</FONT>, with default body text, followed by <FONT SIZE="4">Font Size="4"</FONT>.

Font Size="3"

For the record, I can't take all the credit (or blame) for my sudden expertise; Kathy helped me out a lot along the way mostly by gently reminding me that "that is an unsupported feature of [my] web page," to look at Netscape's Creating Net Sites section, or to leave her alone. In return, my goal is to make sure that my home page is always better than hers.

Font Size="2"

In the spirit of competition, or if you're just into doing a good deed, keep my home page on your hotlist. Soon, I'll be uploading some pictures of my new sofa. Interactive ones. With randomly generated transparent throw pillows.

Font Size="1"

Can you read that ok up there? If you want, I'll type it over for you…

<FONT SIZE="3">Font Size="3"</FONT>, <FONT SIZE="2">Font Size="2"</FONT>, and <FONT SIZE="1">Font Size="1"</FONT>, with default body text.

Netscape Navigator: <FONT SIZE> settings relative to the BASEFONT default setting of 3.

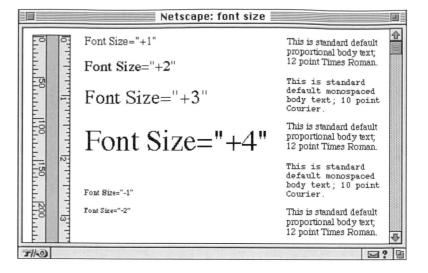

Microsoft Internet Explorer: <FONT SIZE> settings relative to the BASE-FONT default setting of 3.

The FONT SIZE attribute doesn't automatically wrap text to the next line, like the heading styles do. That's because it merely affects the appearance of the text, not the actual significance of the text.

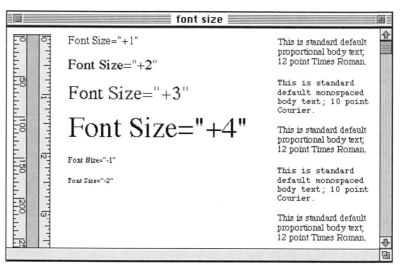

character styles

Just like with heading tags and font size tags, other tags that affect type appearance also fall into two different categories: logical and physical. Logical type style tags affect the look of type as well as the *meaning* of type, whereas physical type style tags simply affect the appearance of the type within.

logical type style tags

<DFN>definition</DFN>, although it doesn't appear different in some browsers, is used as a tag on a word that is being defined.

<EM>emphasis</EM> shows a word or phrase's significance, and generally appears in italics.

<CITE>citation</CITE> is used for names of books, movies, and other quotations or references.

<CODE>code</CODE> displays in a monospaced font and is meant to signify computer code.

<KBD>keyboard</KBD> signifies where a user should enter something from the keyboard, such as a password or e-mail information, and also appears in a monospaced typeface.

definition

emphasis

citation

code

keyboard

sample

strong emphasis

variable

The logical type style tags shown in Netscape Navigator.

<SAMP>sample</SAMP>, yet another computerish code that appears in monospaced type, is used to signify a succession of literal feedback characters.

<STRONG>strong emphasis</STRONG>, usually shows up as bold text, and is used to signify the importance of a phrase.

<VAR>variable</VAR>, shows up in italics, and is used to signify where a number or letter should be replaced, such as in an equation (8 + n =14), or when showing someone an example such as "using FONT SIZE=n will change your type appearance."

physical type style tags

<B>bold text</B>, changes the appearance of the enclosed text to appear bold.

<I>italic text</I>, changes the appearance of the enclosed text to italics.

<TT>typewriter text, or teletype</TT>, changes type to a monospaced typeface.

<U>underlined text</U>, underlines the enclosed text.

bold text

italic text

`teletype text`

<u>**underlined text**</u>

other text appearance tags

<ADDRESS>address</ADDRESS> changes the appearance of text—in most browsers—to italics, and signifies a reference to a person or that person's contact information.

Fred Jones 123 Smith Street San Francisco, CA 94000

<BLOCKQUOTE>blockquote</BLOCKQUOTE> signifies an extended excerpt from another source, and is generally indented about an inch from either margin of the browser window width. Some browsers render the type italicized.

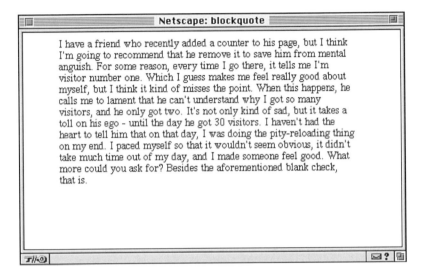

<PRE>preformatted text</PRE> appears in a browser's default monospaced typeface, and maintains the literal typed spacing.

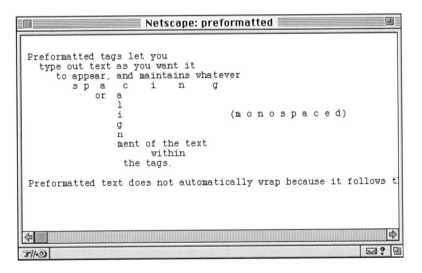

```
<PRE>
Preformatted tags let you
  type out text as you want it
     to appear, and maintains whatever
        s p a c        i     n    g
          or   a
               l
               i                          (m o n o s p a c e d)
               g
               n
               ment of the text
                       within
                  the tags.
</PRE>
```

^{superscript} and _{subscript} are generally used for referencing other works, or footnotes and end-notes. Superscript appears above the enclosed line of text; sub-script drops below.

> If we could superscript text, we would. If we could subscript text, we would.

<BIG>big</BIG> and <SMALL>small</SMALL> tags simply make the enclosed text larger or smaller than the default defined type size.

looks the same to me

A lot of the tags, both the descriptive-function logical tags (head-ings, emphasis, and so on) and the purely physical-appearance tags (font size, italic, ans so on.), end up looking the same on-screen. There are also a lot of tags mentioned here, specifically logical tags for things such as variables and sample tags, that many designers will probably have no need for. So why would you choose to use one over the other?

From the purely aesthetic value, it really makes no difference. Any designer can use any tag that suits their creative purpose and make the page look like they want it to look.

However, after reading through chapter 12, "the importance of html," it should be obvious that if you want to follow the *ideal* of HTML as a true cross-platform and multi-browser construct, then using tags for the logical function for which they were assigned ensures that those who rely on these logical functions can better navigate and understand your pages.

Another benefit in using logical tag structures is the parallel that they have to the concept of a style sheet in a word processor—if you've used heading tags throughout your document to separate sections and then your viewers decide to change the typestyle of your heads and subheads, once the definition of the style has been changed, all occurrences of that particular heading will automatically change.

Some browsers, such as NCSA Mosaic, give the user the option to change many of the physical appearance aspects (size, color, amount of spacing before and after) of logical structure tags.

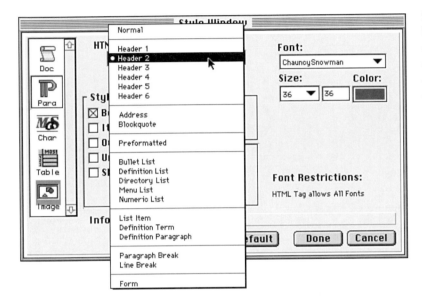

Unfortunately, if you're worried that your viewers may have set up their styles to, for example, show <EM>emphasis</EM> by making that text bright red, 36-point scripted type (we'll pray that they haven't, but you never know), and you want the type to merely be italicized (which is the <EM></EM> default appearance), go with a physical style—in this case, <I>italic</I>. If the appearance of the text doesn't have a specific function related to it, such as the desire for a screen reader to read text aloud with an emphasis on a certain phrase, then choosing physical style tags to preserve your control (or more control) over the aesthetics of your site may be in order. Either way, maintain a coherence of the kind of styles that you choose throughout your document.

220

However, just because the type looks different, doesn't mean that its function has changed. An <H2> tag is still a second-level heading tag, no matter what it looks like. Changing its style aspects once changes its appearance on any viewed site.

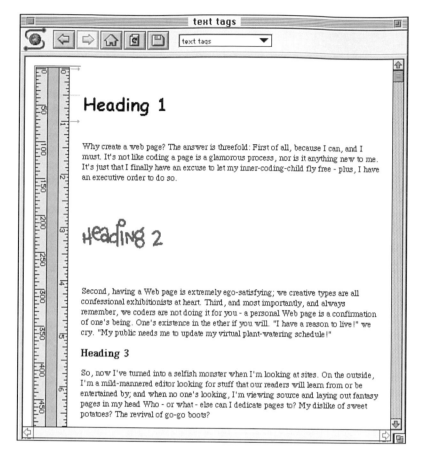

coloring fonts

The FONT tags may also include a color choice reference, in the form of <FONT COLOR="#*nnnnnn*">. Including a hexadecimal color code within the tag gives the enclosed text the color specified. For example, specifying the following will give you red text that is two sizes above the BASEFONT specified size:

```
<FONT SIZE="+2" COLOR="#CC3300">Take me out to the ball
game.</FONT>
```

paragraphs defined

Although lots of designers simply use the paragraph break tag <P> all by itself without a closing tag </P> as a method of adding an extra line space between paragraphs, using the set of tags gives you the option to include paragraph alignment tags. As with heading tags, these are ALIGN=LEFT, ALIGN=CENTER, and ALIGN=RIGHT.

The code structure for a paragraph tag that puts line spaces between paragraphs is as follows:

```
This is the first paragraph.
<P>
This is the second paragraph.
<P>
This is the third paragraph.
```

> This is the first paragraph.
>
> This is the second paragraph.
>
> This is the third paragraph.

To align text either left, center, or right, you need to include para-graph end tags:

```
<P ALIGN=LEFT>This is the first paragraph.</P>

<P ALIGN=CENTER>This is the second paragraph.</P>

<P ALIGN=RIGHT>This is the third paragraph.</P>
```

> This is the first paragraph.
>
>   This is the second paragraph.
>
>   This is the third paragraph.

The results of paragraph tags utilizing end tags and enclosing an alignment attribute.

more breaks

Similar to the <P>paragraph</P> tag is the <DIV>document division</DIV> set of tags. Used to separate blocks of text, as does the paragraph tag, DIV can be used with ALIGN attributes RIGHT, LEFT, and CENTER, as well. Unlike the paragraph tag, the document division tag must always have an end tag.

getting listed

There are a number of text list definitions that are useful for various purposes, such as for highlighting points or tables of contents for sections of a document, listing products by rank or preference, or simply indenting a section of text.

unnumbered, or unordered, lists

```
What to bring on a camping trip:
<UL>
        <LI>backpack
        <LI>sleeping bag
        <LI>mosquito repellent
        <LI>toothbrush
        <LI>marshmallows
</UL>
```

What to bring on a camping trip:

- backpack
- sleeping bag
- mosquito repellent
- toothbrush
- marshmallows

You'll generally get the same visual results with directory (<DIR></DIR>) and menu (<MENU></MENU>) lists as with unnumbered lists. However, if your list contents happen to be a directory of items (a program guide, for example), or a menu of items (for a restaurant or choices of products), then use the appropriate list tags.

numbered, or ordered, lists

```
Make boiled water in four easy steps:
<OL>
        <LI>put water in a pan
        <LI>turn stove on "high"
        <LI>put pan on stove
        <LI>wait
</OL>
```

Make boiled water in four easy steps:

1. put water in a pan
2. turn stove on "high"
3. put pan on stove
4. wait

definition lists

Definition lists give you the option to include a definition term <DT> along with a selection of definition definitions <DD> (by the way, that's not a typo). The definition term is useful for adding subheadlines for each section of definitions within the list.

```
Colleges and Universities in the United States:
<DL>
        <DT>New York
                <DD>Columbia University
                <DD>Hunter College
                <DD>New York University
        <DT>Vermont
                <DD>Bennington College
                <DD>Champlain College
                <DD>University of Vermont
</DL>
```

Colleges and Universities in the United States:

New York
    Columbia University
    Hunter College
    New York University
Vermont
    Bennington College
    Champlain College
    University of Vermont

nested lists

Each of the previous lists can be nested inside one another for specific organizational arrangements, such as numbered lists within unnumbered lists.

```
What to bring on a camping trip:
<UL>
        <LI>hiking gear
        <OL>
                <LI>backpack
                <LI>boots
        </OL>
        <LI>shelter
        <OL>
                <LI>tent
                <LI>raincoat
        </OL>
        <LI>food
        <OL>
                <LI>marshmallows
                <LI>carrot sticks
                <LI>gorp
        </OL>
</UL>
```

What to bring on a camping trip:

- hiking gear
    1. backpack
    2. boots
- shelter
    1. tent
    2. raincoat
- food
    1. marshmallows
    2. carrot sticks
    3. gorp

Tip

Keep up with the structure of cascading style sheet tags and its status as a proposed standard at the World Wide Web Consortium (W3C) site, http://www.w3.org/pub/WWW/TR/WD-css1.

Microsoft's site includes two handy sections for learning and sampling CSS:

Typography on the Web (http://www.microsoft.com/truetype/hottopic.htm)

Cascading Style Sheets Gallery (http://www.microsoft.com/truetype/css/gallery/entrance.htm)

cascading style sheets

Cascading style sheets (CSS) is a proposed method of coding that will enable you to specify definitions of logical text tags defined previously, such as headings and paragraphs. CSS gives more control of the text display to the designer because within a CSS, the designer has the option to define the properties of fonts, backgrounds, text alignment, and other specific page layout controls.

Not only can you change the attributes of existing tags, but you can create your own style sheets for easier coding and styling of your overall site.

At the time this is being written, only Microsoft Internet Explorer version 3.x supports cascading style sheets, but Netscape is promising support of CSS in its next release.

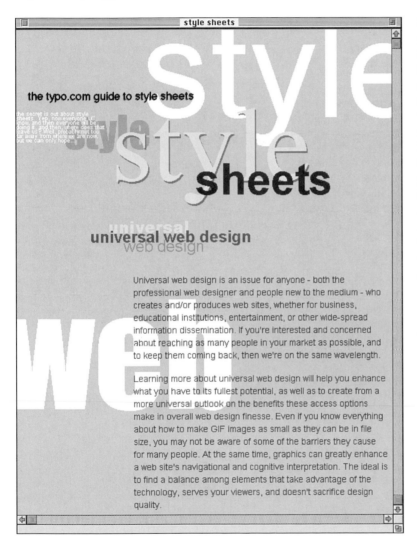

One of the features of using cascading style sheets is to precisely align text on the page pixel by pixel until it appears as you want it to—even off the edges of the pages or overlapping one another. Another feature is also obvious: font size, color, and style are much more flexible than standard text.

What's not so obvious? This entire page is only 6k. If the same design were attempted using graphics—even though, in this case, this site uses only a few browser-safe colors, therefore cutting down on overall potential graphic file size—the overall size and download time would be at least three times bigger. And unless the entire page were made into a graphic, or the word "web" were part of a very large background tile, we'd lose the impact of the background graphic.

So if it's not a standard, and only one browser supports it right now, why am I mentioning it in a book about making web pages accessible? Because the best thing about cascading style sheets is that designers can, for example, specify that a logo font show up on the page in 200-point type (rather than be limited to the current text sizes), and via another tag, they can place menu text in a specified typestyle on *top* of that logo and end up with a very cool-looking web page. This sounds like no big deal because a designer could create the same effect in an image manipulation program like Photoshop, but with CSS taking control, all the effects are carried out with text. The same size graphic effect would be significantly larger in file size than one that is solely made out of text that is rendered on the viewer's screen.

Note

Here's a sampling of the code that is within the previous cascading style sheet image. A major benefit in using CSS is that the designer can define a style once at the beginning of a document, and need only refer to that style later on, rather than having to type all the attributes each time the style is called upon. Before any of the <BODY> content is entered, the styles must be defined. Note that the style definitions are within an HTML comment field (<!-- comment -->). This is a workaround so that those non-CSS browsers that come to the site will still be able to access content, and will ignore all of the enclosed style tags. Otherwise, all the coding will show up in the non-CSS supporting browser.

```
<HTML>
<HEAD>
<TITLE>style sheets</TITLE>
<STYLE>
<!--
BODY { background: #ccccff }
.text { font-size: 14px; line-height: 20px; margin-top: -220px; margin-left: 180px;
color: darkblue; font-family: Arial }

.ban { font-size: 220px; line-height: 10px; margin-top: -68px; margin-left: 194px;
color: white; font-family: Arial }

.ban1 { font-size: 70px; line-height: 80px; margin-top: -48px; margin-left: 70px; color:
orange; font-family: Impact }

.ban2 { font-size: 170px; line-height: 80px; margin-top: -26px; margin-left: 148px;
color: gray; font-family: Times }

.ban2a { font-size: 170px; line-height: 80px; margin-top: -83px; margin-left: 146px;
color: yellow; font-family: Times }

.ban3 { font-size: 70px; line-height: 80px; margin-top: -58px; margin-left: 280px;
color: blue; font-weight: bold; font-family: Arial }
...
```

The words after the periods, such as .text and .ban2, are the names of the styles within the document. Font size refers to the point size of the text; line height is the spacing between lines; margin top refers to its distance from the previous line of text; margin left is its distance from left-hand margin (note that they can be negative numbers); color refers to that style type's color; font family is the typeface chosen for each style.

```
...
-->

</STYLE>
</HEAD>

<BODY>

<DIV CLASS=ban>style</DIV>
<DIV CLASS=ban1>style</DIV>
<DIV CLASS=ban2>style</DIV>
<DIV CLASS=ban2a>style</DIV>
<DIV CLASS=ban3>sheets</DIV>
<DIV CLASS=ban4>the typo.com guide to style sheets</DIV>
<DIV CLASS=ban5>the typo.com guide to style sheets</DIV>
<P>
<DIV CLASS=whisper>
        the secret is out about style <br>
        sheets. Yep, now everyone will <br>
        know, and then everyone will be<br>
        doing it, and then, where does that<br>
        leave us? Well, probably not too<br>
        far away from where we are now,<BR>
        but we can only hope...</DIV>
<DIV CLASS=head1>universal</DIV>
<DIV CLASS=head2>universal web design</DIV>
<DIV CLASS=head3>web design</DIV>
```

```
<DIV CLASS=bgtext>web</DIV>
<DIV CLASS=text>
Universal web design is an issue for anyone - either the professional web designer or
people new to the medium - who creates and/or produces web sites, whether for business,
educational institutions, entertainment, or other wide-spread information dissemination.
If you're interested and concerned about reaching as many people in your market as pos-
sible, and to keep them coming back, then we're on the same wavelength.
<p>
```

After the styles have been defined, they can then be referred to within the document. The <DIV> text break tag is used to separate each section of text, and the CLASS attribute refers to the defined style name, and the text within the tag then takes on the attributes of the style defined with the <STYLE></STYLE> tags; that is, ban, *ban1*, *text*, and *whisper*.

228 The style-sheeted page, which looks cool in Explorer, looks less than spiffy in Netscape Navigator.

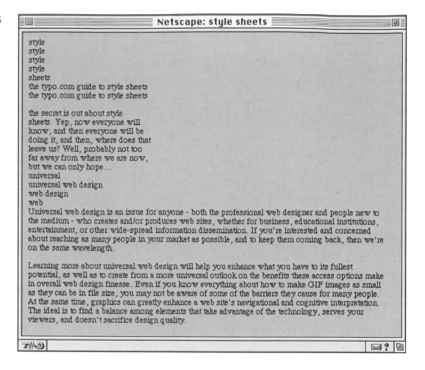

There are limitations to using cascading style sheets, besides the fact that only Explorer, at this point, will let you see these pages properly. First and foremost, the people viewing your page must have the same fonts available and loaded onto their computer in order to view what you have in mind when you design the page. This is no problem if you: 1) design only with fonts you know that your audience already has, and 2) you know they are using a current version of Explorer, which has a number of typefaces available for use and distribution (both Macintosh and PC versions of the same typefaces, as well).

You can always provide the option for site visitors to download the typefaces that your page uses. However, make sure that the typefaces are either public domain or those that you have permission to freely distribute. If possible, choose typefaces that are available for multiple platforms.

summary

ASCII may be dry, but type doesn't have to be boring. Combining and contrasting styles of text gives depth to an otherwise boring text page, and may also contribute to its navigability if logical style tags are used to describe sections of a document accurately. All browsers can access text; it's up to you to make the text itself accessible, understandable, and easy to find one's way through.

CHAPTER 14

> *"I have noticed that the people who are late are often so much jollier than the people who have to wait for them."*
> — *E. V. Lucas*

downloadables

choose the right file format

Offering a library of freely downloadable files—graphics, funny sound clips, a text document that itemizes the site's contents, or whatever—is a great way to get people on your site and keep them coming back. If the files are in a format they can't read, however, you've just wasted their time. And that's a common occurrence on the web. How many times have you rummaged through various software libraries, labored over FAQ lists, and spent hours downloading a bunch of utilities you didn't really need, just to open some random file? No matter how much of a hassle it is for you, it's always in your best interest to offer files in the most common format that you can. The time you spend avoiding angry e-mail messages from weary passersby alone will make it worth the extra effort.

This sounds simple, but leads to a dilemma: Which formats are common and which serve a niche? For the answer, remember to look beyond the technically savvy realm of designers. If a graphic you like is in EPS format, get over it. Although you and most of your fellow professionals have copies of Photoshop on your hard drives, most people don't. Why kill yourself converting a small sound file into a Shockwave plug-in when it will be easier for everyone to simply download it as an AU sound file? You get the point.

Not to slam things that require special viewing tools, but VRML files, streaming audio files, Adobe Acrobat files, and plenty more present a message that can be conveyed well in their particular format only. If that's the case with your content, so be it. It's not web blasphemy to require your audience to go get a fairly common plug-in to view a majority of your site's content. Just make sure it's easy for them to *get* the plug-in. On the other hand, don't throw up a few random, exotic sound and video files just for the status. That's so… Webmaster 1995.

Honestly, nearly any type of content you'd want to offer up can be done through a common file format that anyone, on any computer platform, can read with no problems. Of course, there are plenty of media types out there, so let's run through the big ones.

compressed downloadables

Why are there so many compression standards? Far more than a dozen exist among the Unix, Mac, and PC platforms. You could as easily ask why the sky is blue. Fans of any compression program can argue until they're blue why one algorithm is better than the next. True, certain types of compression work better for different media types, but the difference is usually minimal. Don't try to memorize which type is best for which format. You have better things to do.

For the most part, compression is used for two things: compacting file sizes and holding several files in one nice and tidy package. Both are equally important. It saves your audience download times two-fold because there's less data and fewer files to download. The best part is that the latest round of compression utilities are so simple to use and fast, that compressing all of your downloadables isn't a bad idea. With a few distinct exceptions.

the exceptions

Say you have one sound file that's about 50k. There's really no reason to compress it at all, even if it cuts the file's size by half (which it probably wouldn't because sound files don't compress well at all). In the time it takes someone to download the file, open up a decompression utility, decompress the file, throw away the original—you get the point. The same goes for graphics, especially if they're JPEG or GIF graphics, because they can be viewed directly in your browser; not to mention, JPEG and GIF are two image compression methods, so the images should be of relatively small size anyway). There's no viewer to mess with and no deciding where to download the graphic. When you decide on file formats, obviously keep your audience in mind. What will be the simplest for them to open? Which will keep them closest to your site?

finding the right format

You definitely know you need to compress your unwieldy files, so which format do you choose? The ZIP standard is probably the most widely supported. It compresses most media types well and there are dozens of freely downloadable Mac and PC utilities to compress and decompress the ZIP format. Although the StuffIt (SIT) standard is far more popular on the Mac, fewer PC users can decompress SIT files than Mac users can ZIP files. In fact, the free utility called UnStuffIt, which is available on Aladdin Systems' web site (http://www.aladdinsys.com/), can unstuff ZIP files and SIT files, among several others, on either Macs or PCs. UnStuffIt is probably the utility you want to link to from your site if you're offering up ZIP files.

WinZip from Nico Mak Computing is developing a Netscape unzipping plug-in that you may like to try out. The company offers a demonstration version of most of its utilities from its home page at http://www.winzip.com/.

PKZip from PKWare (http://www.
pkware.com/) is another shareware
utility for DOS and Windows computers that offers a number of
compression and decompression
options, including creating self-
extracting EXE files.

If you know that you have primarily either Mac or PC audiences,
an even easier way for them to read compressed archives is for
you to make self-extracting archives. For Macs, the format is
known as SEA (self-extracting archive), and on PCs it's EXE
(executable). Unfortunately, you're going to have to pick one or
the other, or provide two choices, because each works on only
one platform. But nothing is easier to use; all you have to do is
download the file and double click. For Macintosh, StuffIt is again
going to be your best pick for creating SEAs. For the PC, take
your pick. There are dozens of programs to choose from.

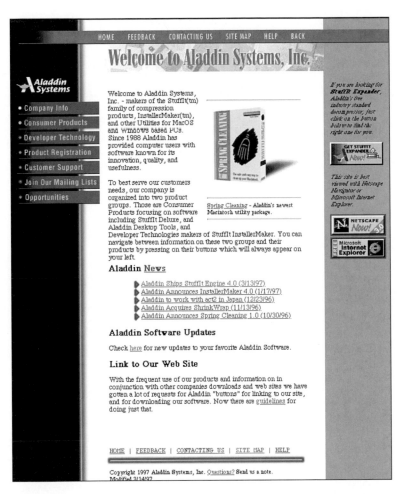

On the Mac side, StuffIt utilities from Aladdin Systems (http://www.aladdinsys.com/) come in both commercial and shareware flavors.

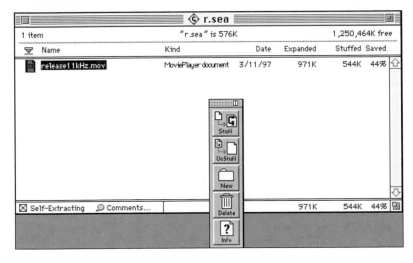

StuffIt Lite, from Aladdin Systems, is flexible enough for most compression needs on the Mac side. It lets you create SIT and SEA files, as well as encode (and decode) BinHex and MacBinary files, among others.

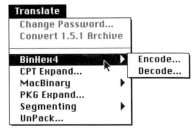

As for the rest of the compression formats—BinHex, UUEncode, MIME, Binary, and so on—there's really no point in using them unless you really need to reach people on platforms other than Mac and Windows. Many decompression utilities such as WinZip and UnStuffIt can handle countless compression formats, but why risk it?

Are you on the Macintosh platform and wondering how to give your Windows visitors ZIP files as an option? ZipIt, a shareware utility by Tom Brown (http://www.awa.com/softlock/zipit/zipit.html), gives Macintoshers access to both creating and accessing the contents of ZIP archives.

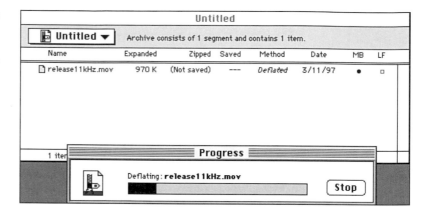

the great debate: graphics

Graphics files are where people start to get really defensive. Most graphic artists have their own favorite graphics format that they'll swear by. Believe it or not, there are even overcrowded newsgroups that hold vicious debates on which is better, GIF or JPEG. In some situations, the format that a graphic comes in does make a difference. For instance, if you had a digital map that had great detail, you'd probably want it in the EPS format so that people could zoom in and see exact street names. But for most things, you're going to want to use either GIF or JPEG. Which one of those two doesn't really matter (to most people anyway). The important reason why you should use one of these two is simple: you know that anyone surfing your site is going to be able to read either format because they're using a web browser. The general "rule" is that GIFs are better for line art (or "flat" art), and JPEGs are better for photographs. On this, most people can agree.

Unless it's for a specific fan group, there's really no reason at all to put a file in BMP, PCX, PICT or any of the other formats because they bring nothing but cross-platform woes. Windows 95 comes ready to read BMP files, but not PICT. Macs come ready to read PICT but not PCX. They all basically do the same thing, so it's best to just generalize. If you want high quality, simply jack up the resolution in either a GIF or JPEG format.

moving right along: video

The web's next big thing is video, so they say. So far, web-based streaming video has been a pretty big mess. A small army of formats have come out in the past year, each completely different from the next. Each one requires a different plug-in, each one claims to be the absolute best, and most of them really don't work at all if the user is hooked up to a 28.8 Kbps modem. In fact, streaming video is another book entirely. For now, avoid it.

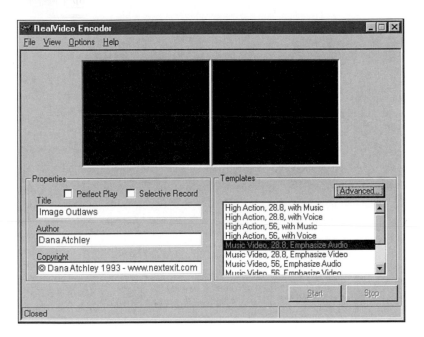

The RealVideo Encoder from Progressive Networks, Inc. (http://www.real-audio.com/), the creators of RealAudio, lets you translate AVI and QuickTime movies into the RealVideo streaming-video format. At the time this book went to press, the RealVideo Encoder was available on the Windows platform only.

At this point, it sure seems like making streaming video files is a lot easier than getting them. Although receiving live video news streams is a great idea, it is nearly impossible to receive either consistent sound or video via a 28.8 Kbps connection. Without fail (so to speak), the error message "Net congestion, Rebuffering..." would appear every few seconds when accessing CSPAN and other's streaming RealVideo feed.

For standard, downloadable video files, your choices are fairly straightforward. The big ones are AVI, QuickTime (MOV), and MPEG. Of the three, the most widely supported is AVI, but that doesn't mean it's the best one around. The reason it is the most supported is simple. Most PCs come with Media Player, which can play AVI files, but not QuickTime. Most Macs come with QuickTime Player, which can handle several movie formats, one of which is AVI. From the development end, you're going to need a video capture card, and nearly every capture card around comes with some kind of software that makes simple AVI video clips.

QuickTime is far more flexible, and QuickTime Player is easily more powerful and should even be supporting MPEG video by the time you read this. There are QuickTime players for both the Mac and PC, so if you're creating on the Mac, you may want to go with the QuickTime format. Anyone who's had their PC for a while, and is any kind of game or multimedia fan, will most likely already have a QuickTime player as well. As far as file size and quality goes, it's comparable to AVI, but using QuickTime Player, you can do a lot more, like play QuickTime VR and MIDI files.

Finally, it seems that MPEG is going to be huge in the near future, thanks to DVD (digital video disc). Because DVD uses the

MPEG-2 format, plenty more people will have an MPEG player on their machine, and there are several MPEG Web browser plug-ins in the works. It's going to be fascinating to see how DVD and the web meld together, but for now, you can probably bet that most people coming by your site are going to have to go download a player to get a look at MPEG.

sound and fury: audio

For the whole low-down on sound, be sure to read chapter 9, "sound bytes." On the web, the most supported format is AU. Although AU format was created on the Unix platform, both of the major browsers on both Macs and PCs will play it. It's not the greatest sound format around, but there's no guesswork because there's no player or helper application to configure. After you've downloaded an AU file, a Play button simply pops up.

Both WAV and AIFF files are also commonly supported (WAV more on the PC, and AIFF more on the Mac). Common players exist for each, and both formats are simple to create and edit. Take your pick; there are plenty of shareware applications on the web.

For music, however cheesy it may sound, most computers are equipped to play MIDI files. And for streaming audio, you'll want to go with either RealAudio or Shockwave.

words to the wise: documents

Obviously, documents are what the web is all about. Forget fancy fonts and overly complex tables. Nine times out of ten, your message can be perfectly conveyed through good old HTML. That is, unless it's something that you want your audience to download and read offline. Then HTML isn't such a great option, especially if there are graphics involved, because most web browsers save only the HTML text, not the graphics, when you save a web page locally.

If you want to offer a downloadable document that can hold all of its design integrity (fonts, formatting, and graphics) and be readable by nearly anyone, you'll probably want to go with Rich Text Format (RTF). Although it's not an amazingly popular format, it's one of those surprising things that works for PCs and Macs while keeping nearly everything intact. You can even embed playable sound and video files into it. Think of it as HTML lite,

One word to the wise: if you're offering straightforward, downloadable video, compress the file as much as you can. Digital video files are still huge; and the smaller the initial file is, the more likely someone will download it.

There are lots of shareware sound players available to your audience, but keep in mind that the latest versions of Netscape and Internet Explorer have WAV, AIF, and MIDI file players included with their browsers.

but everything comes in one nice and simple package. And nearly any full-fledged word processor, such as Microsoft Word or WordPerfect, on any platform will read it.

Unfortunately, RTF's one big problem is that whoever reads the file must have the right fonts installed in their system, or everything will look amiss. If you want to do some really fancy design work, use any font you want, and have a sophisticated navigational system throughout the document, you'll want to use Adobe's Acrobat (PDF). It includes the fonts and everything else within the document, which—as you can guess—makes for bigger files for people to download). You can also build a hot, clickable Table of Contents. Even certain words can be live-linked to other parts of the document or other web sites. The Acrobat Reader is free and is available for both Macs and PCs. But to make Acrobat files, you need the full-blown version of Acrobat, which costs around $295. The Acrobat Reader is a common web helper application, and many larger companies have devoted a good chunk of their web publishing to the Acrobat format.

Adobe Acrobat lets viewers who have it installed see the fonts, images, and layout as you intended. However, because files have to include so much information, they tend to be quite large.

If you just have a large text-only document, a regular text (TXT) file will do fine, and anyone can read it. Or, if you're in a gambling mood, you could just put all your documents in Microsoft Word format. Although not everybody owns a copy of Word, most people have a word processor that can convert Word files into readable documents. Of course with Word, you run into the same problem you do with RTF documents. Your font choice is limited. But if you're making simple documents available, you'll probably want to keep your font choices to a minimum anyway. Not many people want to read much in the English Script font.

best bets

In all cases, the best rule of thumb is to fight the urge to do something needlessly fancy. Although the most commonly supported formats may not be the flashiest, you know they're going to work, and they cause far less confusion with your audience. Depending on your needs, here are the default formats that will probably work the best:

ZIP	Compression
GIF or JPEG	Graphics
AVI	Video
AU	Audio
RTF	Documents

For a more detailed look at your main format choices, see the following table.

common file formats found on the web

file extension	file type	primary platform	viewable on mac and windows	good viewer application for windows	good viewer application for mac
AIFF	Sound	Macintosh	Yes	Windows Media Player	Macintosh Sound Player
ASCII	Text	Unix	Yes	Notepad	TeachText
AVI	Video	PC	Yes	Media Player	QuickTime Player
ARJ	Compression	PC	Yes	WinZip	DeArj
AU	Sound	Unix	Yes	Netscape Navigator	Netscape Navigator
BIN	Compression	Macintosh	No	n/a	UnStuffIt
DOC	Document	PC	Yes	WordPad	Microsoft Word
EPS	Graphic	Macintosh	Yes	??	??
EXE	Compression	PC	No	Self-Extracting	n/a
GIF	Graphic	n/a	Yes	Any Web Browser	Any Web Browser
GZ	Compression	Unix	Yes	WinZip	UnStuffIt
HTML	Document	Unix	Yes	Any Web Browser	Any Web Browser
HQX	Compression	Unix	Yes	UnStuffIt	UnStuffIt
JPG/ JPEG	Graphic	n/a	Yes	Any Web Browser	Any Web Browser
MIME	Compression	n/a	Yes	Xfer Pro	??
MOV	Video	Macintosh	Yes	QuickTime Player	QuickTime Player
MPEG	Video	PC	Yes	NetToob	Sparkle
PCX	Graphic	PC	Yes	Lview Pro	JPEGView
PDF	Document	Macintosh	Yes	Acrobat Reader	Acrobat Reader

file exten-sion	file type	primary platform	viewable on mac and windows	good viewer application for windows	good viewer application for mac
PICT	Graphic	Macintosh	Yes	Lview Pro	Apple's Clipboard
PNG	Graphic	n/a	Yes	Any Web Browser	Any Web Browser
RTF	Document	PC	Yes	WordPad	Any word processor
SEA	Compression	Macintosh	No	n/a	Self-extracting
SIT	Compression	Macintosh	Yes	UnStuffIt	UnStuffit
TAR	Compression	Unix	Yes	WinZip	Tar
TIFF	Graphic	Macintosh	Yes	Lview Pro	JPEGView
TXT	Document	n/a	Yes	WordPad	Text Pad
UUE/UU	Compression	Unix	Yes	UnStuffIt	UnStuffIt
WAV	Sound	Windows	Yes	Windows Sound Player	Macintosh Sound Player
ZIP	Compression	Windows	Yes	WinZip	UnStuffIt

estimated download times

file size	9600	14.4	28.8	ISDN	T1
1 MB file	45 min	19 min	9 min	2 min	< 1 min
2.5 MB file	1.5 hours	45 min	22 min	4 min	2 min
3.5 MB file	2.5 hours	70 min	35 min	7 min	3 min
5 MB file	3.25 hours	90 min	45 min	9 min	4 min
10 MB file	7.5 hours	3.25 hours	90 min	20 min	10 min

download options

How many times has this happened to you? You're downloading a gigantic file; you're 25 minutes into the download, with only three minutes left to go; and you lose your connection because you forgot to disable call waiting or your ISP's server went down. Your download is lost, and you have to start all over again. Few things are more annoying.

Do your audience a great service and offer your files in various sets—especially if you have a large library. For example, if you have 20 graphic files that are freely downloadable, you can offer them in three ways: one by one (uncompressed of course), in three compressed sets of five, or all 20 in one compressed file. This way, your forgetful visitor has a better chance to receive a complete file before the phone rings.

summary

Among lots of other things, the web has become the breeding ground for new and obscure file formats. What you need to remember the most is common sense. Whenever you want to offer downloadables, such as VRML, streaming video, or a Java application, always remember to have another page that explains to viewers what they need to download in order to view your content. Obviously, supply links to any plug-ins, players, or helper applications that are needed, and whenever possible give a second option. You should also try to keep the amount of add-on applications needed to see everything on your site to a minimum. It's also a good idea to state at the bottom of your opening page everything that visitors will need in order to get the "full effect" of your web site. And to keep visitors from surfing away, reassure them that you also have a low-bandwidth site that doesn't require anything special.

You shouldn't penalize visitors who don't have the right browser or operating system by making the majority of your downloadables inaccessible. Just like many sites have the frames and no-frames versions, do the same for your specialized content. For instance, if you have a document for people to download, why not offer it in Acrobat and plain text formats, just so you know that everyone will be able to read it? Otherwise, all of your hard work building outstanding content may go to waste.

accessibility review & resources

41 things to check, fix, or try

Just as it's crucial to test products before you buy them, it's imperative to review your site before it goes live to your audience. Here are a number of checklist items, tips, resources, and suggestions to get you on your way to making your site as accessible as possible.

upload and test

One common problem affecting both the usability and navigability of your site is pages not showing up where they are expected (or supposed) to be once they have gone live. This most likely is due to the designer setting up the site structure differently on the home drive than on the remote server. When you're creating a site that has links to images or pages in other folders or directories, the anchor tags to those links must match once your pages are on the other system. For example, if your background image is called "tile.gif," and you kept—and referred to—it in a separate folder/directory called "images," then there must also be a folder /directory on your server called "images," in the same relative position as on the drive on which you designed the site.

Your site may work great when it's running off your hard drive, but how will it work from your server or your service provider's server? The only way to find out is to upload it and try it.

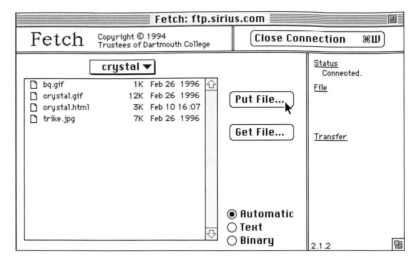

try your site with images off

Some people prefer to cruise the web with image-loading turned off so that they can get around faster. When they hit a site of interest, they then turn on image loading. Others are unable to view images. So how does your site look when there are no images showing? Do your pages come up as blanks with no navigational tools to be found?

If you have inserted <ALT> tags, do they make any sense? If they contain simply the name of the graphic, or one-word non-navigation explanations (that is, "graphic.gif" or "this is an image map"), then they do very little to help out your visitors.

how's it look in other browsers?

Netscape Navigator and Microsoft Internet Explorer give the most flexibility and options in web site design, but what if, by chance, some poor soul comes wandering to your site using another browser?

If you've gone to the trouble of creating multiple versions of your site, say, one for browsers that support frames and one that doesn't, check to make sure your alternative site works in its applicable browser. You may be surprised at what you're seeing.

There are still a good chunk of people who use text-only browsers. Even if you don't create a text-only design, testing your site with a text-only browser is a great way to test the overall navigability and "understandability" of your site.

If you haven't put <ALT> tags in your image codes, now's the time. This tag inserts a line of text if the image doesn't load, so at least people can hopefully get an idea of where that link will take them or what the image contains.

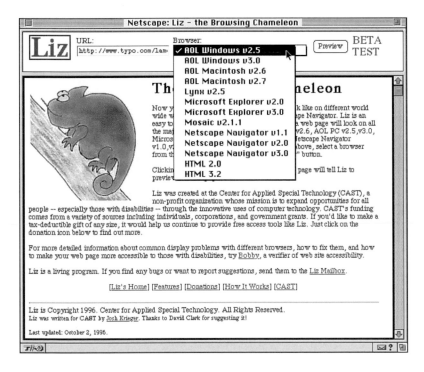

"Liz - the Browsing Chameleon," written by Josh Krieger, (http://www.cast.org/liz/) is a site maintained by the Center for Applied Special Technology (CAST) that lets you preview what a site will look like in a number of browsers, on various platforms. Just type the URL, choose the browser from the pop-up menu, and click Preview.

This window will load the URL you entered in an approximation of the browser display that you chose.

Check out what your URL looks like in Lynx at the "What does your HTML look like in Lynx?" page created by Steven L. Baur (http://www.miranova.com/~steve/LynxView.html).

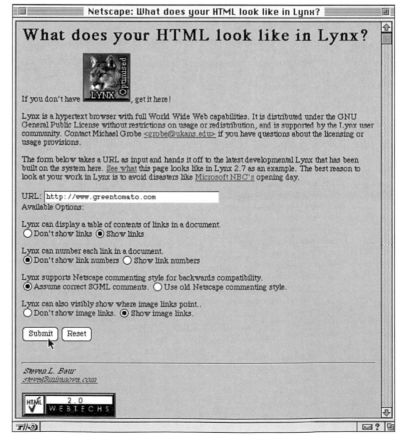

how's it look on other platforms?

You may think that if you've designed your site on a Macintosh and tested everything on Netscape Navigator for the Mac, that everything will look hunky-dory on the Windows version of Navigator. T'aint always so.

Graphics, for example, often show up darker on a Windows monitor. You may want to go back to your graphics application and alter your images' contrast so that they are more easily viewed on various platforms.

check your code

If you want to make sure that your code is cool with various browsers, stop over at Bobby (http://www.cast.org/bobby/). Also written by Josh Krieger for CAST, Bobby checks for accessibility factors (such as missing <ALT> tags) and browser compatibility. Bobby also gives an analysis of page and image load times, which you can use to determine whether your page loads too slowly for an average user.

Note 247

A resource for practical information on designing a site for multiple browsers is *Hybrid HTML Design: A Multi-Browser HTML Reference* by Kevin Ready and Janine Warner (1996 New Riders Publishing, ISBN: 1-56205-617-4). You'll find more than 400 pages that show examples of sites in a variety of browsers, in-depth reviews of HTML editors and how they rate in the tags department, and what seems like every HTML tag known, dissected for your designing pleasure.

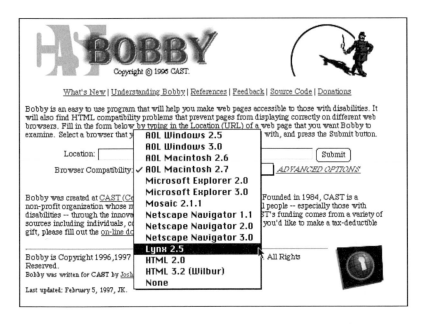

keep text and links readable on the background

This is a very easy thing to check, and it's very logical to figure out what's wrong and what has to be done. If you can't read the

text, the people coming to your site won't be able to, either. The most important key to readability is contrast. If your type color is light, make your background dark, and vice versa. For more information on color choices and legibility, see chapter 11, "color & contrast."

If you use background tiles that have both light and dark colors in them, neither light or dark text will read very easily over it. Make sure your tiles are either overall light or overall dark—the opposite of whatever color text you're using.

color by numbers

A lot of people prefer to work in their graphics programs or browse the web using the highest monitor setting that their computer supports. But there are still quite a few people whose computer's color limit is 256, especially on older systems. Before you set your site loose on the world (ideally, you did this when developing the graphics in the first place), give it a look-through with your monitor set at 256 colors and the lowest resolution your video card supports.

are images as small as they can be?

Did you save all of your GIFs in GIF89a format? Whether or not you decided to make a color of your image transparent to make it seem as though it's floating above the background, saving your image in GIF89a format could cut your image size down by as much as half. Test your JPEGs at different levels of compression— the higher the quality, the bigger the file.

title bar matching

Do the titles in your title bars match the contents of your page? If you've cut and pasted code from other pages (even your own), to save time and because the basic structure of each page is the same, make sure to change the words within the <TITLE> </TITLE> tags.

It's especially important to make your title bars descriptive because when someone bookmarks your page, the title bar words are what show up as the site description in the bookmark listing. For example, instead of calling your home page "Welcome" or "My Home Page," consider titling it "Acme Home Page" or

Note

For the ultimate resource on color for the web, pick up a copy of *Coloring Web Graphics* by Lynda Weinman and Bruce Heavin (1996 New Riders Publishing, ISBN: 1-56205-669-7). This book takes web color and color combinations to their limits.

"Bob Smith's Web Site" or "Zebra Museum Site Main Index"—
anything to differentiate it from the possibly hundreds of other
listings in someone's bookmark file.

spelll czech!!!

Spell check your pages! Whenever I go to a web site that claims
to be a professional organization and it's full of spelling errors
(especially if they misspell their own company or product names),
I'm less likely to go back to the page, and I certainly wonder how
professional the organization really is. Those users who come to
your page using a speech reader or talking browser will also have
difficulty understanding your message if their computer can't figure out how to pronounce an unfamiliarly spelled word.

If your HTML editor doesn't have a spelling checker, cut and
paste the text into your word processor to check for obvious
errors, take note of the errors, and then go back to your editor to
fix them.

If you don't have a spelling checker anywhere in your arsenal, after you've loaded your pages to your web server, load your browser and click over to Doctor HTML (http://www2.imagiware.com/RxHTML/). The Doctor will spell check any URL you enter, as well as check images, form structure, test your links, give you an estimate of page download time, and more.

Netscape: Doctor HTML v5

Doctor HTML™

Please select which tests you wish the **Doctor** to perform, and enter the URL
that you wish the **Doctor** to examine. Please be patient while **Doctor HTML**
examines the page.

Introduction

Single Page
Analysis

Site Analysis

Feedback

FAQ

Help

HTML
Resources

Whats New

Accolades

URL: http://www.typo.com/   [Go!]

Report Format: ○ Short   ○ Do All Tests
      ◉ Long   ◉ Select from list below

☒ Spelling   ☐ Image Analysis   ☐ Document Structure

☐ Image Syntax   ☐ Table Structure   ☒ Verify Hyperlinks

☒ Form Structure   ☐ Show Commands

☐ Show Page (Javascript Only)

Advanced Options

Authorization Information

Username: [＿＿＿＿]   Password: [＿＿＿＿]

Copyright 1995,1996 Thomas Tongue and Imagiware, Inc.

how fast is fast?

As much as we might not be able to understand why the rest of the world hasn't purchased 28.8 modems yet, it remains a statistical fact that a high percentage of modem owners still use their trusty 14.4 to access the web. Another thing to remember, however, is not just potential slow access because people don't want to buy another modem after spending money on a 14.4 a year ago, but that there are still many areas in the U.S. (and in other countries, too) where local-access dial-up does not exist. These people are spending at least seven cents a minute on a 14.4 waiting for pages to load. Depending on your goals for your site and your target audience, this could influence your site design.

navigation

Do viewers have navigational options? Your home page imagemap may win a cool-web-art award, but is it the only option you give for people to navigate your site? Adding a simple text navigation bar on the page will assist those who don't load graphics, use a text browser, or can't utilize an imagemap.

> artsy | bizarre | friends | kidz | literature | starting points | other

It's crucial to include alternate forms of navigation on your site. Adding text menus, such as these, to the top or bottom of each page doesn't take up much room and guarantees access to links that might otherwise be unavailable (such as those in an imagemap or in frames that some people may not be able to access).

> tack | saddles | gifts | bookstore
> woodworks | linens | gear | links

Do you continue to provide navigation tools throughout the site? If someone has wandered into the depths of your content, can they find their way back using the options you've provided? True, every browser I've seen has a "back" button, but don't count on the browser's navigational tools for users to find their way—especially if your site uses frames. Using the browser's "back" button will suck viewers right out of your site altogether.

alignment

Are images falling into the places you thought you told them to? Is text wrapping around the images where you want it to wrap? This is especially important to check within other browsers because many don't support certain alignment tags.

> Contents could include events announcements, notification of site updates,
> Lamott's-books-wanted/for sale, and perhaps open discussion of her work. Interested? Please
> **write to lamott@typo.com** if you are. I'll let you know when/if the list gets started. **crooked**
> **little heart cover** *NE FF !*
>
> Crooked Little Heart
>
> The long-awaited *sequel to Rosie* will be appearing in bookstores in late spring (April 1, 1997),
> but you can **order it now**, at a 10% discount! Amazon.com will ship it to you when it is released
> by the publisher. *Hardcover - $21.60 ('You save $2.40)*
> *CONFERENCES*
>
> [INLINE] Anne Lamott is one of the instructors for the **The Sun Valley Writers'**
> **Conference**'s Advanced Fiction Writing Workshop, *June 18-21*, 1997. The Sun Valley
> Writers' Conference "takes place in the picturesque area of Ketchum/Sun Valley, Idaho, where
> Ernest Hemingway lived and wrote, where sports enthusiasts flock to trout streams, white-water
> adventures and limitless hiking trails."

A misplaced <CENTER> tag can render a page nearly impossible to read. Although this text may not be overly difficult to read, large blocks of centered text can be because each line starts in a different place, and our eyes have a more difficult time finding the beginning of each subsequent line.

Within tables and frames, is it text in the proper position that makes it the easiest to read? Remember, simple tips like making sure large bodies of text aren't affected by an orphaned <CEN-TER> tag that got left behind highly increase readability.

window resizing

Do people have to widen their browser window to get a full look at your site? If you ask them to widen it one time, do they have to widen it again when they hit another page?

Don't make your visitors resize windows to get all of the information on each page.

item	stock number	quantity	price (each)	amo
Evergreen tomato seeds	4126		$2.59	
GreenTomato.com Sauce (32 oz jar)	3264		$3.69	
our very own Green Tomato Cook Book	2854		$19.95	
fried green tomato batter mixins (8 oz bag)	1399		$3.99	
expert tomato growing kit	5586		$39.99	
			subtotal	
overnight $12		shipping & handing		
			sales tax	
			TOTAL	

Netscape: Green Tomato order form — what can we get you?

Yes, I've been to sites where I need to open my window maybe an inch more than the default size. This isn't so bad, but then I click to go to another page in the site and it's just enough wider that I have to either scroll sideways or open my window wider again.

Sure, opening a browser window a little isn't much work, but viewers shouldn't have to keep doing it for every page they visit.

is your "cool stuff" gratuitous?

One reason the web has become so popular is because it can show us pretty pictures rather than just straight text. But before you slather your pages with special effects and big images, make sure they serve a purpose. If the purpose is to show off your art-work or JavaScript finesse, then fine. But if you're putting little JavaScript scrolling messages across the bottom of the screen just because you can, you'll end up annoying more people than impressing them: especially after their browsers crash.

do all links work?

It's frustrating to go to a site where you think you're going to be able to find what you want, only to be greeted with an error message because a link doesn't work. Test each and every text link, imagemap, and image link that you have.

Cool stuff, such as JavaScripts and Shockwave files, can greatly enhance a page. But if the person visiting your site can't use a plug-in on his system, or if the Shockwave file takes a long time to download and is just a piece of eye candy that serves no informational or enter-tainment value, then everyone's time has been wasted.

making contact

Can you imagine handing out a business card that had only your name on it—no contact information? Make sure all relevant infor-mation is included somewhere on your site that's easily accessible. MAILTO: tags are easy to insert, and by now you should be famil-iar with your company's mailing address, phone numbers, and fax numbers, so that will take 15 seconds to type. If you usually tell customers your street address, put it in. If you'd rather have them call you than e-mail you, say that. If there's more than one person people can write to for a specific purpose, specify the role of each addressee, for example, "e-mail Sue for sales information" and "e-mail Anne for technical specifications."

If you want people to be able to contact you, make sure you provide all necessary contact information, such as phone, street address, specific e-mail contacts, and so on (if you want them to be able to contact you in these ways!). If you don't want to put all contact information on each page, at least offer a link on each page to a "how to contact us" page that includes all relevant information.

are links and icons consistent?

Use the same link names and icons throughout your site. For example, if you use a compass icon on one page to give people the option to view your site map, use the same icon for the same purpose on other pages.

catalog || order form || recipes || contact us || home

home || order form || catalog || contact us || recipes

our stuff || order here || cook and eat || where are we? || main

When you provide links to the areas on your site, be sure to maintain both consistent labeling of the links and the same order in which the links appear in each case. Changing the name of a link, say from "catalog" to "our stuff" or "products," is confusing. And changing the order of links forces your visitors to reread the menu bar to make sure they're clicking on the right one. This is especially important if you provide a large number of links or icons that lead to a number of different areas on your site.

Besides using the same icons, be sure that the <ALT> tags you've added to an image remain the same for those who aren't viewing or can't view images. Also, don't forget consistent placement: if you've decided to put your menu bar on the bottom of pages, make sure it stays at the bottom of pages so that people don't have to work to find it.

size warnings

Got a humdinger of a piece of artwork or a long, long text file that your site just can't do without? You don't have to get rid of them, just warn visitors as much as possible about what's coming up. If it's a 100k image, add whatever "warning" information you can to its link, for example, "100k JPEG; approx. 2 minutes loading time at 28.8."

Long text files also have a pain-in-the-butt quotient. Any file larger than 20k can be a hassle to wait for, but a 20k text file takes up more room on a page than an image, and so can seem more overbearing.

The <LOWSRC> tag that can be used within an image tag to load a lower-resolution representation of the higher-resolution image (<IMG SRC="tomatomenu.gif" LOWSRC="gtomlow.gif">). If the browser supports LOWSRC, the low-resolution image you specify will load first, and then the higher-resolution image will load on top of it.

If you can't break up your text files among separate pages because your customers may need to print out a full document from their browser (it's inconvenient to have to print info from a number of separate pages), at least give viewers a warning before they click into a deluge of ASCII.

```
recommended   listening   formats

14.4 modem              28.8 modem              ISDN & faster

release.wav 1.8M        release.wav 3.7M        release.wav 7.5M

release.mov 984K        release.mov 1.9M        release.mov 7.5M

RealAudio (14.4) 96K    RealAudio (28.8) 224K   RealAudio (ISDN+) 888K

release.au 712K
```

If you're offering large files for viewing or download, give your visitors a hint of a file's size so they know what they're getting into.

turn off blinking

Although blinking text seemed really cool three years ago, now most people would agree it's fairly annoying. Blinking text can also be misread by screen readers, and can be difficult to focus on for some people with visual impairments.

clarity factors

Is it clear throughout your text where the start of a new section or paragraph is? Don't forget to include subheads where necessary—ones that stand out from the main body of text—and either indent new paragraphs or add <P> paragraph breaks to text. Horizontal rules, while the bane of some web designers, also serve to break up big chunks of text into more readable, discernible sections.

caption jpeg images

JPEG images are able to include comments in their files that are readable by some text browsers and screen readers. Include these comments when you can. Some image editors, such as GifConverter for the Mac, enable you to type in JPEG image comments in a pop-up dialog window.

GifConverter for the Mac lets you type comments that are readable by some browsers and viewers to an accompanying a JPEG.

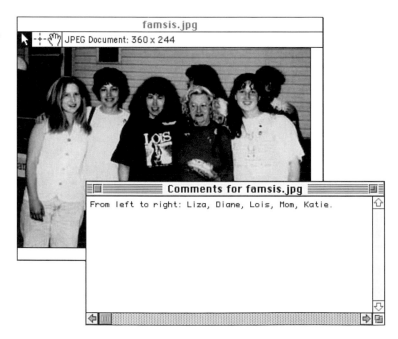

provide sound & movie transcripts

Include a transcript of any audio or narrated movie files you include on the site. Even if you don't have the person-power to transcribe each and every audio file, try to at least provide a synopsis for those who are unable to hear the files on your site.

limit links

Use the minimum number of links per sentence as possible for easier understanding of the text content, better readability, and navigation throughout the site. Consider putting all relevant links at the end of a story, in a sidebar, or below paragraphs that refer to the links.

html purity

Using HTML tags for specific title, subtitle headings, paragraph breaks, lists, and so on is ideal for those who access the web via screen readers, or those who use Braille displays or translation applications. HTML, when used with these document-structure tags, alerts Braille translation software to the formatting necessary for a section of text based on the construct of the HTML code. In short, the code tells us "this is a heading" or "this is a subhead" so that the page is easier to navigate or reconstruct.

D tagging

Detailed image descriptions, or D tagging, is a proposal by The National Center for Accessible Media (http://www.boston.com/wgbh/ncam) for making images more accessible to those with disabilities or those who can't view images. It's an option for people who want to see an image's description for larger images that take a while to download.

noframes

Did you remember to include an informative or helpful NOFRAMES option for those who can't access your framed site? Offering links to download frame-capable browsers is better than nothing, but it's not enough.

The Web Access Symbol, available from the CPB/WGBH National Center for Accessible Media (NCAM), is available for display on those sites that contain "accessibility features to accommodate the needs of disabled users." For specific requirements and information about how to include this symbol on your site, visit http://www.boston.com/wgbh/pages/ncam/symbolwinner.html.

sound choices

If you're offering music clips and sound bytes from your site, try to keep file size down by experimenting with various formats. Full stereo sound is wonderful, but it takes up a lot more space than a mono sound byte. For narrative only, low-end RealAudio files are fine for most purposes.

Also, if you're not sure of what platform your viewers use, stick to sound formats that most of the newer popular browsers can handle: RealAudio, WAV, AU, and QuickTime.

forms

If you have forms on your site for correspondence, order filling, survey taking, or other purposes, give your audience the option of sending the form or requested information in an alternative way, such as via e-mail or by printing out the form and faxing or mailing it to you. Include all necessary contact information, such as a snail-mail address, fax number, and e-mail address on the form page itself, so that when printed or copied, the necessary information is always available to the user. You don't want to force users to go digging around for your fax number if they've printed out your form and just want to get around to ordering.

multilingual

| Australian Site |
| Brazilian Portuguese Site |
| Danish Site |
| Dutch Site |
| French Site |
| German Site |
| Italian Site |
| Japanese Site |
| Korean Site |
| Spanish Site |
| Swedish Site |
| ✓ U.S. English Site |

Having a public web site means that you now have a potential worldwide audience. The web is an international forum for information exchange. To purposely reach as many people as possible, creating sites specific to an audience who speak other languages may be worth your while.

If you sell products via your web site, be aware of any shipping restrictions or charges that are specific to various countries, as well as any monetary exchange and tax requirements.

site map

Have you provided a site index or map to the areas of your site? Creating a detailed list or diagram, separated by categories of information, assists visitors in finding what they want to find in an efficient manner.

Site maps or site indexes assist visitors in seeing your site's contents at a glance.

summary

Everything comes down to giving your viewer choices in what they want to see, hear, experience, read, and access. The more options available, the greater the variety of people with their variety of knowledge, experience, abilities, and equipment that can access your material.

CHAPTER 16

WebTV

designing for the TV generation

The world is web-happy, perhaps even web-bonkers. I doubt anyone can miss seeing the multitude of advertisements on the air and in print—even on the sides of buses—touting web addresses. I bet that in most industrialized countries, even if people don't know what the web *is,* they've at least heard the word and noticed that nearly every article, ad, business card, and radio show has one of those http://www thingies. Now, WebTV is the first mass-marketed technology that enables people to view the web on their television. Will this be the big break we've all been looking for—the one that brings our pages to every home?

arguments about televising the web

More often than not, the argument I hear against WebTV and other television-based web access methods is, "If someone owns a computer, why would they want to buy a set-top box to see the web?" Good question. Personally, I own three computers that I use to access the web; why would I want to go out and spend another $300+ to see the web on my television? Okay, because I'm a geek who buys this stuff because I'm curious and because it's what I write about and even do for fun. Most of WebTV's customers, however, will come from the other end of the spectrum—people who don't want a computer (gasp!).

Even though hyper-speedy computers can be found relatively inexpensively, their starting prices of around $1,200 are still much higher than a WebTV box's $300+ price tag. If all a person wants

is web access and e-mail, then $300 to $400 is a lot easier to justi-fy. Plus, even self-proclaimed computer illiterates are probably masters of the remote control.

So, will the web be the next big thing with the U.S.'s 90 million television viewers? Another good question. With all the media hype, not to mention the big ad campaigns by WebTV Networks and its hardware cohorts Sony and Philips Magnavox, WebTV is at least catching the attention of many web designers who are wondering how to design for this viewing medium.

how WebTV works

WebTV is a combination of hardware, software, and a subscrip-tion service that allows users to access the web and to send and receive e-mail. At this writing, the WebTV "box," which looks similar to a VCR or laser disc player, costs about $320 in con-sumer electronics stores. The subscription fee for unlimited online access is just under $20 a month.

The unit has a built-in 33.6 Kbps modem and comes with a remote control for page navigation. The unit plugs into an exist-ing analog phone line and into the sound in/video in ports of your VCR or television. Optional hardware (recommended, espe-cially if you plan to type a lot of e-mail) includes a standard-sized wireless keyboard, which runs about $100. If you already have a spare PC keyboard, you might be able to save some money: the WebTV box includes a port for a standard PS/2-compatible key-board. Just keep in mind that you'll have to sit pretty close to the TV to stay connected.

After you've plugged the unit in, it automatically dials into a local number (not too many are available yet, by the way, but more are promised) and takes you through the registration process. Once that's done, you're logged onto the WebTV home page as your starting point every time you turn on the unit.

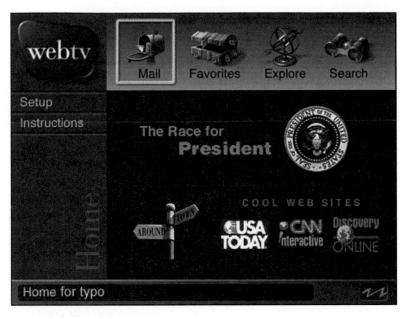

Once you've connected to WebTV, you're taken directly to its proprietary home page for WebTV members.

accessibility issues

Jim Tobias, a principle with Inclusive Technologies (a research firm dedicated to evaluating the accessibility features of hardware and software), graciously allowed me to share his assessment in regard to the specific access issues regarding WebTV. Tobias is somewhat visually impaired (corrected to 20/40 with slight astigmatism), and tested the WebTV on a standard 19-inch television screen. Overall, Tobias is excited about WebTV, but he finds it "still a long way from accessible." The following italicized sections are Tobias's comments.

the remote and keyboard

"The remote control is a bit slimmer than the average TV remote, it sports (from the business end down) four directional buttons in a circular pattern, with a small central Go button. Outside the circle in the NW, NE, SW, and SE positions, are four small triangular buttons: Scroll Up, Go Back, Scroll Down, and Go Home, respectively. Below this complex are five buttons (a column of three and a column of two): Options, Recent, Search, Favorites, and TV/Web. The long power button lies below these.

 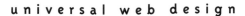

Note

A keyguard is a hard plastic cover with holes for each key that assists those with unsteady hands or pointing devices with pressing the desired keys.

"All these buttons are soft chiclets, with the small buttons about .25 inches in diameter and standing about .125 inches high. They are a bit stiff and wobbly. Having the crucial Go button in the center of the directional arrows will definitely pose problems for people with hand coordination problems. A keyguard could improve things.

"The 11.5- by 5.5-inch keyboard is light, with a pretty good action. For some reason, they put flip-out back feet on it, as if it were a desktop keyboard. (What it needs, suggests Jim's wife, is a cup holder and a chip bowl.) The keyboard makes the product so much more usable—no more hunting and pecking with the remote to simulate typing. It has all the regular keys, plus all the remote's function keys: Search, Back, Home, etc. Having one-key access to these features improves WebTV's accessibility for people with cursor-finding or cursor-control difficulties.

"The downside of the keyboard is the key size (regular keys are okay at about .5 inches, but the function keys are only about .375 inches), and the key labels are printed in "mustard" on dark gray. This color combination is death to read in regular living room lighting."

navigational interface

"Only some navigational actions yield an audible tone and a visible screen change. At start-up, the system shows a connecting screen and plays a little jazzy number until you're connected. Then the tune and the screen both change. However, after this there is a long delay before the main screen appears, and there is no tone to indicate its arrival. So blind users would not know when they could begin browsing.

"A yellow outline box moves from one link to another as you control via the remote, but there is no tone to indicate you have moved. This is a problem because the keys themselves give no physical feedback and are not reliable if there is glare or if you are more than 10 or 15 degrees off line with the box.

"When you select a link by pressing Go, there is both a tone and two screen changes: a progress bar appears, and the outline box changes to green. Trying to scroll up at the top or down at the bottom of a screen yields a tone, but no visual effect.

"Error messages occur occasionally and are presented both as text in a box and as a 'sad' tone."

visually impaired access

"Considering that the display is on a TV, WebTV's readability is high. WebTV uses some patented technologies (WorldScan and TVLens) that optimize the presentation. On my 19-inch set, I had little trouble reading text at 12 feet in average light. I had no trouble getting to any sites, either directly or via the default Excite search capability."

cognitively impaired access

"WebTV may be useful to someone with a cognitive impairment, as it appears easier to set up and use than the regular computer/modem/ browser/Internet provider combination. Since the Favorites (bookmarks) choice appears on the main screen, the easiest session procedure is: turn on the TV, turn on WebTV, wait for the main screen, scroll right once to Favorites, press Go, and select among the links shown there. The Recent key takes you to a screen that shows thumbnails of your most recently visited screens, which is also easier to navigate than the textual history feature of both Netscape Navigator and Microsoft Internet Explorer."

hearing impaired access

"I could not find any features that put a deaf or hard-of-hearing user at a disadvantage. The graphical display is consistent, except for the lack of a visual cue that you are at the end of a line of links."

design issues

Just like web designers who have to design with cross-platform issues and browser differences in mind, WebTV designers have constraints to work within as well. The following sections discuss some of the considerations designers have to take account when designing for WebTV.

available real estate

The most distinct difference between the computer screen and the television screen is the size of the window. Netscape Navigator's default browser window is 490 by 337 pixels, whereas WebTV's default is 544 by 376 pixels. This allows for a slightly larger design, but don't forget that if you design for WebTV, others may not be able to see the layout that you intended.

The WebTV window is 544 pixels wide by 378 pixels high.

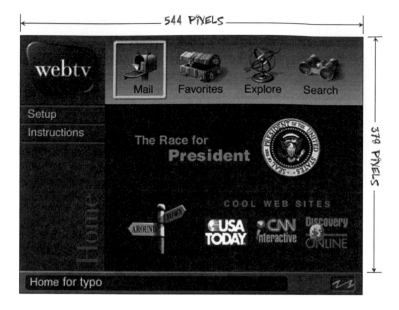

Because TV viewers aren't used to scrolling to get more information, avoid making your pages larger than the recommended dimensions of the WebTV screen. The WebTV interface allows scrolling vertically only (it doesn't have horizontal, or side-to-side scrolling), so no matter what your design, it will be forced to fit horizontally within the 544 pixels allowed for the WebTV screen.

Any of your images that have been created to fit a wider-than-544-pixel screen will be squished down to 544 pixels wide in order to appear in the WebTV screen. This has its good and bad points: It's good that images aren't cut off and that WebTV users don't have to scroll horizontally in order to see the entire graphic; however, it's bad if menu bars and imagemaps are rendered too small for easy readability.

color challenge

The other major difference is the way that television shows color on-screen. The WebTV folks suggest that for best results, you shouldn't use "full" red or "full" white because full red or white backgrounds will appear to bow the edges of the page. A suggested hex value for a BGCOLOR is #EFEFEF for those who want a light-colored background, and #191919 is recommended for those who want to use a dark-colored background. Note, however, that neither of these hex values belong to the 216 colors within the browser-safe color palette, so the results may be different from what you want within standard browsers.

Peter Duke, creator/proprietor of http://www.dukemedia.com/, has dedicated a good deal of his site's content to the discussion and evaluation of WebTV and its color palette. He's graciously created a cross-platform palette that includes those colors that are compatible among the Macintosh, Windows, and NTSC. This palette is limited to 163 colors.

The cross-platform and NTSC color palette can be found at http://www.dukemedia.com/ntscpalette.html. Included are both the hexadecimal values for each compatible color, as well as the RGB values for each.

font size

Most people have their default browser font size set at 12-point Times Roman (proportional) and 10-point Courier (fixed font), so that's what we end up designing around—usually. WebTV gives the option only to the user to change font size among the choices small, medium, and large. You can override the user's preferences by using the values "small," "medium," or "large" within the body tag (<BODY FONTSIZE=*value*>...</BODY>). The type used by WebTV as its default body text is an Arial-like sans-serif typeface.

To test for readability of your site within the WebTV browser, increase your typefaces to 18 points, and change the typeface to Arial or Helvetica, or some other rounded sans-serif typeface. It'll make a *big* difference in the appearance of your page, especially if you have narrow columns or lots of wraps around graphics, or use fixed layouts (such as with the <PRE> tag or tables). Basically, the screen allows for 40-character lines, or 20 lines per "page."

Note

NTSC stands for National Television Systems Committee, a broadcast engineering advisory group that determined the NTSC color television standard. This standard is used in the U.S., Canada, Mexico, and Japan. The PAL (Phase Alternating Line) standard is used in most of Europe and most of the rest of the world. An excellent resource for digital and television information and definitions can be found at The Quantel Digital Fact Book: http://www.quantel.com/dfb/index.html.

268

Before starting the testing of my page in Netscape, or other browsers, to see how it would roughly look on WebTV, I created a 544×376 pixel-high GIF image—the same size as a WebTV screen.

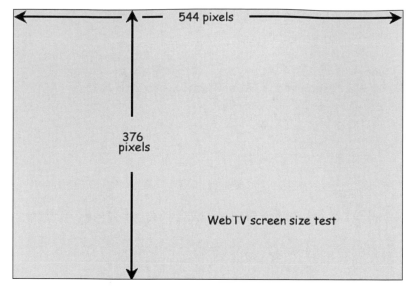

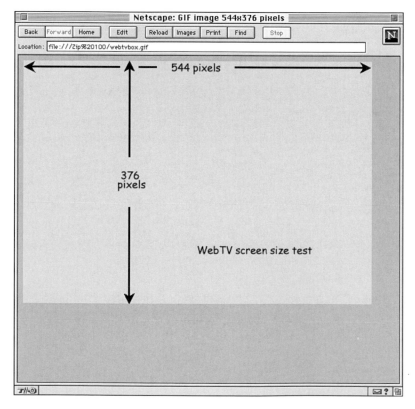

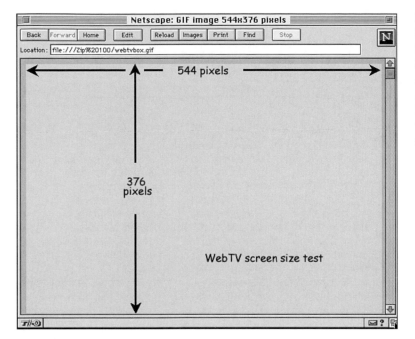

I opened my 544×376 pixel image in the browser so that I'll know how tall and wide to make the browser window in order to approximate the WebTV screen. Although each browser has a slightly different buffer around the content of a page, this test is close enough for most purposes.

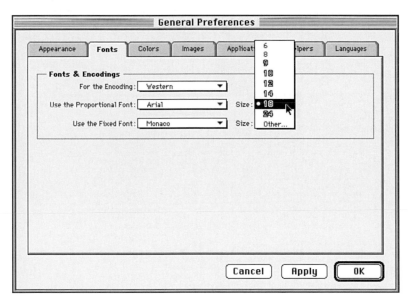

In your browser's settings, change your proportional typeface to Arial or Helvetica 18 point, and your monospaced type to Monaco or Courier 18 point.

Here are the regular Netscape versions and WebTV mock-up versions of the Old Fairgrounds Tackshop Classifieds…

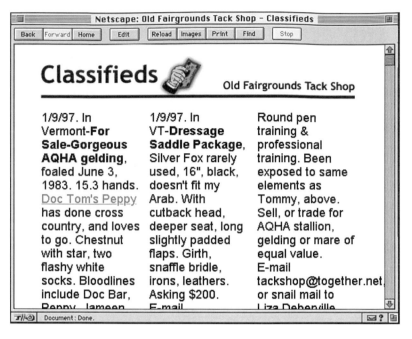

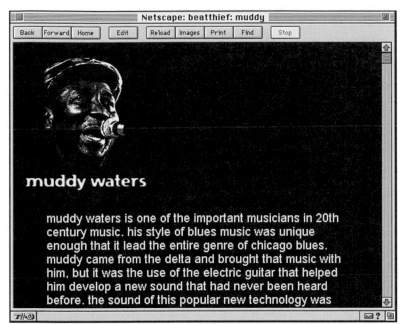

...and beatthief's Muddy Waters page (http://www.beatthief.com).

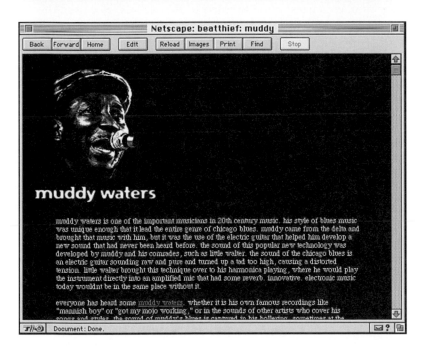

Remember that if you include graphical text (such as text on top of a button or within an imagemap) and it appears small on your computer screen, it will be even harder to read on a television screen. Consider creating new graphics or including larger text links for easier viewing and navigability.

shuddering lines

Television screens wreak havoc with one-pixel lines or horizontal rules; they'll appear to shake or quiver on-screen and, subsequently, distract your audience from the content of the page. If horizontal rules or thin lines are necessary to your design, add a pixel of width to the <HR> tag (<HR SIZE=2>, for example), or anti-alias lines that are graphical in nature (anti-aliasing adds at least a couple of pixels to the width of a line).

downloadables

Because there is no way to download software into a WebTV unit (because there's no computer involved), pages designed for WebTV users should avoid links to downloadable objects.

image size

Although the WebTV unit is equipped with a 33.3 Kbps modem, television audiences unaccustomed to the web are not used to having to wait for images to appear on their television screens. For this reason alone, it's crucial to keep images as small as possible for the quickest downloads. Physical dimensions of images should also fit well inside the WebTV screen size to avoid having to scroll. The use of image <HEIGHT> and <WIDTH> tags is encouraged so that text will load up first on the screen while the images are downloading.

WebTV-specific html tags

There are a number of tags specific to WebTV that are ignored by other browsers but add functionality to the WebTV layout. Some of them are pretty cool, and all can be viewed on the WebTV Networks development documentation pages (http://webtv.net/devdocs/htmlref/htmlref-1.html). Here are a couple examples.

<sidebar>...</sidebar>

Anything within this tag set will appear in a nonscrolling section on the left side of the television screen, much like a static frame. Although it's ignored by other browsers, the content within the tags doesn't disappear; it simply appears at the top of the body of the web page in which you've placed the tag. This has the potential to look pretty awful, so if you're planning on using this function often, you may want to set up a separate WebTV version of your site.

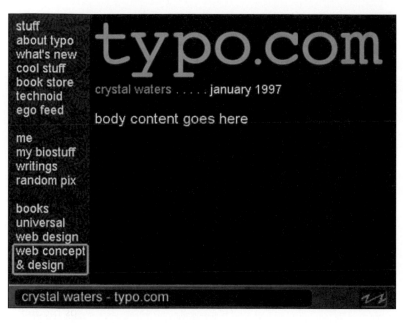

To structure a WebTV sidebar, the code for the sidebar must be placed before the <BODY> tag of the rest of the document. The resulting page has a similar look to a framed page. The left-hand sidebar, in this case, is specified to take up 20 percent of the window width, stays fixed, and doesn't scroll. The sidebar can have its own background color or image, font color, and link color.

```
<TITLE>crystal waters - typo.com</TITLE>
</HEAD>

<SIDEBAR WIDTH=20% BGCOLOR="#660000" BACKGROUND="greys.gif"
➥TEXT="#CCCCCC" LINK="#CCCCCC" VLINK="#999999">

<FONT SIZE=5 COLOR=#FFCC66">stuff</FONT><BR>
<A HREF="./about.html">about typo</A><BR>
<A HREF="./new.html">what's new</FONT></A><BR>
<A HREF="./cool/cool.html">cool connections</A><BR>
<A HREF="./store/store.html">book store</A><BR>
<A HREF="../technoid/technoid.html">technoid</A><BR>
<A HREF="./kudos.html">ego feed</A>
<P>
<FONT SIZE=5 COLOR=#FFCC66">me</FONT><BR>
<A HREF="../crystal/crystal.html">my biostuff</A><BR>
<A HREF="./writings/writings.html">writings</A><BR>
<A HREF="./pix/pix.html">random pix</A>

<P><FONT SIZE=5 COLOR=#FFCC66">books</FONT><BR>
<A HREF="../uwd/uwd.html">universal web design</A><BR>
<A HREF="./wcd/wcd.html">web concept & design book</A>

</SIDEBAR>

<BODY BGCOLOR="#000000" TEXT="#CCCCCC" LINK="#CCCCCC"
➥VLINK="#999999">
...body stuff goes here...
</BODY>
```

274 Unfortunately, the previous code that was specified for WebTV doesn't come out all that great in other browsers. Here's what it looks like in Netscape Navigator. All the links are there, but the structure is completely gone.

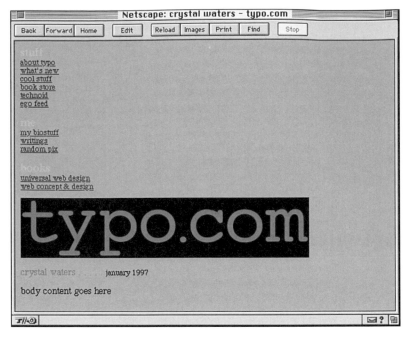

<nosmartquotes>

WebTV automatically changes all straight quotes (") into smart quotes (" "), sometimes known as curly quotes. If you don't want your quotes to change, simply add the <nosmartquotes> tag to your page.

The official WebTV developers documentation can be downloaded in Adobe Acrobat Reader PDF format from http://www.webtv.net/ corp/devdocs/home.devdocs.html, or read online in HTML format at http://www.webtv.net/corp/dev-docs/htmlref/htmlref-1.html.

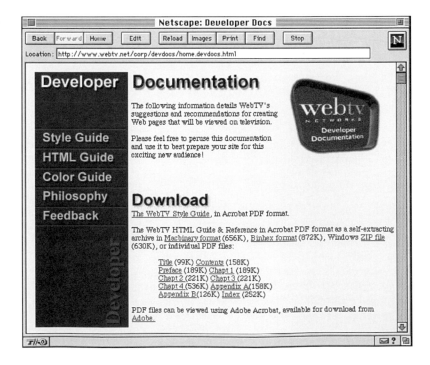

summary

Although it's yet to be seen whether WebTV will sweep the nation into the arms of the web, there certainly is a lot of enthusiasm from both the industry and consumers that have taken the bait and tried the product—enough to get the attention of web designers. Take advantage of WebTV Networks' regularly updated developer's documentation, and most of all, keep in mind that the television viewing community is largely different from the computer community. They aren't used to interacting with their televisions—other than to change the channel—and they are used to having all content fit on one screen. Most of all, they are used to being entertained. The less work you can make them do the better, including avoiding small text that is hard to read and small visual elements. Hey, it could just be that the easiest way to study up on web design for television is to watch television.

CHAPTER 17

> *"One way or another, we all have to find what best fosters the flowering of our humanity in this contemporary life, and dedicate ourselves to that."*
>
> — *Joseph Campbell*

assistive technology & legislation

are you legally olbigated to make your site accessible?

Probably the last thing on your mind when you first created your web site was the possibility that the law might require you to include different acccss features and functions. At the time this book went to press, there weren't any cases of a web site being sued for not following the guidelines set forth in the Americans with Disabilities Act. However, because web sites are publicly accessible documents—and because, at least in the U.S., businesses serving the public are responsible for making their services and businesses public—it's my opinion that it's only a matter of time before legislation steps in to make sure anyone who wants information from a site can get it.

Americans with Disabilities Act

The Americans with Disabilities Act (ADA) is a comprehensive civil rights law that benefits people with disabilities, and seems the most likely law to be expanded to include elements to affect web design and functionality. To understand why the ADA may effect the web, here's a bit of information about the ADA and what its intended purpose is for people with disabilities.

The requirements the ADA enacts first went into effect on January 26, 1992 and are applicable to both for-profit and non-profit organizations. The Department of Justice enforces the ADA's requirements in three areas:

Title I: Employment practices by units of state and local government

Title II: Programs, services, and activities of state and local government

Title III: Public accommodations and commercial facilities

for your employees

Intranets are becoming a prevalent tool for communications and information exchange within private businesses, and we'll probably see a greater push toward issues of web accessibility for employees with disabilities. There are already laws in place that ensure accessibility, or "reasonable accommodation," for these employees in the workplace, and it wouldn't be surprising at all if these laws begin to be applied to information access via the Internet and intranets. According to the ADA, the term "reasonable accommodation" includes

(A) making existing facilities used by employees readily accessible to and usable by individuals with disabilities

and

(B) job restructuring, part-time or modified work schedules, reassignment to a vacant position, acquisition or modification of equipment or devices; appropriate adjustment or modifications of examinations, training materials, or policies; the provision of qualified readers or interpreters, and other similar accommodations for individuals with disabilities.

Thanks in part to Title I of the ADA, employers may not discriminate against an individual with a disability in hiring or promotion if the person is otherwise qualified for the job. Employers can ask about one's ability to perform a job, but cannot inquire whether someone has a disability or subject a person to tests that tend to screen out persons with disabilities.

Employers need to provide "reasonable accommodation" to individuals with disabilities. This includes actions such as job

restructuring and modification of equipment. Employers do not need to provide accommodations that impose "undue hardship" on business operations. Those who need to comply: All employers with 25 or more employees must comply, effective July 26, 1992. All employers with 15–24 employees must comply, effective July 26, 1994. (*Americans With Disabilities Act Requirements Fact Sheet*, U.S. Department of Justice Civil Rights Division Coordination and Review Section CRD-20 GPO : 1990 0 – 273-184)

So if you have developed an intranet for your employees, or a site that serves both your company's employees and the public, accessibility issues may become more than just a consideration—they may become a requirement. Depending on the employee's disability, reasonable accommodation for web site design could mean creating text versions of sites or enhancing a site for easier screen-reader accessibility (for those with visual impairments); improving navigational cues or making them easier to click on (for cognitive or physical impairments); or providing transcripts of sound and movie files (for those with hearing impairments).

government availability

Title II of the ADA, as mentioned, covers programs, services, and activities of state and local government. This covers everything from the local public school to libraries to the State Capitol. As a matter of fact, in January 1997 it was debated in Congress whether or not government information would be made available on the Internet. If so, then the biggest factor that decides whether a citizen receives government documents becomes whether or not they have a computer with Internet access.

But we should get back to you and your web site. If web sites are determined to be covered under ADA regulations, you may be required to make your information accessible to public libraries and schools. In order to do so, you may have to take into account the fact that many public facilities have equipment that can't handle the latest browsers. Providing a text-based site may be required in order to (nearly) guarantee access by all public facilities.

access to the world

The web is a vast and continually growing public information resource. It's highly probable that there will be some sort of ADA

Note

"Public accommodations" are considered to be private businesses that provide goods or services to the public, including stores, restaurants and bars, theaters, hotels, recreational facilities, museums, and schools.

(or other) legislation for fair accessibility to this public information, and businesses will have to comply. In this sense, the section in effect is Title III, public accommodations and commercial facilities.

According to ADA literature, nearly all types of private businesses that serve the public are included, regardless of the size of the business; and if you own, operate, lease, or lease to a business that serves the public, then you are covered by the ADA and have obligations to comply when a facility is altered or a new facility is constructed. In short, if you're involved in a matter with a business that is open to the public, you've got to make sure that every customer can access the facility and the products and services that you sell or provide for public usage.

The law states that if you own or operate a business that serves the public, you must remove physical "barriers" that are "readily achievable"—meaning within your financial and physical means. The determination of a business's "readily achievable" requirement is based on the size and resources of the business in question. Big businesses with large amounts of resources are expected to remove barriers faster than a tiny boutique with a single owner and a small income. However, it is also expected that as a business's resources increase, its efforts to remove barriers will also increase.

The ADA was written with physical barriers in mind, namely, to tackle barriers such as steps, inaccessible parking spaces, restroom door widths, door handles that are hard to grasp, sales counters that are too high, restaurant tables that are too low, and so on.

It also covers topics such as you and your employees making every effort to communicate with a person who is deaf, and your obligation to help customers if they request assistance—for example, via writing notes back and forth with pen and paper, or by communicating through an interpreter. According to the law, seeing-eye dogs are given admittance to businesses with their owners, and the store's employees are required to assist in visual descriptions of a product if so requested.

the big question

Because the web is not a facility (in the sense that there are no buildings to enter), is it still covered under the jurisdiction of the ADA? The original law went into place in 1992, so it's obvious

that its compilers had no idea of the amazing growth of businesses that don't have a physical building with the need for a wheelchair ramp and parking places. Nowadays, you can find almost anything on the web, and more companies are turning to the web as a major or even sole marketing and distribution method for their services and products.

As a web designer or owner, the only answer I can offer you is to keep your eyes open for whispers (or shouts) about new regulations. Sites that provide information on the Americans with Disabilities Act and other legislation in this vein include:

- U.S. Department of Justice Americans with Disabilities Act ADA HOME PAGE
  http://www.usdoj.gov/crt/ada/adahom1.htm

- The American with Disabilities Act Statute (full text of the ADA)
  http://www.usdoj.gov/crt/ada/statute.html

- The ADA and Disability Info page
  http://www.public.iastate.edu/~sbilling/ada.html

- The ADA Information Center Online Homepage
  http://www.idir.net/~adabbs/index1.html

- Job Accommodation Network
  http://janweb.icdi.wvu.edu/

- ADA Compliance Guide
  http://www.thompson.com/tpg/person/able/able.html

summary

Forty-nine million people in the United States have a legal disability. Many of these people are in the workforce and have technology available to them that assists in making the web accessible. There are many techniques in this book to guide you toward making a more accessible web site; and many of the people out there trying to access your site will appreciate your efforts. So with luck, if there's a law passed that requires you to overhaul your site to make it accessible, then you'll be prepared.

Keep tabs on these and other resources by visiting the author's site at http://www.typo.com.

connections

**The Center for Universal Design:
Environments For People Of All Ages And Abilities**
http://www2.ncsu.edu/ncsu/design/cud

**The CPB/WGBH National Center for Accessible
Media (NCAM)**
http://www.boston.com/wgbh/ncam

typo.com by crystal waters
http://www.typo.com

The Britannica Guide to Black History
http://blackhistory.eb.com/

BrowserWatch
http://www.browserwatch.com

BrowserWatch Plug-In Plaza
http://browserwatch.iworld.com/plug-in.html

C|NET Browser Troubleshooting
http://www.cnet.com/Help/browserhelp.html

C|NET Navigation Help
http://www.cnet.com/Help/navehelp.html

C|NET The World Wide Web
http://www.cnet.com/Help/web.html

**CommerceNet/Nielsen Internet Demographic Analysis
of Postratification Weighting Procedures**
http://www.commerce.net/work/pilot/nielsen_96/position.html

DejaNews: The Source for Newsgroups
http://www.dejanews.com/

Digital Dreams Talk Media
http://www.surftalk.com/

GVU's World Wide Web User Surveys
http://www.cc.gatech.edu/gvu/user_surveys/

Liszt: The Mailing List Directory
http://www.liszt.com/

Netscape Communications
http://www.netscape.com

New Networks Institute
http://www.newnetworks.com/

Nielsen Media Research Interactive Media
http://www.nielsenmedia.com/

Shockwave Technical Support
http://www.macromedia.com/support/technotes/shockwave/
browser/win/index/html

YAHOO! Search Engine
http://www.yahoo.com

Bank of America
http://www.bankamerica.com/

Family TreeMaker Online
http://www.familytreemaker.com/

Microsoft Accessibility Resources
http://microsoft.com/enable

The Archimedes Project
http://kanpai.stanford.edu/arch/arch.html

Coloring Web Graphics Browser-Safe Color Palette
http://www.lynda.com/hex.html

Jeff Gates: In Our Path
http://www.tmn.com/iop/index.html

Web Access '97: Sixth International World Wide Web Conference
http://www-csli.stanford.edu/arch/GUI

Western Blind Rehabilitation Center
http://www.-csli.stanford.edu/arch/GUI/wbrc.html

WEBDEVELOPER Online
http://www.webdeveloper.com/

The Compendium of HTML Elements: Page Description
http://www.synapse.net/~woodall/icons/table.htm

DISCOVERY CHANNEL Online
http://www.discovery.com

Trace Research and Development Center
http://trace.wisc.edu

Crescendo: Live UpDate
http://www.liveupdate.com/

The Cross-Platform Page: Audio Formats
http://www.mcad.edu/Guests/EricB/xplat.aud.html

EmeraldNet, Inc.
http://www.emerald.net/

The InterVU Network
http://www.intervu.com/

Macromedia
http://www.macromedia.com/

NET TOOB Stream 3.1: The Ultimate Multimedia Solution for the Web
http://www.duplexx.com/

See Hollywood and Vine
http://www.hollywoodandvine.com/

StreamWorks NOW
http://www.xingtech.com/sw_now.html

Talker 2.0
http://www.mvpsolutions.com/PlugInSite/Talker.html

VoxWare: The Voice in Software
http://www.vaxware.com/

YAHOO! Search Engine for Voice Recognition
http://www.yahoo.com/Business_and_Economy/Companies/
Computers/Software/Voice_Recognition

Yamaha Midi Plug-in
http://www.ysba.com/midplug_index.html

The Caption Center at WGBH
http://www.boston.com/wgbh/caption

The Caption FAQ: Frequently Asked Questions About Closed Captioning
http://www.caption.com/capfaq/

Closed Captioning Web
http://www.erols.com/berke/

The CPB/WGBH National Center for Accessible Media: Captioning and Audio Description on the Web
http://www.boston.com/wgbh/pages/ncam/captionedmovies.
html

Next Exit: Interactive Multimedia Theatrical Performance
http://www.nextexit.com/html_gif/nextexit.html

turn table
http://www.turntable.com/

**216-color, browser-safe CLUT (color lookup table)
for the Mac**
ftp://ftp.adobe.com/pub/adobe/photoshop/mac/3.x/
web216m.sit
for Windows
ftp://ftp.adobe.com/pub/adobe/photoshop/win/3.x/
web216w.zip

Lynda Weinman's Browser–Safe Color Charts
http://www.lynda.com/hex.html

Browser By Design's HTML Resource pages
http://www.browserbydesign.com/resources/appa/apa1.htm

Bobby
http://www.cast.org/bobby/

Chemnitz University of Technology, HTML-Prüfung mit weblint (German interface)
http://www.tu-chemnitz.de/~fri/www/html-test.html

Composing Good HTML
http://www.sil.org/sgml/sgml.html

Doctor HTML
http://imagiware.com/RxHTML.cgi

EWS Weblint Gateway
http://www.fal.de/cgi-bin/WeblintGateway

FAL Weblint Gateway v3.0b3
http://www.fal.de/cgi-bin/WeblintGateway

HTML 2.0 Standards
ftp://ds.internic.net/rfc/rfc1866.txt

The HTML 3.0 Hypertext Document Format
http://www.w3.org/pub/WWW/Arena/tour/start.html

Masayasu Ishikawa's Japanese Weblint Interface
http://saturn.aichi-u.ac.jp/~mimasa/jweblint/

Microsoft's HTML Authoring Tips for Internet Explorer 2.0
http://www.microsoft.com/workshop/author/other/
ie20tips-f.htm

Netscape Extensions to HTML 2.0
http://www.netscape.com/assist/net_sites/html_extensions.html

Netscape Extensions to HTML 3.0 Proposals
http://www.netscape.com/assist/net_sites/html_extensions_3.html

Sandia National Laboratories
http://www.sandia.gov/sci_compute/elements.html
http://orion.postech.ac.kr/~handol/www/html/html_elem.html
http://www.sandia.gov/sci_compute/html_ref.html

SGML Basics
http://www.sil.org/sgml/sgml.html

University of South Australia, Weblint Checking by URL
http://www.netspot.unisa.edu.au/weblint/

W3C (World Wide Web Consortium)
http://www.w3.org

Weblint
http://www.khoros.unm.edu/staff/neilb/weblint.html

Weblint Gateways Listing
http://www.cre.canon.co.uk/~neilb/weblint/gateways.html

WebTechs
http://www.webtechs.com/html-val-svc/

Microsoft's CSS—Typography on the Web
http://www.microsoft.com/truetype/hottopic.htm

Microsoft's Cascading Style Sheets Gallery
http://www.microsoft.com/truetype/css/gallery/entrance.htm

World Wide Web Consortium (W3C)
http://www.w3.org/pub/WWW/TR/WD-css1

Aladdin Systems, Inc.
http://www.aladdinsys.com/

PKWare, Inc: The Data Compression Experts
http://www.pkware.com/

Progressive Networks RealAudio Video
http://www.realaudio.com/

WinZip: Nico Mak Computing, Inc.
http://www.winzip.com/

ZipIt Home Page
http://www.awa.com/softlock/zipit/zipit.html

Liz – The Browsing Chameleon
http://www.cast.org/liz/

The National Center for Accessible Media
http://www.boston.com/wgbh/ncam

The Web Access Symbol
http://www.boston.com/wgbh/pages/ncam/symbolwinner.html

What Does Your HTML Look Like in Lynx? Page
http://www.miranova.com/~steve/Lynx-View.html

Beatthief's Muddy Waters Page
http://www.beatthief.com

Dukemedia
http://www.dukemedia.com/

Dukemedia's Cross-Platform and NTSC Color Palette
http://www.dukemedia.com/ntscpalette.html

The Quantel Digital Fact Book
http://www.quantel.com/dfb/index.html

WebTV Networks Development Documentation Pages
http://webtv.net/devdocs/htmlref/htmlref-1.html

ADA and Disability Information
http://www.public.iastate.edu/~sbilling/ada.html

Americans with Disabilities Act: Kansas Commission on Disability Concerns
http://www.idir.net/~adabbs/index1.html

JAN on the Web: The Job Accommodation Network
http://janweb.icdi.wvu.edu

U.S. Department of Justice: Americans with Disabilities Act: ADA Home Page
http://www.usdoj.gov/crt/ada/adahom1.htm

U.S. Department of Justice: Americans with Disabilities Act of 1990
http://www.usdoj.gov/crt/ada/statute.html

ADA Compliance Guide
http://www.thompson.com/tpg/person/able/able.html

The Audio Description HomePage
http://www.artswire.org/Artswire/ad/index.html

Braille Translation with MegaDots from Raised Dot Computing
http://ww.rdcbraille.com

caption.com: Directory of Captioning Information
http://www.caption.com/caption-info.html

CSLI: Certified Sign Language Interpreting
http://www.cslisd.com/csli

Deaf World Web
http://deafworldweb.org/dww

Dyslexia 2000 Network
http://www.futurenet.co.uk/charity/ado/index.html

Gus Communications, INC.
http://www.gusinc.com/

HTML to ICADD Transformation Service
http://www.ucla.edu/ICADD/html2icadd-form.html

The Library of Congress: National Library Service for the Blind and Physically Handicapped
http://lcweb.loc.gov/nls/nls.html

My Handi-Capable Reporter
http://mhcr.com

PC WholeWare
http://www.pcww.com/index.html

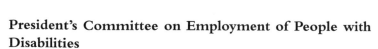
President's Committee on Employment of People with Disabilities
http://www.pcepd.gov/contents.htm

The Rights of Disabled Persons
gopher://asa.ugl.lib.umich.edu:80/hGET%20/chdocs/rights/
Disabled.html

Yuri Rubinsky Insight Foundation: WebABLE
http://yuri.org/webable/index.html

Index

A

accessibility
  disabilities, 279-280
  functions,
    web sites, 277-281
  to Intranet
    employees, 278-279
  time, cost of, 24
accessing, *see* activating
accomodations
  (public), 279-280
Acrobat Reader, 238-239
activating
  forms, 106-108
  Internet, 24-25
  web sites
    information, 252-253
    methods, 16
    modems, 19
ActiveX, 158
ADA (Americans with Disabilities
  Act), 25, 277-279
  governments, 279
  physical
    impairments, 25
ADD (Attention Deficit
  Disorder), 81, 98
/ADDRESS tag, 216
ADDRESS tag, 216
AIFF (Audio Interchange File
  Format), 147-150, 157
Aladdin Systems
  web site, 231, 233
ALIGN tag, 120
aligning text
  CSS (Cascading Style Sheets), 225
  manually, 130-132
alignment tags, 221, 250-251

ALT tag, 26-28, 44-45, 200,
  244-245, 247, 254
  graphics, 60-61
  imagemaps, 63
  NCAM (National Center for
    Accessible Media), 27
Americans with Disabilities Act,
  see ADA (Americans with
  Disabilities Act)
animations, GIF (Graphics
  Interchange Format), 161
anology, 42-43
appearances
  tags on-screen, 218-220
  text, 207-209, 216-218
applications,
  shareware, 157
AREA tag, 202
areas, text, 110
arranging, *see* organizing
ASCII (American Standard Code
  for Information Interchange),
  196, 255
Attention Deficit Disorder, *see*
  ADD (Attention Deficit
  Disorder)
attributes, columns/rows, 118-120
attribution tags
  (fonts), 212-214
AU (SunAudio), 147-150, 157, 239
audiences
  shareware players, 237-238
  web sites
    designing, 19-36
    for disabilities, 25
    dislikes, 25
    text features, 81-101
  see also viewers
audio files, transcripts, 257

Audio Formats web site, Cross-Platform Page, 150
AVI (Audio Video Interleaved), 236, 239
AXES tag, 132
AXIS tag, 132

B

/B tag, 216
B tag, 216
backgrounds
    multicolored, 183-185
    sounds, embedding, 151
    text, viewing, 188-191
Bank of America web site, 44
banners, 99
bars
    navigation, 44
    titles, matching, 248-249
BASEFONT tag, 215
Beatthief's Muddy Waters web site, 271
BGSOUND tag, 151
/BIG tag, 218
BIG tag, 218
Binary, 234
BinHex (compression formats), 234
blindness, color, 192-193
BLINK tag, 202
blinking text, turning off, 255
/BLOCKQUOTE tag, 217
BLOCKQUOTE tag, 91-93, 97, 217
Bobby, CAST (Center for Applied Special Technology), 202-206
/BODY tag, 267
BODY tag, 273
bookmarks, 100
borders, frames, 143
BORDERS tag, 141-143
BR tag, 79, 208-209
    cells, 121-123
breaking up, *see* separating
breaks
    lines, inserting, 73-74
    paragraphs, 73-74

The Britannia Guide to Black History web site, 28
browser-safe color palettes, 53
browsers
    alignment tags, 250-251
    Bobby, CAST (Center for Applied Special Technology) web site, 206
    colors, downloading palettes, 187
    forms, 33, 103-112
        printing, 112-115
    frames, 137-139
    graphical, 16
    help, c|net web site, 31-33
    HTML (HyperText Markup Language) tags, 195-196
    JavaScript, 74-78
    NCSA (National Center for Supercomputing Applications), 128
        Mosaic, 219
    plug-ins, 26-27
    PowerBook, 67
    tables, 117-126, 128-132
        rendering, 121-125
    text
        appearances, 207-209
        tags, 127
    text-only, 128
    time limits, 24
    typefaces, 79, 208
    web, 79
    web sites, 244-246
    WebTV (pixels), 269
    windows
        resizing, 251-252
        sizes, 18
        sizing, 65-67
BrowserWatch web site, 37
buttons
    Back (browsers), 139-140
    Quote (Netscape), 106
    Radio, 108-109
    Reset, 111
    Send, 112
    Submit, 111-112
bytes, sound, 145-160

C

capital letters (text), 90-91
The Caption Center at WGBH web site, 179

The Caption FAQ web site, 179
CAPTION tag, 123, 125
captions
    cells, 124
    graphics, 63
    inserting
        graphics, 123-125
        movies, 161-163
    movies, 165-178
    types, selecting, 174-178
CAST (Center for Applied Special Technology), 245
    web site, 245, 247
    Bobby, 202-206
CD-ROM (Compact Disk-Read Only Memory), 40
CELLPADDING tag, 118
cells, 117-120
    captions, 124
    extra spaces, inserting, 123-125
    tables, 118-120
    tags
        BR, 121-123
        P, 123
CELLSPACING tag, 118
Center for Applied Special Technology, *see* CAST (Center for Applied Special Technology)
CENTER tag, 128, 195, 251
CGI (Common Gateway Interface) scripts, 103
characters
    reading, 83
    tags, styles, 215-216
    writing, 83
charges for access time, 24
check boxes, 108-109
choosing, *see* selecting
chromatic hues, 182
circles, 42
/CITE tag, 215
CITE tag, 215
classifieds home page, 84-88, 91-92, 270
clicking options, 46-47
client-side imagemaps, 44-45, 63
clips
    low-resolution, 161-162
    sounds, 157-158
Closed Captioning Web site, 179
CLUT (Color Lookup Table), 187

c|net web site, 29-33
/CODE tag, 215
CODE tag, 215
codes
    CSS (Cascading Style Sheets)
    graphics, 226-228
    fonts, coloring, 220
    tags
        ALT, 244
        HTML (HyperText Markup
        Language), 257
        NOFRAMES, 138
        paragraphs, 221-222
    web sites, testing, 247-251
coding
    CSS (Cascading Style
    Sheets), 224-227
    HTML (HyperText Markup
    Language), 198
Color Lookup Table, *see* CLUT
    (Color Lookup Table)
colors
    backgrounds, 183-185, 187
    blindness, 192-193
    browser-safe palettes, 53
    contrast (web sites), 181-190, 192
    dithered, 187
    fonts, 220
    monitor settings, 183
    neutral, 182
    numbers, 248
    selecting, 186-187
    viewing
        combinations, 191
        comibations, 187-190
        type sizes/styles, 192
    WebTV, 266-267
    see also graphics
COLSPAN tag, 118
columns, 117-120
    attributes, 118-120
    layout, 84-85, 91-93
    reading, 89
    screen readers, 88
    tables, creating, 93
    text, 84-93
combinations of colors,
    viewing, 187-191

commands
    File menu (Netscape)
        Open File, 59-60
        Save Frame As, 140
    Movie menu (MoviePlayer), Get
    Info, 167
comments
    JPEG (Joint Photographic Experts
    Group), inserting, 256
    text areas, 110
CommercialNet/Nielsen Internet
    Demographic Study web site, 37
Common Gateway Interface, *see*
    CGI
Compact Disk-Read Only
    Memory, *see* CD-ROM
components of tables, 117-120
compressing
    files, 230
        standards, 231-234
        videos, 237
    graphics, 50-53
computer screens
    dimensions, 66
    sizing, 67-68
concepts, teaching
    symbols, 42-43
connecting web sites, 19
constructs, HTML (HyperText
    Markup Language)
    resources, 199
costs
    access time, 24
    Internet, activating, 24
creating, *see* designing
cropping graphics, 54-56
CSS (Cascading Style Sheets),
    224-227
    codes, graphics, 226-228
    features, 225
    fonts, 225-226
    Internet Explorer, 228
cues, navigation, 27-29
cultural services, Yahoo! web
    site, 22-23

D

D tag, 62
D tagging, graphics, 257
DD tag, 223
default
    font sizes, 208
    typefaces, browsers, 208
    windows, WebTV,
        265-266
defining graphics,
    height/width, 59-60
definition lists, 223
DejaNews web site, 35-36
descriptions inserting
    (movies), 161-163
designing
    for WebTV, 265-272
    forms, 106, 108-111
    icon links, 41
    navigation, 40
    screens versus papers, 69-74
    table columns, 93
    text, 207-208
    transcripts from movies, 163-165
    web sites, audiences, 19-36
desktop icons, 40
/DFN tag, 215
DFN tag, 215
Digital Dreams Web
    site, 33-35
Digital Video Disc, *see* DVD
dimension screens, 66-68
Directory of Symbols, 43
disabilities
    access to WWW (World Wide
        Web), 279-280
    ADA (Americans with Disabilities
        Act), 277-278
    D tagging, 257
    intranet employees, 278-279
    see also impairments
dithered colors, 187
/DIV tag, 222
DIV tag, 222
DL tag, 91
Doctor HTML (HyperText
    Markup Language), 249
    Web site, 200
documents, RTF (Rich Text
    Format), 239

downloading
  files, 229-242
  WebTV, software, 272
dpi (dots per inch), 55-56
/DT tag, 223
DT tag, 223
**DVD (Digital Video Disc),
 151, 236**
dyslexia, 81
  reading text, 98

E

**editors, HTML (HyperText
 Markup Language), 249**
elements
  forms, 108-111
  navigation, designing, 40
/EM tag, 215
EM tag, 215, 219
EMBED SRC tag, 149
EmeraldNet web site, 148
employees, intranets, 278-279
encoders
  RealAudio,
   downloading, 154
  RealVideo, 235
**environments, forced
 quiet, 159**
**errors, spelling
 (web pages), 249**
**examples, teaching
 symbols, 42-43**
EXE (Executable), 232

F

Family Tree Maker web site, 46
**FAQs (Frequently Asked
 Questions), 35-36**
features
  CSS (Cascading Style Sheets), 225
  web sites, text, 81-101
fields
  passwords, 110
  text, 110
File menu commands (Netscape)
  Open File, 59-60
  Save Frame As, 140
files
  compressing, 230
   standards, 231-234
  downloading, 229-242

formats
  selecting, 229-230
  videos, 235-237
  graphics, 234-239
   sizing, 53
  JavaScript, 252
  Shockwave, 252
  size warnings, 254-255
  sounds, 157
   formats, 258
   *.WAV
   (Waveform), 156*
  thumbnails, movies, 163
  transcripts
   audio, 257
   movies, 257
  .TXT (Text), 239
  .WAV, 145
  .ZIP, 231
focus groups, 35
FONT SIZE tag, 195, 212-214
fonts
  attribution tags, 212-214
  coloring, 220
  CSS (Cascading Style Sheets),
   225-226
  sizes
   default, 208
   WebTV, 267-271
**forced quiet
 environments, 159**
formats
  files, 234-239
   graphics, 234-239
   selecting, 229-230
   sounds, 258
   videos, 235-237
  MPEG (Moving Picture Experts
   Group), 151-152
  multipage, 100-101
  selecting web pages,
   239-241
  SGML (Standard Generalized
   Markup Language), 196
  sounds, 156-157
   clips, 157-158
   *MIDI (Musical Instrument Digital
   Interface), 150-151*
   MOD (Modulo), 151
  tables, one-column, 93

forms
  activating, 106-108
  browsers, 33
  designing, 106, 108-111
  elements, 108-111
  Internet Explorer, 104, 106-108
  Navigator, 104, 107-108
  printing, 112-115
  text, 106
   areas, 110
  troubleshooting, 106
  viewers guiding through, 111
  web sites, 103-112, 258
FRAME tag, 46
FRAMEBORDERS tag, 141-143
frames, 133-143
  browsers, 137-138
  navigating, Back
   button, 139-140
  printing
   Internet Explorer, 140-142
   Navigator, 140-142
  scroll bars, 134-136
  subwindows, 134-136
  web sites, 134-136, 142-143
   borders, 143
FRAMESET tag, 135-136
Frequently Asked Questions, *see*
 **FAQs (Frequently Asked
 Questions)**
functions, *see* **methods**

G

**Get Info. command (Movie
 menu), MoviePlayer, 167**
**GIF (Graphics Interchange
 Format), 50-53, 230, 234, 239**
  animations, 161
  interlaced, 51
  saving, 51
  single-pixel
   transparent, 74
**GIF89 format, saving
 graphics, 248**
GifConverter for the Mac, 256
**governments, ADA (Americans
 with Disabilities Act), 279**
**graphical browsers,
 updating, 16**
Graphical User Interface, *see* **GUI**

graphics

ALT tag, 60-61

codes, 244

captions, 63

inserting, 123-125

colors

browser-safe color palettes, 53

contrast, 181-190, 192

cropping, 54-56

CSS (Cascading Style Sheets), 226-228

D tag, 62

D tagging, 257

files, 234-239

GIF (Graphics Interchange Format), 50-53

Gif Converter for the Mac, 256

height/width, defining, 59-60

JPEG (Joint Photographic Experts Group), 52-53, 56

saving

as 72 dp (dots per inch), 55-56

GIF89 format, 248

sizing, 53, 56

thumbnails, 57-60

web sites, 49-63, 252

loading, 244

WebTV, 266, 272

see also colors

Graphics Interchange Format, *see* GIF

groups, focus, 35

GUI (Graphical User Interface), 40, 60

guidelines

forms, designing, 111

navigating, 39-47

text

length, 82

links, 257

gutters, 87

GVU WWW User Survey web site, 18, 24, 37

H

H1 tag, 196, 210

H2 tag, 196, 210, 220

H3 tag, 196, 210

H4 tag, 210

H5 tag, 210

H6 tag, 211

hardware, web sites, 17

headings

settings, 211-212

web pages, 209-212

headlines, seperating text, 94-96

hearing impairment

WebTV, 265

web sites, sounds, 159

help

browsers, 31-33

navigation, c|net web site, 29-33

horizontal lines (WebTV), 272

HR tag, 272

HTML (HyperText Markup Language), 195-196, 237

coding, 198

screen readers, 197-198

SGML (Standard Generalized Markup Language), 196

standards

resources, 199

W3C (World Wide Web Consortium) web site, 197

structures, logic, 196-197

tags

/ADDRESS, 216

ADDRESS, 216

ALIGN, 120

ALT, 26-28, 44-45, 200, 244-245, 247, 254

AREA, 202

AXES, 132

AXIS, 132

/B, 216

B, 216

BASEFONT, 215

BGSOUND, 151

/BIG, 218

BIG, 218

BLINK, 202

/BLOCKQUOTE, 217

BLOCKQUOTE, 91-93, 97, 217

/BODY, 267

BODY, 273

BORDERS, 141-143

BR, 79, 121-123, 208-209

browsers, 195-196

CAPTION, 123, 125

CELLPADDING, 118

CELLSPACING, 118

CENTER, 128, 195, 251

/CITE, 215

CITE, 215

/CODE, 215

CODE, 215

codes, 257

COLSPAN, 118

D, 62

DD, 223

/DFN, 215

DFN, 215

/DIV, 222

DIV, 222

DL, 91

/DT, 223

DT, 223

/EM, 215

EM, 215, 219

EMBED SRC, 149

FONT SIZE, 195, 212-214

FRAME, 46

FRAMEBORDERS, 141-143

FRAMESET, 135-136

H1, 196, 210

H2, 196, 210, 220

H3, 196, 210

H4, 210

H5, 210

H6, 211

HR, 272

/I, 216

I, 216, 219

interpreting, 198-199

/KBD, 215

KBD, 215

LOWSRC, 254

MAILTO, 33-35, 106-107, 252

MARQUEE, 202

MAXLENGTH, 110

/MENU, 222

MENU, 222

NOFRAMES, 136-139

NOSMARTQUOTES, 274

/OL, 223

OL, 223

/P, 221

P, 79, 208-209, 221, 256

/PRE, 217-218

PRE, 126-132, 217-218, 267

ROWSPAN, 118

/SAMP, 216

SAMP, 216
/SIDEBAR, 272-274
SIDEBAR, 272-274
/SMALL, 218
SMALL, 218
/STRONG, 216
STRONG, 216
TABLE, 126-127, 132
/TITLE, 248-249
TITLE, 248-249
TR, 120
TT, 126-132
/U, 216
U, 216
/UL, 222
UL, 222
VALIGN, 120
/VAR, 216
VAR, 216
WebTV, 272-274
WIDTH, 118
validation programs, 200-206
HTML Editor, 249
hues, 182
Hybrid HTML Design: A Multi-Browser HTML, 247
HyperText Markup Language, *see* **HTML**

I

/I tag, 216
I tag, 216, 219
icons, 40-42
designing links, 41
desktop, 40
text, writing, 98-99
web sites, 253-254
labeling, 253-254
Wood Works, 122
imagemaps, 44-46, 63
images, *see* **graphics**
impairments
ADA (Americans with Disabilities Act), 25
D tagging, 257
web sites
physical, 25
visual, 197-198
WebTV, hearing, 265
see also disabilities

information on web sites, activating, 252-253
inserting
captions, 123-125, 161-163
comments, JPEG (Joint Photographic Experts Group), 256
descriptions to movies, 161-163
extra spaces into cells, 123-125
line breaks, 73-74
links (plug-ins), 158
sounds, 146-147, 156-158
Inter-NOT: Online & Internet Reality Check New Networks web site, 37-38
interfaces
GUI (Graphical User Interface), 60
navigational, WebTV, 264
Interlaced GIF (Graphics Interchange Format), 51
Internet
activating time limits, 24-25
costs, 24
see also web sites; WWW (World Wide Web)
Internet Explorer
CSS (Cascading Style Sheets), 228
FONT SIZE tag, 214
forms, 104, 106-108
printing, 112-113
frames
printiing, 140-142
headings
settings, 211
Internet Explorer 3.0
accessibility
functions, 46
sounds, embedding, 151
Internet Service Providers, *see* **ISPs**
interpreting HTML (HyperText Markup Language) tags, 198-199
InterV web site, 152
Intranet employees, 278-279
ISPs (Internet Service Providers), 24
italics, 91

J

JavaScript
browsers, resizing, 74-78
files, 252
monitors, testing, 77-78
Jeff Gate's: In Our Path web site, 57-58
JPEG (Joint Photographic Experts Group), 50, 52-53, 230, 234
comments, inserting, 256
graphics, 56
captions, 63
saving, 55-56

K-L

/KBD tag, 215
KBD tag, 215
keyboards (WebTV), 263-264
keyguards, 264

labeling forms, 111
languages
translating requirements, 20-23
Yahoo! web site, 22-23
layout
columns, 84-85, 91-93
three, 86-88
tables, 128-132
web pages, 69-70, 72-74
length of text, guidelines, 82
letters, capitals, 90-91
lines
breaks
BR tag, 121-123
inserting, 73-74
text, 95-96
horizontal (WebTV), 272
links
icons, designing, 41
plug-ins, inserting, 158
sentences, 101
text, *98-99*
guidelines, 257
web sites, 252-254
reading, 247
viewers, 100-101
lists
definitions, 223
nested, 224
numbered, 223

text, 222-224
unnumbered tags, 222
Liszt Directory of E-mail Discussion Group web site, 35
LiveAudio plug-ins, 149
LiveUpdate web site, Crescendo, 151
Liz:CAST (Center for Applied Special Technology) web site, 206
loading
tables, 126-127
web sites, graphics off, 244
locations of web sites, 19
logic structures, HTML (HyperText Markup Language), 196-197
logical type style tags, 215-216
long forms, 108
low-resolution clips, 161-162
LOWSRC tag, 254

M

Macintosh
PowerBook, 66
RealAudio, 154-155
SEA (Self-Extracting Archive), 232
SIT (StuffIt) standard, compressing files, 231
sounds
AIFF (Audio Interchange File Format), 147
SND format, 147
SoundApp, 157
Macromedia web site, Shockwave, 156
MAILTo tag, 33-35, 106-107, 252
mapping web sites, 258-259
marketing research resources, 36-38
GVU WWW User Survey, 37
markets, targets (web sites), 29
MARQUEE tag, 202
matching title bars, 248-249
MAXLENGTH tag, 110
/MENU tag, 222
MENU tag, 222
menus
multiple-choice, 109
pop-up, 108-109
command choices, 112
text, 250

metaphors, 40-42
methods
color blindness, 192
compressing files, 230
web sites
access, 277-281
activating, 16
Microsoft Internet Explorer 3.0, *see* Internet Explorer 3.0
MIDI (Musical Instrument Digital Interface), 145-147, 150-151
Midplug web site, 151
MIME (Multipurpose Internet Multimedia Extensions) types, Live Audio plug-ins, 148, 234
MOD (Modula), 150-151
modems, web sites, 19, 250
monitors
colors, setting, 248
sizing, 79
testing, 77-78
web sites, 17-18
monochromatic colors, 182
mouse
forms, without, 106-107
navigating, 134-136
Movie menu commands, Get Info (MoviePlayer), 167
MoviePlayer, plug-ins, 165-178
movies
captions, 165-178
inserting, 161-163
descriptions, 161-163
Outlaws web site, 166-178
QuickTime, 159, 161-162
NCAM (National Center for Accessible Media), 166
thumbnails, 163
transcripts
creating, 163-165
files, 257
MPEG (Moving Picture Experts Group), 151-152, 236
MPEG-2 (Moving Picture Experts Group), 152
multicolored backgrounds, 183-185
multilingual web sites, 258
multipage format, 100-101
multiple-choice menus, 109

Musical Instrument Digital Interface, *see* MIDI

N

National Center for Accessible Media, *see* NCAM
National Center for Supercomputing Applications, *see* NCSA
National Television Standards Committee, *see* NTSC
navigating
with frames, 133-143
guidelines, 39-47
imagemaps, 44-45
with mouse, 134-136
text, 45-46
web site options, 250
navigation
bars, 44
cues, 27-29
designing, 40
help (c|net web site), 29-33
web pages, sizing, 80
Navigator, 59
FONT SIZE tag, 214
forms, 104
frames, printing, 140-142
headings, 211
NCAM (National Center for Accessible Media)
ALT tag, 27
QuickTime movies, 166
web access symbol, 257
NCSA (National Center for Supercomputing Applications), 117, 128
Mosaic, 112, 117, 128, 212
nested lists, 224
Net Toob web site, 152
Netscape
forms, 107-108
printing, 112-113
Navigator, *see* Navigator
plug-ins, 156
web site, translating languages, 20-21
windows, 68
WinZip (Nico Mak Computing), 231

Netscape 3.0, LiveAudio plug-in, 148-149
neutral colors, 182
New Networks web site, 37
    Inter-NOT: Online & Internet
    Reality Check, 37-38
newsgroups, DejaNews web site, 35-36
NOFRAMES
    option, 257
    tag, 136-139
        codes, 138
        Web pages, visual impairments, 138-139
NOSMARTQUOTES tag, 274
notebooks (screens), 65-67
NTSC (National Television Standards Committee), 267
    color palettes, 267
numbered lists, 223
numbers, color of, 248

O

/OL tag, 223
OL tag, 223
Open File command (File menu), Navigator, 59-60
options
    clicking, 46-47
    files, downloading, 242
    navigational, 39-47
    NOFRAMES, 257
    radiation, 42
    web sites
        navigating, 250
        text, 209-214
    wildcards, 136
ordered lists, *see* **numbered lists**
organizing
    layout (web pages),
    69-70, 72-74
    web sites, 25-29
Outlaws (movie) web site, 166-178

P

/P tag, 221
P tag, 79, 208-209, 221, 256
    cells, 123
pages, numbers, 82-83

pages, *see* **web pages**
PAL (Phase Alternating Line), 267
palettes, browser-safe colors, 53, 187
paragraphs
    breaks, 73-74, 123
    tags, 221-222
password fields, 110
PCs (Personal Computers), 147
    .EXE (Executable), 232
    .WAV (Waveform), 147
.PCX (file extension) graphics, 235
Phase Alternating Line, *see* **PAL (Phase Alternating Line)**
physical
    appearances, NCSA Mosaic, 219
    file size
        graphics, cropping, 54-56
    type style tags, 215-216
picking out, *see* **selecting**
PICT (graphics file format), 235
pixels
    tables, 70-74
    WebTV, 268-271
PKWare web site, 232
PkZip (shareware utility), 232
platforms
    display capabilities, 18
    features, 16
    web sites, 245, 247
    WebTV, designing for, 265-272
    Windows, RealVideo Encoder, 235
players
    QuickTime, 236
    RealAudio, 154-155
plug-ins
    browsers, 26-27
    links, inserting, 158
    LiveAudio, 148-149
    MoviePlayer, 166-178
    MPEG (Moving Picture Experts Group), 152
    Netscape, 156
    RealAudio, 153-155
    Shockwave, 155-156
    sounds, 153

    video formats, 235-237
    Voxware ToolVox, 156
    web sites, features, 17
pop-up menus, 108-109
    command choices, 112
PowerBook screens, 65-67
/PRE tag, 217-218
PRE tag, 126-132, 217-218, 267
printing
    forms, 112-115
    frames, 140-142
programs, validation, 200-206
public accomodations, 279-280
punctuation of text (web pages), 84

Q

Quantel Digital Fact Book web site, 267
QuickTime, 236
    movies, 159, 161-162
        captions, 165-178
        NCAM (National Center for Accessible Media), 166
Quote button (Netscape), 106

R

radiation options, 42
radio buttons, 108-109
reader screens, 101, 132
    columns, 88
    HTML (HyperText Markup Language), 197-198
    tables, 88
reading
    characters, 83
    columns, 89
    text
        ADD (Attention Deficit Disorder), 98
        difficulties, 89
        dyslexia, 98
    web sites, 183, 247
        links, 247
    see also viewing
RealAudio (Progressive Networks), 145-147, 153-155
    Encoder, 154
    web site, 145, 153
RealVideo, 235

regulations, governments (disabilities), 279
remotes, WebTV, 263-264
rendering tables (browsers), 121-125
reports, marketing research, 36-38
requirements, translating languages, 20-23
Reset button, 111
resizing
    browsers (JavaScript), 74-78
    windows, 251-252
resources
    HTML (HyperText Markup Language) standards, 199
    marketing research, 36-38
reviewing accessibility of web sites, 243-259
Rich Text Format, *see* RTF
rows, 117-120
ROWSPAN tag, 118
RTF (Rich Text Format), 237-239
rules, *see* guidelines

S

/SAMP tag, 216
SAMP tag, 216
Sandia National Laboratories web site, HTML Reference Manual, 198
saturation (colors), 182
Save Frame As command (File menu), Netscape, 140
saving
    GIF (Graphics Interchange Format), 51
    graphics
        as 72 dpi (dots per inch), 55-56
        GIF89 format, 248
        JPEG (Joint Photographic Expert Group), 55-56
screens
    designing paper versus screen, 69-74
    dimensions, 66-68
    notebooks, 65-67
    PowerBook, 65-67

readers, 101, 132
    columns, 88
    HTML (HyperText Markup Language), 197-198
    tables, 88
    sizing, 67-68
    tags, appearances of, 218-220
scripts, CGI (Common Gateway Interface), 103
scroll bars (frames), 134-136
SEA (Self-Extracting Archive), 232
selecting
    caption types, 174-178
    colors, 186-187
    formats
        files, 229-230
        web pages, 239-241
Self-Extracting Archive, *see* SEA
Send button, 112
sentence links, 101
separating text, 84-96
services, cultural, 22-23
settings
    browsers (WebTV), 269
    headings, 211
    monitor colors, 183
tables, 117-126, 128-132
SGML (Standard Generalized Markup Language), 196
shareware
    applications, 157
    sounds players, 237-238
sheets, CSS (Cascading Style Sheets), 224-227
Shockwave, 145-147, 155-156, 161, 252
shots, still-image, 161
/SIDEBAR tag, 272-274
SIDEBAR tag, 272-274
similes, 41
SimpleText, 165-178
SIT (StuffIt), compressing files, 231
sites (web)
    accessibility of, 243-251
    ADA (Americans with Disabilities Act), 280-281
    Aladdin Systems, 231, 233
    Audio Formats, 150
    Bank of America, 44

Beatthief's Muddy Waters, 271
The Britannica Guide to Black History, 28
browsers, 244-246
BrowserWatch, 37
The Caption Center at WGBH, 179
CAST (Center for Applied Special Technology), 202-206, 245, 247
Closed Captioning, 179
c|net, 29-33
color contrast, 181-190, 192
CommercialNet/Nielsen Internet Demographic Study, 37
DejaNews, 35-36
Digital Dreams, 33-35
Doctor HTML, 200
EmeraldNet, 148
Family Tree Maker, 46
forms, 258
frames, 142-143
graphics, 49-63, 252
GVU WWW User Surveys, 18, 37
icons, 253-254
InterVU, 152
Jeff Gate's: In Our Path, 57-58
links, 252-254
LiveUpdate, 151
Macromedia, 156
mapping, 258-259
Microsoft, 47
Midplug, 151
modems, 250
multilingual, 258
Net Toob, 152
Netscape, 20-21
New Networks, 37-38
NTSC (National Television Standards Committee), 267
organizing, 25-29
Outlaws (movie), 166-178
PKWare, 232
platforms, 245, 247
Quantel Digital Fact Book, 267
RealAudio, 145, 153
RealVideo, 235
Sandia National Laboratories, 198
sounds, 145-160
Stanford University, 60
StreamWorks, 152
Talker, 156
testing, 243-244, 246
text, 207-208

Turntable Media, 162
uploading, 243-244
Voxware ToolVox, 156
W3C (World Wide Web
 Consortium), 197, 224
Weblint, 200-201
WebTechs, 200
WebTV, 274
WinZap, 231
Yahoo!, 22-23, 160
sizes
 file warnings, 254-255
 fonts
  default, 208
  WebTV, 267-271
 graphics (WebTV), 272
 windows, 18
sizing
 graphics, 53, 56
  defining, 59-60
 monitors, 79
 screens, 67-68
  *designing paper versus screen,
  69-74*
 web pages, 65-80
 windows, 69
/SMALL tag, 218
SMALL tag, 218
smart quotes (""), 274
SND format
 (Macintosh), 147
software
 speech-to-text, 160
 to-text, 160
 voice-recognition, 160
 WebTV, downloading, 272
SoundApp (Macintosh), 157
SoundEdit (Macromedia) 16, 147
sounds
 backgrounds,
  embedding, 151
 clips, 157-158
 files, 157
  formats, 258
  WAV (Waveform), 156
 formats, 156-157
 MIDI (Musical Instrument Digital
  Interface), 150
 MOD (Modula), 151
 plug-ins, 153
 RealAudio (Progressive
  Networks), 145, 153-155
 Shockwave, 155-156

SND format (Macintosh), 147
 text, transcribing, 159-160
 Voxware ToolVox, 156
 web sites, 145-160
  alternatives, 159
  inserting, 146-147, 156-158
spaces, extra, 123-125
specifying, *see* defining graphics
speech-to-text software, 160
spelling errors (Web pages), 249
Standard Generalized Markup
 Language, *see* SGML
standards
 forms, printing, 112-115
 files, compressing, 230-234
 HTML (HyperText Markup
  Language)
  resources, 199
  *W3C (World Wide Web
   Consortium) web site, 197*
Stanford University web site, 60
still-image shots, 161
StreamWorks web site, 152
/STRONG tag, 216
STRONG tag, 216
structures
 CSS (Cascading Style Sheets)
  tags, 224
 logic, HTML (HyperText Markup
  Language), 196-197
StuffIt, *see* SIT (StuffIt)
styles
 colors, types, 192
 tags, 215-216
subheads (text), 256
 seperating, 94-96
Submit button, 111-112
subwindows, 142-143
 frames, 134-136
surveys, GVU WWW User
 Survey, 37
symbols, 42
 circles, 42
 Directory of Symbols, 43
 radiation, 42
 teaching concepts, 42-43

T

TABLE tag, 126-127, 132, 195
tables, 132
 cells, 118-120
  captions, 124

columns, 85
 designing, 93
components of, 117-120
layout, 128-132
loading, 126-127
one-column, 93
pixels, 70-74
rendering browsers, 121-125
screen readers, 88, 132
setting, 117-126, 128-132
three-column, 128-132, 141
web sites, 143
tags
 /ADDRESS, 216
 ADDRESS, 216
 ALIGN, 120
 alignment of, 250-251
 ALT, 26-28, 44-45, 200, 244-245,
  247, 254
  graphics, 60-61
  *NCAM (National Center for
   Accessible Media), 27*
 appearances on-screen, 218-220
 AREA, 202
 attribution fonts, 212-214
 AXES, 132
 AXIS, 132
 /B, 216
 B, 216
 BASEFONT, 215
 BGSOUND, 151
 /BIG, 218
 BIG, 218
 BLINK, 202
 /BLOCKQUOTE, 217
 BLOCKQUOTE, 91-93, 97, 217
 /BODY, 267
 BODY, 273
 BORDERS, 141-143
 BR, 79, 208-209
  cells, 121-123
 CAPTION, 123, 125
 CELLPADDING, 118
 CELLSPACING, 118
 CENTER, 128, 195, 251
 /CITE, 215
 CITE, 215
 /CODE, 215
 CODE, 215
 COLSPAN, 118
 CSS (Cascading Style Sheet), 113,
  224, 228
 D, 62
 DD, 223

/DFN, 215
DFN, 215
/DIV, 222
DIV, 222
DL, 91
/DT, 223
DT, 223
/EM, 215
EM, 215, 219
EMBED SRC, 149
FONT SIZE, 195, 212, 213-214
FRAME, 46
FRAMEBORDERS, 141-143
FRAMESET, 135-136
H1, 196, 210
H2, 196, 210, 220
H3, 196, 210
H4, 210
H5, 210
H6, 211
headings (web pages), 209-212
HR, 272
HTML (HyperText Markup
  Language)
    browsers, 195-196
    codes, 257
    interpreting, 198-199
    WebTV, 272-274
/I, 216
I, 216, 219
/KBD, 215
KBD, 215
lists, 222-224
logical type style, 215-216
LOWSRC, 254
MAILTO, 33-35, 106-107, 252
MAXLENGTH, 110
/MENU, 222
MENU, 222
NOFRAMES, 136-139
NOSMARTQUOTES, 274
/OL, 223
OL, 223
/P, 221
P, 79, 208-209, 221, 256
    cells, 123
paragraphs, 221-222
physical type style, 216
/PRE, 217-218
PRE, 126-132, 217-218, 267
ROWSPAN, 118
/SAMP, 216
SAMP, 216
/SIDEBAR, 272-274

SIDEBAR, 272-274
/SMALL, 218
SMALL, 218
STRONG, 216
styles, 215-216
TABLE, 126-127, 132, 195
text
    appearances, 216-218
    browsers, 127
/TITLE, 248-249
TITLE, 248-249
TR, 120
TT, 126-132
/U, 216
U, 216
/UL, 222
UL, 222
VALIGN, 120
/VAR, 216
VAR, 216
WIDTH, 118
Talker, 153
  web site, 156
targets, markets, 29
teaching symbols, concepts, 43
televisions
  NTSC (National Television
    Standards Committee), 267
  WebTV, 261-272
testing
  monitors, 77-78
  web sites, 243-244, 246
    codes, 247-251
text
  aligning
    *CSS (Cascading Style
      Sheets), 225*
    manually, 130-132
  appearances, 207-209
    tags, 216-218
  areas, 110
  blinking, turning off, 255
  browsers, 127
  capital letters, 90-91
  characters, 83
  clarity factors, 256
  columns, tables, 85
  comprehension disorders, 81
  designing, 207-208
  fields, 110
  forms, 106
  gutters, 87
  italics, 91
  length guidelines, 82

line breaks, 95-96
link guidelines, 257
lists, 222-224
menus, 250
navigating, 45-46
options, 209-214
punctuation, 84
reading
    *ADD (Attention Deficit
      Disorder), 98*
    difficulties, 89
    dyslexia, 98
    web sites, 247
  seperating, 84-96
  transcribing sounds, 159-160
  viewing backgrounds, 188-191
  web sites, 207-208
    features, 81-101
  windows, sizing, 69
  writing, 97-99
    icons, 98-99
    links, 98-99
text-only browsers, 128
three-columns
  layout, 86-88
  tables, 128-132, 141
thumbnails
  graphics, 57-60
  movies, 163
time limits for browsers, 24
title bars, matching, 248-249
/TITLE tag, 248-249
TITLE tag, 248-249
TR tag, 120
**transcribing text (sounds),
  159-160**
transcripts
  audio files, 257
  creating, 163-165
  movies
    files, 257
    web pages, 165
**translating languages,
  requirements, 20-23**
troubleshooting forms, 106
TT tag, 126-132
Turntable Media web site, 162
.TXT (Text) files, 239
typefaces, browsers, 79, 139, 208
types
  MIME (Multipurpose Internet
    Multimedia Extensions), 148
  sizes, columns, 88-89

U

/U tag, 216
U tag, 216
/UL tag, 222
UL tag, 222
Uniform Resource Locator, *see*
 URL
Unix, sounds, 147
unnumbered list tags, 222
UnStuffIt (file utility), 231
updating graphical browsers, 16
uploading web sites, 243-244
URL (Uniform Resource
 Locator), 133-143
users, *see* audiences; viewers
UUEncode (compression
 formats), 234

V

validation program, HTML
 (HyperText Markup
 Language), 200-206
VALIGN tag, 120
values (colors), 182
/VAR tag, 216
VAR tag, 216
videos
 DVD (Digital Video Disc), 151
 files, 235-237
 MPEG (Moving Picture Experts
  Group), 151-152
 streams, 236
viewers
 blinking text, turning off, 255
 check boxes, 108-109
 forms, 108-111
 text, clarity factors, 256
 web sites, indicating links,
  100-101
 see also audiences
viewing
 colors, 192
  blindness, 192-193
  combinations, 187-191
  type sizes/styles, 192
 text backgrounds, 188-191
 see also reading
visual impairments
 frames, web pages, 138-139
 WebTV, 265
 see also impairments

voice-recognition software, 160
VoxWare, 153, 156

W-Z

W3C (World Wide Web
 Consortium) web site, 197, 224
warnings (file sizes), 254-255
WAV (Waveform), 145, 147-150
 files, 145, 156-157
WEB ACCESS 97 conference, 60
web access symbol, NCAM
 (National Center for Accessible
 Media), 257
web browsers, *see* browsers
web pages
 column spacing, 88-89
 formats
  multipage, 100-101
  selecting, 239-241
 frames, 138-139
 headings, 209-212
 layout, 69-70, 72-74
 movie transcripts, 165
 page numbers, 82-83
 sizing, 65-80
 spelling errors, 249
 visual impairments, 197-198
 writing text, 98-99
web sites
 accessibility, 243-259, 277-281
 activating
  methods, 16
  modems, 19
 Aladdin Systems, 231, 233
 audiences, designing, 19-36
 Audio Formats, Cross-Platform
  Page, 150
 Bank of America, 44
 Beatthief's Muddy Waters, 271
 The Britannica Guide to Black
  History, 28
 browsers, 244-246
 BrowserWatch, 37
 The Caption Center at
  WGBH, 179
 CAST (Center for Applied Special
  Technology), 245, 247
  Bobby, 202-206
  Liz, 206
 Closed Captioning web, 179
 c|net, 29-33
 codes, testing, 247-251

colors
 blindness methods, 192
 contrast, 181-190, 192
 selecting, 186-187
CommercialNet/Nielsen Internet
 Demographic Study, 37
connecting to, 19
DejaNews, 35-36
Digital Dreams, 33-35
Doctor HTML, 200
EmeraldNet, 148
Family Tree Maker, 46
forms, 103-112, 258
frames, 134-136, 142-143
graphics, 49-63, 252
 thumbnails, 57-60
GVU WWW User Surveys, 18, 37
hardware features, 17
icons, 253-254
image-loading, 244
information
 activating, 252-253
 ADA (Americans with Disabilities
  Act), 280-281
InterVU, 152
Jeff Gate's: In Our Path, 57-58
links, 252-254
 reading, 247
Liszt Directory of E-mail
 Discussion Groups, 35
LiveUpdate, Crescendo, 151
Macromedia Shockwave, 156
mapping, 258-259
Microsoft, Accessibility Page, 47
Midplug, 151
modems, 250
monitors, 17-18
multilingual, 258
navigating options, 250
Net Toob, 152
Netscape, translating
 languages, 20-21
New Networks, 37
 Inter-NOT: Online & Internet
  Reality Check, 37-38
NOFRAMES option, 257
NTSC (National Television
 Standards Committee) color
 palettes, 267
options, clicking, 46-47
organizing, 25-29
Outlaws (movie), 166-178
PKWare, 232

platforms, 245, 247
  features, 16
plug-ins, 17
Quantel Digital Fact Book, 267
reading, 183
RealAudio, 145, 153
RealVideo, 235
Sandia National Laboratories,
  HTML Reference Manual, 198
sounds, 145-160
  alternatives, 159
  files, 157
  formats, 156-158
  inserting, 146-147, 156-158
Stanford University, 60
StreamWorks, 152
tables, 143
Talker, 156
testing, 243-244, 246
text
  features, 81-101
  options, 209-214
  reading, 247
text-only, 207-208
time limits, 24
Turntable Media, 162
uploading, 243-244
viewers
  disabilities, 25
  indicating links, 100-101
Voxware ToolVox, 156

W3C (World Wide Web
  Consortium), 197, 224
Weblint, 200-201
WebTechs, 200
WebTV, 261-264, 274
WinZap, 231
Yahoo!
  languages, 22-23
  voice-recognition software, 160
  see also Internet; sites; WWW
  (World Wide Web)
web, *see* **WWW (World Wide Web)**
Weblint web site, 200-201
WebTechs web site, 200
WebTV, 261-272
  accessibility of (impairments),
    263-265
  arguments, 261-262
  colors, 266-267
  designing for, 265-272
  font sizes, 267-271
  graphics, 266, 272
  horizontal lines, 272
  keyboards, 263-264
  navigation interface, 264
  overview, 262-263
  pixels, 268-271
  remotes, 263-264
  software, downloading, 272
  tags, 272-274
  web site, 274
  windows, 265-266

WIDTH tag, 118
wildcard options, 136
Windows
  browsers, 65-80
    resizing, 251-252
    sizes, 18
  frames, scroll bars, 134-136
  Netscape, 68
  platforms, RealVideo
    Encoder, 235
  RealAudio, 154-155
  sizing text, 69
  WebTV, 265-266
**WinZap (Nico Mak Computing)
  web site, 231**
Wood Works icon, 122
writing
  characters, 83
  text, 97-99
WWW (World Wide Web), 108
  accessibility of (impairments),
    279-281
  form elements, 108-111
  help, c|net web site, 32-33
  WebTV, 261-272
  see also **Internet; web sites**

Yahoo! web site, 22-23
  voice-recognition software, 160

ZIP format, 231, 239
ZipIt, locating, 234